The Kurds in Iraq

Also available

The Kurds in Iran
The Past, Present and Future
Kerim Yildiz

The Kurds in Syria
The Forgotten People
Kerim Yildiz

The Kurds in Turkey
EU Accession and Human Rights
Kerim Yildiz

Kurdish Human Rights Project
11 Guilford Street
London
WC1N 1DH
United Kingdom
Tel: +44 20 7405 3835
Fax: +44 20 7404 9088
Email: khrp@khrp.org

The Kurdish Human Rights Project (KHRP) is an independent, non-political, non-governmental human rights organisation founded and based in London, England. KHRP is a registered charity and is committed to the promotion and protection of the human rights of all persons living in the Kurdish regions, irrespective of race, religion, sex, political persuasion or other belief or opinion. Its supporters include both Kurdish and non-Kurdish people.

The Kurds in Iraq

Past, Present and Future

Revised edition

Kerim Yildiz

Pluto Press

in association with

KURDISH HUMAN RIGHTS PROJECT

First published 2007 by Pluto Press
345 Archway Road, London N6 5AA
and 839 Greene Street, Ann Arbor, MI 48106

www.plutobooks.com

British Library Cataloguing in Publication Data
A catalogue record for this book is available from the British Library

Hardback
ISBN-13   978 0 7453 2663 4
ISBN-10   0 7453 2663 3

Paperback
ISBN-13   978 0 7453 2662 7
ISBN-10   0 7453 2662 5

Library of Congress Cataloging in Publication Data applied for

10 9 8 7 6 5 4 3 2 1

Designed and produced for Pluto Press by
Chase Publishing Services Ltd, Fortescue, Sidmouth, EX10 9QG, England
Typeset from disk by Stanford DTP Services, Northampton, England
Printed and bound by CPI Group (UK) Ltd, Croydon, CR0 4YY

To my Wife Bridget and my Son Dara

Contents

Acknowledgements

This book was written by Kerim Yildiz, who would like to thank Merin Abbass and Sayran Sulevani for their invaluable research assistance.

Foreword

With the demise of the rule of the Ba'ath party in Iraq, the country's Kurdish population faces a new chapter in the political and regional development of its region. For over a century the Kurds have been subject to the grand schemes of other powers, denied autonomy, and have faced the onslaughts of military assaults, economic embargoes, and the destruction of their native regions.

This publication is intended to provide an outline of some of the issues affecting the Kurds in Iraq. It provides a brief exploration of the past's effect on the present, and of how both the Kurds and the international community may avoid repeating previous mistakes, laying the foundations for an internationally recognised autonomous region committed to pluralistic democracy and human rights. Such a region would require a commitment to the rule of law and internationally recognised human rights standards.

In the intervening years between the First Gulf War and the 2003 US-led war against Saddam, the Kurds established a democratic administration, which has persevered despite a lack of assistance from the international community to facilitate its establishment or indeed any international recognition. Iraqi Kurdistan serves as a role model not only for Iraq but also for the rest of the Middle East, particularly with regard to adherence to human rights principles, including women's rights and freedom of expression. The study proposes that the Kurds should continue to have full and equal participation in the reconstruction of Iraq. The study also details a range of human rights policies to the Occupying Powers, the international community and the Kurds themselves. The publication highlights the international initiatives possible to ensure the economic and social development of Iraqi Kurdistan, including equitable distribution of the revenues of oil and the Oil-for-Food Programme.

This publication provides a scholarly analysis of the urgent and as of yet unanswered question: what is to be the future of the Iraqi Kurdistan bearing in mind what was achieved after the First Gulf War in 1992? In BHRC's view, unless the rule of law is quickly established throughout post-war Iraq, the future of the whole region remains bleak.

The research and writing of this publication was undertaken by Kerim Yildiz, Executive Director of the Kurdish Human Rights Project. The advice and assistance of KHRP staff members and other experts is gratefully acknowledged, including that of Tom Blass, freelance journalist and researcher, Clodaghmuire Callinan and Rochelle Harris. This publication was made possible by the financial support of the Sigrid Rausing Trust.

Mark Muller
Vice President,
Bar Human Rights Committee of England and Wales

Map of the area inhabited by Kurds

Introduction

Since the downfall of Saddam Hussein's regime in 2003, the Kurds of Iraqi Kurdistan have made significant achievements in securing their rights, perhaps signalling a milestone towards a new culture of human rights in the Middle East. Nonetheless, the Kurds have faced enduring hardship over the past century, including military attacks, economic embargoes, human rights violations and the destruction of their native regions.

Some of the landmarks in the history of Iraqi Kurdistan – perhaps most notably the chemical and gas attacks at Halabja, the 1991 uprising and the subsequent flight of over 2 million refugees – have been so egregious as to have become imprinted on the consciousness, and sometimes conscience, of the outside world. Other events are less well known and less well understood: such as US and Iranian involvement in Iraqi Kurdistan in the 1970s, Turkish intervention, the nascent democracy of the autonomous area and the double embargo effect of Saddam Hussein's economic siege and United Nations (UN) sanctions. This publication is intended to provide an outline of some of the issues affecting the Kurds in Iraq. It provides a brief exploration of past history's effect on the present, and of how both the Kurds and the international community may avoid repeating previous mistakes, laying the foundations for an autonomous region committed to a pluralistic democracy and human rights.

There are no exact ethnological or linguistic criteria by which the Kurds can be defined. There are a number of Kurdish dialects. There is no single religion that binds them, and they are to be found in numerous countries. Paraphrasing Benedict Anderson, one might say that Kurds are those that believe themselves to be so.[1] Kurdish identity, however, is not monolithic. While some Kurds believe passionately in the existence of a pan-Kurdish nation, others are bound more closely to other identities; tribal, national or religious.

Standing at the crossroads of so many powerful nations, the Kurds have always, inadvertently or otherwise, been subject to or caught up in the vicissitudes of their allegiances and altercations. This publication looks at the ways in which the Kurds in Iraqi Kurdistan have been subjected to sustained violence and oppression by several Iraqi regimes. This is not unique to Iraq. In Turkey, as in Iran, Syria

1

and the former Soviet Union, Kurds have been the victims of village destructions and evacuations, killings, torture, rape in custody, arbitrary detentions, censorship and other human rights violations. On several occasions, governments – the outlooks of which are otherwise opposed – have sought to collaborate in their efforts to suppress the Kurds.

Behind the pattern of victimisation lies the fear of the Kurds breaking away from the states in which they live to create their own nation. The dream of an independent Kurdistan is not universally perceived in the same way. Some regard it as a dream, perhaps realisable in generations to come, but unfeasible for the moment. Others regard the right to self-determination as a fundamental right guaranteed *inter alia* by the UN Charter. It is little surprise that anti-secessionist measures taken by some states have had a tendency to alienate Kurds, fuelling a radicalism which might not otherwise carry itself with such fervour.

This publication was written with the purpose of introducing the Kurds to a readership in some cases newly wakened to their existence by media reports arising out of the US-led invasion of Iraq. Much of the research was undertaken in London.

In August 2003, a KHRP fact-finding mission to Iraqi Kurdistan arrived soon after the bombing of the UN building in Baghdad, which had severely dented the morale of international agencies and non-governmental organisations (NGOs).[2] Many expatriate staff were leaving or had left Iraq. Still others were arriving in the comparatively safe north from the nation's capital. The sense of post-liberation jubilation was muted. The Kurds living above the 'green line' separating 'Saddam' Iraq from 'Kurdish' Iraq had been 'free', with all the qualifications and hardships that that entailed for over ten years. The end of the war had brought new forms of relief. Many were visiting family members in Mosul and Kirkuk for the first time in years. As one man in Erbil described, 'For twelve years we've lived with Saddam's guns trained on us just across the border; just knowing they've gone means we can breathe more easily.'[3]

The end of Saddam's rule also brought with it disappointments. Many families still clung to the hope that when the Ba'athists fell, mothers, fathers, children and siblings that had disappeared years before would reappear.[4] With the passage of time and the continuing discovery of mass graves around the country, those hopes are fading and some are grieving for the second time. Others, living in impoverished conditions and without access to the wealth and luxuries visible in bazaars and shops, decry the inability of the international community and of their own government to improve their condition overnight.

The political climate, and its tensions created by the rights or wrongs of the war, has constituted an interesting backdrop against which to write about the Kurds in Iraq. The question as to whether war was 'justified' created unlikely allies and unlikely foes. The arguments for and against seemed to be at odds with any clearly definable ideological lines. The new front created in the battle for ideas concerns the respective roles of the UN and the US-led administration. In all these issues, the Iraqi Kurds sided more closely with the hawks of the US than the doves of 'Old Europe' or the UN. Their perspective did not necessarily vindicate the decision to go to war. Only time will tell what effect the end of Ba'athism has had on Iraq. Many Kurds are disenchanted with the provisions of multilateralism, being better disposed toward any potential ally promising action over deliberation. Kurds will admit that circumstance has often forced them into choosing their friends before fully considering the wisdom of having done so. For the first time in their history, however, the Kurds may have backed the winning horse.

Part I
The Past

1
The Kurds

'KURDS' AND 'KURDISTAN'

The Kurds are native inhabitants of their land and as such there are no strict 'beginnings' for Kurdish history and origins.[1] In modern times, Kurds as an ethnic group are the end product of thousands of years of evolution stemming from tribes such as the Guti, Kurti, Mede, Mard, Carduchi, Gordyene, Adianbene, Zila and Khaldi,[2] and the migration of Indo-European tribes to the Zagros mountain region some 4,000 years ago.[3] The Kurds are similar to the Highland Scots in that they have a clan history, with over 800 tribes in Kurdistan.[4] At the time of the Arab conquest of Mesopotamia in the seventh century AD, the name 'Kurd' was used to describe these nomadic people who lived in this region.

The term 'Kurdistan', meaning 'the land of the Kurds', first appeared in the twelfth century when the Turkish Seljuk prince Saandjar created a province with that name. This province roughly coincides with the area of Kurdistan (Kordestan) situated in modern Iran. It was not until the sixteenth century, however, that the phrase 'Kurdistan' came into common usage to denote a system of Kurdish fiefs generally, and not just the Saandjar-created province. The range of land which Kurdistan encompasses has fluctuated historically, but it was and remains predominantly the geographical region that spreads across the mountainous area where the borders of Iraq, Iran, Syria and Turkey meet. Claims as to the exact dimensions of Kurdistan vary but its backbone is the Taurus and Zagros mountain chains, and it stretches down to the Mesopotamian plain in the south and, in the north and north-east, up to the steppes and plateaus of what was Armenian Anatolia. The small Kurdish-populated areas just inside the Armenian and Azerbaijani borders with Turkey and Iran respectively are sometimes included as part of Kurdistan depending on the commentator. These areas have, however, been known as 'Red Kurdistan'. Smaller minority communities, including Christians, Turcomans, Assyrians and Armenians, also inhabit Kurdistan as a whole.

Although Kurdistan has appeared on some maps since the sixteenth century, it is clear that it should be more than a geographical term as it also refers to a human culture, which exists in that land.[5] Kurdistan has no fixed borders, and claims to the territory that it comprises vary between different organisations, groups and individuals. No map of Kurdistan can be drawn without contention as, for all practical purposes, Turkey has always denied Kurdistan's existence, while Iran and Iraq remain reluctant to acknowledge that it is as extensive as many Kurds purport, and Syria denies that it extends into its territory.[6]

LANGUAGE

The Kurds do not have a single common language but speak a number of different dialects. The biggest group, as regards the number of people who speak it, is called 'Kurmanji'. This dialect is spoken by Kurds living in Turkey, Syria and the former USSR; it is also spoken by Kurds living in the northern part of Iran and down to the Greater Zab river in Iraq.[7] The other chief dialect is Sorani (or Kurdi), which is spoken by Iraqi Kurds living south of the Greater Zab and by Iranian Kurds living in the Kordestan province. A speaker of one of these dialects can usually understand a speaker of the other, although someone from a remote area may find it difficult. Sub-dialects include Kirmanshahi, Leki, Gurani and Zaza. Some of these sub-dialects are not easily learnt or understood by fellow Kurds. As is the case with the Irish language and most minority languages, the official languages spoken around Kurds influence Kurdish modern dialects.[8] Thus, Kurdish in Turkey contains a large number of Turkish words and Kurdish in Iraq contains an overlay of Arabic words.[9]

RELIGION

The Kurds are not homogeneous religiously. The majority of Kurds are Sunni Muslims, who were converted between the twelfth and sixteenth centuries, and adhere to the Shafi'i school rather than the Hanafi school which was the official religion of the Ottoman Empire. There are a number of other different religious affiliations among the Kurds, however, and they include Jews; Christians; Alevis, who follow an unorthodox form of Shi'ism; adherents to the 'established' faith of Iran – Ithna'asheri Shi'i Islam; the Ahl-i Haqq (People of Truth), a small sect found in the south and south-east of Kurdistan; and Yazidis.[10]

POPULATION

There are no official population figures for Kurds but it is accepted that they are the largest ethnic group without a state in the world. Estimated figures indicate that the highest numbers of Kurds are to be found in Turkey, but it is in Iraq where they constitute the largest proportion of the overall population. There are believed to be over 15 million Kurds in Turkey (20 per cent of the population); 4 million in Iraq (25 per cent of the population); 7 million in Iran (15 per cent of the population); over 1 million in Syria (9 per cent of the population); 75,000 in Armenia (1.8 per cent of the population; and 200,000 in Azerbaijan (2.8 per cent of the population). These estimates are conservative but indicate that the Kurds are currently the fourth largest ethnic group in the Middle East.

The absence of reliable figures is in part due to the lack of censuses in Syria, Turkey, Iraq and Iran that recognise ethnic identity as a legitimate category of registration. It has suited the countries inhabited by the Kurds to manipulate and downplay the size of their Kurdish communities in order to prevent them from becoming politically powerful.

TOPOGRAPHY OF KURDISTAN

The precipitation in Kurdistan has meant that the area is agriculturally rich and many Kurds are engaged in livestock farming and agricultural production. Tobacco is the main cash crop, as well as cotton and grain in some areas. Other products, such as fruit and vegetables, are mainly for domestic consumption. Once richly forested, the area has suffered from widespread deforestation, which has devastated timber production and caused environmental damage. Oil is also concentrated in the Kurdish regions. There have been regular disputes over its exploitation and revenues from oil have been one of the major causes of conflict between the Kurds and the ruling governments in the region. Other minerals found in the area include chrome, copper, iron, coal and lignite. Water is yet another element that is rich in Kurdistan, with both the Euphrates and Tigris rivers running through it. However, the Kurds do not control the flow of the rivers. There has been little effort made towards industrial development in the Kurdish areas, as economic underdevelopment is a convenient method for the governments in the region of keeping the Kurds under control.

2
The Treaty of Sèvres and the Creation of Iraq[1]

Historically, the Kurds have enjoyed a considerable degree of semi-autonomy under the various regional powers seeking to exercise territorial control over the lands inhabited by Kurdish tribes. Indeed from the sixteenth century the Persian and Ottoman Empires allowed Kurdish autonomy in order to maintain peace on their open borders.

The first opportunity for the Kurds to establish an independent state came with the collapse of the Ottoman Empire and the end of the First World War. In the aftermath of the First World War there was a new preoccupation with the situation of minority groups – albeit driven primarily by strategic political considerations rather than concern for individual and group protection. In his Fourteen Point Programme for World Peace, President Wilson included the statement that the non-Turkish minorities of the Ottoman Empire should be 'assured of an absolute unmolested opportunity of autonomous development'.[2]

This sentiment had champions within each of the great powers – Britain, France and the US – as it did within those 'nationalities' themselves. But there were other aspects to consider, such as the break-up of the Ottoman Empire, the threat posed by the nascent Soviet Union, the status of the Catholic Armenian population, and Britain's desire to preserve stability in and around its colonial possessions. The Kurds' right to self-determination was understood by the British, but qualified by the unsubstantiated belief that a Kurdish leader could not be found that would sacrifice either his own or tribal interest for the greater purpose of the Kurdish nation. Indeed Britain was not even sure that a widespread and cohesive Kurdish identity transcending tribal or other loyalties even existed. Turkey, fearful of further dismantlement of its empire, played on British fears.[3]

Notwithstanding these reservations, the Treaty of Sèvres, signed by the Allied Powers and the Ottoman government in 1920, envisaged an independent Kurdish state. Article 62 of the Treaty provided that a Commission appointed by the French, Italians and British would, within six months of the treaty entering into force, draft a scheme of local autonomy for the Kurdish areas lying east of the Euphrates, south of Armenia and north of Syria and Mesopotamia – with safeguards for other minorities within these areas. Article 64 further provided that if, after one year of the implementation of the treaty, the majority of the Kurdish population in this area called for independence, then subject to recommendation from the Council of the League of Nations, Turkey should agree to renounce all rights to the area. The final sentence of Article 64 referred to the Kurds living in Mosul and stated that, 'If and when the said renunciation is made, no objection shall be raised by the main Allied powers should the Kurds living in that part of Kurdistan at present included in the vilayet of Mosul[4] seek to become citizens of the newly independent Kurdish state.'

This last section of Article 64 referred to the fact that the British were appointed by the League of Nations as the mandate authority over the Ottoman provinces of Mesopotamia (which included Mosul) the same year that the ill-fated Treaty of Sèvres was signed. Initially, British policy appeared to be to keep the Kurdish area separate and autonomous. At the 1921 Cairo Conference, at which a future Arab state of Iraq was discussed, a memorandum from the British government's Middle East Department stated 'We are strongly of the opinion that purely Kurdish areas should not be included in the Arab state of Mesopotamia, but that the principles of Kurdish unity and nationality should be promoted as far as possible by H.M.G.'[5] Winston Churchill, then heading the Colonial Office, predicted that an Arab leader in Iraq 'would ignore the Kurdish sentiment and oppress the Kurdish minority'[6] and it was decided to keep Kurdistan under separate administration headed by a British High Commissioner.[7] The British did in fact carry out a referendum in Mosul in 1921 but based the franchise on property ownership. They then turned the extremely poor poll into a pretext for annexation.[8]

The High Commissioner in Iraq, Sir Percy Cox, had long been convinced of the desirability of incorporating the Kurdish areas into an eventual Arab state. He was supported by the new Arab King of Iraq, Emir Faisal, brought in by the British and anxious to consolidate his fragile support and authority. Cox continued to press the need for incorporation and fuelled by fears of renewed Turkish claims on the area, Churchill capitulated in October 1921. He agreed that the Kurdish areas should be included in Iraq and should participate in the National Assembly, although still on condition of local autonomy.

Progress towards the emergence of Iraq as an independent state was reflected the following year when the 1922 Treaty of Alliance put Anglo-Iraqi relations on a treaty basis. Yet it still appeared that the British might honour their commitment to Kurdish autonomy when they issued a Joint Declaration with the Iraqi government, communicated to the League of Nations in December 1922, recognising the right of the Kurds to form a government within the borders of Iraq.

During this period, the Treaty of Sèvres was not implemented. The treaty was a humiliation for Turkey, which faced chaos and deprivation in the aftermath of war. Mustafa Kemal, the founder of the Turkish Republic, repudiated its provisions and waged a war of national independence. After this conflict, the adversaries negotiated a new accord to settle issues of sovereignty, claims, rights and the like. Kurdish leaders petitioned the League of Nations and Britain for recognition of Kurdish autonomy during negotiations on the 1923 Treaty of Lausanne. However, this instrument completely ignored the claims of the Kurds to any form of independent status and carved up Kurdistan, only recognising the protection of the rights of religious minorities. The area subject to the Treaty of Sèvres was restored to Turkish sovereignty; the rest was divided between Iran and the new state of Iraq.[9]

The League of Nations did, however, reinforce Kurdish claims to autonomy and their need for special protection in 1924. In the context of settling the border between Turkey and Iraq, the League of Nations set up an International Commission of Inquiry that went to Mosul in 1925. It found that five-eighths of the population of the disputed territory was Kurdish. It indicated that this pointed towards an independent state on the basis of ethnicity alone, although it noted that those living north of the Greater Zab were more closely connected with the Kurds of Turkey and those living south had more in common with the Persian Kurds. The Commission finally recommended that the disputed territory of Mosul remain within Iraq. It did, however, express great concern about the stability of Iraq and considered that guidance and protection in the form of a League mandate ought to be maintained for a substantial period of time to enable the consolidation and development of the state. The Commission's recommendation to leave Mosul within Iraq appeared to be predicated on the continuation of the mandate system, since it noted that Turkish sovereignty over Mosul would be preferable to granting it to a new state of Iraq not yet ready for independence.

The League accepted the Commission's recommendation against partition of the area but decided in favour of attaching Mosul to Iraq. However, this was on condition that Mosul remained under the League mandate for 25 years, and that due consideration was given to conferring responsibility for local administration, the justice system and education on Kurdish officials, and having Kurdish as the official language. The British, as the mandate authority, were invited to report to the League on the administration of Mosul, the promulgation of a form of autonomy and recognition of the rights of the Kurds. The 1922 Alliance Treaty was accordingly amended to secure the British mandate for 25 years or until Iraq's admission as a member of the League, whichever was sooner.

The only concrete step towards British fulfilment of the obligations set out in the League's resolution was a 1926 Local Languages Law, allowing Kurds in Erbil and Sulaimaniya to have primary education and to print books in their own language. However, when various Kurdish cultural societies were formed in 1926 and 1927, which took an increasingly political stance, they were dismantled by police operations conducted by the British.

During this time the whole of Iraqi Kurdistan was still refusing to accept an Arab administration and the British were repeatedly involved in measures to suppress opposition and unrest. The British brought Sheikh Mahmud[10] back to Sulaimaniya in 1922 hoping that he would repel any Turkish aggressive moves on the area. Sheikh Mahmud, however, not only declared himself 'King of Kurdistan' and formed an embryonic administration but also attempted to play off Turkey and Britain against each other. The British called for his surrender and launched an offensive in 1923 to prevent him joining forces with the Turks, following which he was forced to flee. His attempts to regain power led to RAF bombing raids. A year later, further unrest in Mosul after legislative elections in 1924 was put down with more bombing raids and led to a resumption of British occupation in Sulaimaniya.

In 1930 another Anglo-Iraq Treaty of Alliance was signed, aimed at ending the British mandate and regulating future British relations with Iraq. The Treaty made no mention of the Kurds, still less did it do anything to secure Kurdish autonomy or basic rights. Leaders in Sulaimaniya sent petitions to the League, recalling its 1925 decision, but these were ignored. Unrest flared again; in September 1930 troops fired directly into protesting crowds in Sulaimaniya, killing dozens of people. Sheikh Mahmud, who was again leading the protests, was severely defeated and forced to surrender to the Baghdad government. He was placed under house arrest and kept there for more than 20 years until his death in 1956.[11]

Iraq attained its independence from Britain in 1932. Iraq's membership of the League of Nations was, however, conditioned on its acceptance of international obligations to protect the civil and political rights of the Kurds and their rights as a minority group. These provisions were expressed to constitute internationally supervised obligations and fundamental laws of Iraq, which could not be undermined by any subsequent laws, regulations, or official action. In practice, the Hashemite monarchy under King Faisal only eroded the protections that Britain had intended for the Kurds. Key legislation, drafted with the aim of ensuring language rights, was implemented half-heartedly or not at all. Faisal's death in 1933 was thought to offer the Kurds a new chance to ameliorate the position in which they now found themselves.

Subsequent history, however, is one of conflict, betrayal and dashed promises. Each of the regime changes punctuating Iraqi governance over the course of the past eight decades has had a significant and violent effect on the fate of both the Kurds and much of the rest of the Iraqi population.

3
The Kurds Under Barzani

REVOLTS

The Iraqi government was beset by factionalism and loss of coherent leadership following King Faisal's death. King Ghazi succeeded him but with the weakness of the central government, naturally new revolts occurred.

By 1935 the Kurds were emboldened enough for Kurdish chiefs to challenge the government on its failure to uphold its obligations under the Declaration. Amongst other demands were the official use of Kurdish language in Kurdish areas, representation in the National Assembly, and a fair share of the nation's resources. But the Kurdish chiefs were unsuccessful. The new government chose not to support the Kurds.

In October 1936, General Bakr Sidgi staged a coup in Iraq. He was of Kurdish origin but not a Kurdish nationalist and had been a commander of the northern region army units during the several years of revolts. General Sidgi was in alliance with the Ahali Group political faction and King Ghazi accepted the coup. In August 1937, however, General Sidgi was assassinated. The Mosul command of the armed forces then turned on the military-led government and toppled Iraq's first government installed by coup, by yet another coup. A further coup in 1938 led to another Ottoman officer becoming Prime Minister.

In 1939, King Ghazi was killed in an automobile accident. His son Faisal II became King although he was only four years old. When Britain went to war with Germany in 1940, the Iraqi regime entered into diplomatic relations with Germany and Italy. Britain wanted to use bases in Iraq to launch a Russian front but when they arrived in Basra the pro-Axis government ordered the RAF to stop all their flights. In response, British aircraft began targeting Iraqi positions, which resulted in their swift defeat.

THE EMERGENCE OF A KURDISH LEADER

The most important occurrence from a Kurdish perspective in this intervening period between Iraq's independence and the revolution

of 1958 was the emergence of a powerful and charismatic political
leader, Mullah Mustafa Barzani. He had started his political life by
organising local revolts in his own Barzan region, for which he was
subsequently exiled to the city of Sulaimaniya. There he was held
under house arrest until his escape in 1943. A new Kurdish revolt
broke out in 1943 which lasted until 1945, following which Barzani
was forced to flee to Iran. His arrival in Iran coincided with the
creation of the Kurdish 'Mahabad Republic' in the north.

This bold attempt at nationhood in Iran was only made possible
by support from the Soviet Union as it controlled the north of Iran
during the Second World War. With the end of the war however,
and the beginning of the Cold War, the Soviet Union was asked by
the western powers to withdraw from Iran. The Kremlin, mindful
of maintaining the composure of the global apple-cart, complied.
Despite its ephemeral span, the 'Mahabad Republic' was significant
for numerous reasons. It was here that the Kurdish Democratic Party
(KDP) was formed in 1945. It was here, also, that a schism emerged
leading to the creation of the Iraqi KDP (with Barzani as president)
in addition to the Iranian KDP (PDKI).

Barzani fled Iran for the Soviet Union in 1947, as following the
Soviet withdrawal he was unsuccessful in coming to terms with an
Iranian government that was determined to show its muscle in the
north-west of the country. There he remained until the overthrow
of the Hashemite monarchy in Iraq by General 'Abd al-Karim Qasim
and his group of Free Officers in 1958.

AFTERMATH OF THE 1958 REVOLUTION

The 1958 revolution was genuinely popular among all sections of
Iraqi society. Among the Kurds it was believed that a new era of
Kurdish–Arab understanding had been established. Barzani and
his associates were allowed to return from exile. A Kurd, Khalid
Naqshabandi, was appointed to a three-man 'sovereignty council',
indicating goodwill towards Kurdish sentiment. But good relations
were short-lived. It became apparent that the Free Officers would
never tolerate Kurdish autonomy in any form. In addition, splits
were apparent within Kurdish opinion – in part, between those that
supported the government, and those, like Barzani, who did not.
Barzani's Kurdish militia, the *peshmerga*,[1] occupied the north of Iraq
from Zakho to the Iranian border. The government responded with

a prolonged but futile bombing campaign, which in one form or another, continued until 1975.

THE BA'ATH REGIMES

In February 1963 the regime of General Qasim was brought to an end by a coup of the Ba'ath party; a new Arabic ideology influenced Iraq, which was socialist and secular in spirit. Within weeks of the Ba'aths seizing power, thousands of Iraqis were killed, tortured or imprisoned as the party attempted to eradicate all remnants of the previous regime and to crush even the possibility of dissent. Once again, the Kurds harboured the aspiration that the new government would prove sympathetic to Kurdish autonomy but the reverse proved true. The KDP did agree to a ceasefire and talks began on Kurdish autonomy. However, the talks collapsed as the Kurds insisted on including Kirkuk and Mosul in the Kurdish autonomous region. With the failure of these talks, the Ba'ath regime initiated a policy of crushing the Kurds through military might and began an 'Arabisation'[2] process that continued until the end of the Ba'athist regime in 2003.

In November 1963, infighting and confusion within the Ba'ath party resulted in the takeover of the Iraqi government by 'Abd al-Salam 'Arif.[3] Within months, 'Arif had negotiated a peace agreement with Barzani leading to a lull in the conflict.

'Arif died early in 1966, to be succeeded by his brother, al-Bazzaz. In June 1966, al-Bazzaz made a Declaration, which clearly recognised the binational (Kurdish/Arab) character of the Iraqi state, and implied regional autonomy as long as it did not undermine Iraqi unity. This, on paper, was an important step for Barzani and the Kurds. However, the reality was that al-Bazzaz did not have the support of his officers, and he fell from power soon after signing the agreement. A military stalemate ensued, and Barzani consolidated his power base until the Ba'ath party seized power again in July 1968.

Recent Kurdish claims to autonomy have never been in any doubt. It was Saddam Hussein that negotiated and then imposed the autonomy agreements of the 1970s.

THE MARCH MANIFESTO OF 1970

That the Kurds as a group have their own linguistic and cultural needs was recognised at the inception of Iraq, and reconfirmed in the Constitution of 1958. Autonomy for Iraqi Kurds as a part of Iraq's political and constitutional equation dates back at least to the March Manifesto of 1970, and has, on paper, been confirmed on numerous occasions since. Had it been adopted, it is possible that many of the Kurds' subsequent conflicts with the central government might have been avoided. While the manifesto stops short of describing Iraq in federal terms, a substantial proportion of its provisions are still regarded by the Kurdish political parties as a blueprint within any new constitutional framework yet to be drawn up.

The March Manifesto was drafted in the wake of the Ba'athists taking power in 1968, as it attempted to consolidate its grip on civil, political and military power within the nation. The Iraqi Communist Party (ICP), while outlawed, still commanded considerable power. Iraq also faced external threats posed by other regional powers, notably Israel and Iran, and indirectly by the US through the agency of the Shah of Iran. A 'solution' to the Kurdish problem was desirable for the Ba'athists to alleviate pressure from the north. In March 1969, the KDP had made a daring attack on Iraqi Petroleum Corporation installations in Kirkuk, highlighting the oilfield's vulnerability and the military capability of Barzani and his followers.[4] That the Kurds were armed by the Iranians heightened the Ba'ath party's desire for conciliation.

The manifesto (negotiated by Saddam Hussein and by Mahmud 'Uthman on behalf of the KDP) was announced on 11 March 1970. On the face of it almost all of Barzani's demands were met; Kurdish, alongside Arabic, was to be an official language in areas where the majority of the population was Kurdish, and taught throughout Iraq as a second language; Kurds would participate fully in government, including senior army and cabinet posts; Kurdish education and culture would be reinforced and all officials in Kurdish areas would be Kurds, or speak Kurdish; Kurds would be free to establish student, youth, women's, and teachers' organisations; funds would be set aside for the development of Kurdistan; pensions would be provided to the families of *peshmerga* killed in battle; agrarian reform (appertaining to ownership of farmland) would be implemented; a Kurd would be one of the vice-presidents of Iraq; and finally, there would be unification of Kurdish majority areas as one self-governing unit.

Had the manifesto been implemented, principal officials, up to the level of Governor, including district officers and chiefs of police and security, would have been Kurdish or Kurdish-speaking. The region was to receive extra investment from Baghdad, in the form of an economic development plan undertaken with regard for Kurdish underdevelopment, extending to relief and assistance of the needy and unemployed. In addition there would be official promotion and promulgation of Kurdish literary, artistic and cultural endeavours, a Kurdish press and a television station, as well as an amnesty for those who had fought against the state from the Kurdish areas.

It is arguable as to whether there was any sincerity on behalf of Baghdad. Kurdish leaders have reportedly declared their foreknowledge that it was little more than a ruse, but a ruse that could not be refused. Nonetheless, preliminary steps taken by the Ba'athists were encouraging. A taskforce consisting of four Kurds and four Arabs was established, and charged with working out the implementation of the manifesto. KDP apparatchiks were appointed to the governorships of Sulaimaniya, Erbil and Dohuk (the latter a new Kurdish governorate, created in the effort to mollify the Kurds). The Interim Constitution was amended so as to state that 'The Iraqi people are composed of two principal nationalisms: The Arab Nationalism and the Kurdish Nationalism.'[5] Villages were rebuilt and *peshmerga* were even paid by the government to act as border guards.

Over the course of the following three years it became clear that Saddam Hussein lacked the will to implement the manifesto. A number of reasons lay behind the failure; Barzani was subject to several failed assassination attempts, possibly government-backed; and the Kurds' choice of vice-candidate, Habib Karim, was rejected by Baghdad. The key sticking point, however, was the failure to resolve the status of Kirkuk. In its drafting, the manifesto neatly sidestepped the issue as to whether the city of Kirkuk and its surrounding oilfield would fit into the autonomous region; instead, it provided for the 'unification of areas with a majority as a self-governing unit'.[6] The government agreed to demarcate the border between the two regions by virtue of population – where a Kurdish population was in the majority, it would be included. This was to be decided by a census.[7]

Barzani accused Saddam of deliberately attempting to alter the demography of the region, bringing in Arab settlers from the south and north of the country. By 1973, clashes had started to break out between the two sides once again, despite continued negotiations.

Four years after the March Manifesto, Saddam Hussein imposed his own Autonomy Law. By this time, Barzani was looking at the opportunities offered by siding with the Iranians.

THE 1974 AUTONOMY LAW[8]

Saddam Hussein gave Barzani two weeks to accept the Law for Autonomy in the Area of Kurdistan (Act No. 33 of 1974). Barzani refused and bitter fighting followed. In some respects the Law appeared almost reasonable. It purported to establish Kurdistan as a self-governing region that had considerable authority over its own social and economic affairs. It also fleshed out in detail the area's administrative and legislative structures. The region was to be defined in accordance with the 1970 Agreement and the 1957 census records, in the absence of a more up-to-date head-count. Nonetheless, it fell far short of Barzani's demands. It did not cede Kirkuk, and more critically, it imposed a vastly more central government control over the region than was envisaged by the March Manifesto.

Act No. 33 of 1974 described the autonomous region as an integral administrative unit with juridical personality and autonomy within the Republic of Iraq, with Erbil as its metropolitan centre. Kurdish and Arabic were to be the official languages, and languages of education. The region was to have its own budget and financial resources derived from local taxation. A Legislative Council, envisaged as an elected legislature, was established, as was an appointed administrative body, the Executive Council. Executive Council members would hold ministerial rank and report directly to the Council of Ministers.

Under the Autonomy Law, the Legislative Council was empowered to adopt decisions relating to the development of the area and promotion of its local, social, cultural and economic aspects. Developments of culture, national characteristics and traditions, and functioning of local departments, institutions and administrative bodies, were also under the Legislative Council's auspices. It was tasked with the ratification of plans and programmes of the Executive Council on economic and social matters, and on development, education and health. It also maintained oversight and control over financial issues.

Most of the main administrative functions of government came under the control of the Executive Council, including education and higher education, works and housing, agriculture and agrarian reform, internal affairs, transport and communications, culture and youth, municipalities and summer resorts, social affairs, and state property. But the Council's responsibility was more restricted with regard to other issues, including matters relating to the administration of justice, security and public order, and the appointment of Kurdish or Kurdish-speaking officials for the Autonomous Area.

Article 1 provided that Kurdistan would enjoy autonomy as an integral unit within the framework of Iraq. Kurdistan was to be defined by the existence of a majority according to the 1957 census; a census that Barzani rejected. Erbil was designated as its metropolitan centre.

Article 13 stated that, 'The President of the Republic shall appoint a member of the Legislative Council to form an Executive Council. The President of the Republic may [sic] dismiss the chairman of the executive council at any time, in which case the Executive Council shall be dissolved.'

Article 17 ensured that state apparatus was firmly embedded into the region: 'Police, security and nationality formations in the area shall be attached to their directorates general at the Ministry of Interior, and their staff subject to the laws and instructions applied in the Republic of Iraq.' Article 19 added, 'Supervision of the legality of the decisions of the autonomous bodies shall be exercised by the Supreme Court of Appeal of Iraq.'

The autonomous region itself (*mintaqat al-hukm al-dhati*) accounted for less than half of the total area of Iraqi Kurdistan. Legal limitations substantially qualified autonomy; central authorities were authorised to give the local administration 'general guidance', and a minister of the state was authorised to attend all meetings of the so-called autonomous bodies. The validity of any decision by the autonomous authorities could be contested by the Minister of Justice, and if contested, the decision could be suspended by a committee of the Iraqi Court of Cassation. In appearance, none of these are necessarily draconian but in the absence of any effective challenge, or check on executive authority, the presidential will could ultimately override any decision.

Subsequent amendments to the law further undermined 'autonomy' by introducing restrictions on who could stand for election to the Legislative Council. A law introduced in 1986 stipulated that candidates must 'believe in the leading role of the Arab Ba'ath Socialist Party and in the principles and aims of the glorious revolution of 17–30 July 1968 and should have played a notable role in the implementation of those principles and aims'. Candidate lists needed the approval of central government – ensuring that the only eventual members of the council were sympathetic to Saddam Hussein and the Ba'ath party. Elections for the Legislative

Council were held throughout the 1980s. Yet even by the time of the government's 1992 withdrawal from the north, it appears that the Executive and Legislative councils were barely functioning if at all.

US AND IRANIAN INVOLVEMENT
IN KURDISH–IRAQI RELATIONS: 1970–75

Barzani had enjoyed the backing of the Soviet Union up until the signing of a friendship pact between Moscow and Baghdad in 1972, by which time Barzani began to shift his trust away from the Russians to the opposite ideological pole. The extent to which other regional players dictated the action of Barzani throughout the 1970s should not be understated. Arguably, Barzani would not have continued his armed struggle against the seemingly insurmountable Iraqi military had it not been for his belief that the US and Iran genuinely supported Kurdish autonomy. In reality, it became clear that Iran and the US used the Kurds as vehicles for their own regional designs. Being so vulnerable, exploitation by the US and the Shah of pre-Revolutionary Iran was inevitable.[9]

Since 1937, Iran had felt humiliated by restrictions on its right to use the Shatt al-'Arab waterway connecting the Persian Gulf to the Iranian port of Abadan and the Iraqi port of Basra. Iran under the Shah was Iraq's major rival, and the Shah found that backing the Kurds financially and militarily was a useful means of putting pressure on Baghdad. Both the US and Iran, in addition, were concerned by Baghdad's increasingly close relationship with Moscow. By 1972 the new relationship between Barzani and Baghdad forged by the March Manifesto of 1970 had effectively broken down. The parties continued to fight, although negotiations continued over Kirkuk, the census and other outstanding sticking points.

The US became increasingly interested in Iraqi affairs after the signing of the friendship pact with the Soviet Union in April 1972. The nationalisation of Iraq's oil facilities in June 1972 also provoked the Shah of Iran into providing the Kurds with increased military and financial aid.

Barzani's confidence was buoyed by the support that he received not only from the Shah, but from the CIA with the backing of Henry Kissinger. Previously, the US's respect for Iraqi territorial integrity, and for the borders of all the nations in which Kurds lived, had dissuaded it from recognising or supporting the Kurds in any capacity. But in 1972, US desires to maintain the Shah's allegiance, not just in the

Middle East but in relation to US policy in south-east Asia, extended to assistance in underwriting the Kurds' war against Baghdad. As Barzani's relations with the Iranians had not always been fruitful, the Shah cajoled the US to make direct contact with the Kurds. Barzani was encouraged by US assurances that the Shah would continue to back the Kurds until they had achieved their own political objectives. In a newspaper interview in 1973, Barzani declared, 'We do not trust the Shah ... I trust America. America is too great a power to betray the Kurds.'[10]

When Barzani refused to accept the terms of the 1974 Autonomy Law it drew both sides into fighting. Barzani's forces numbered some 60,000 *peshmerga*, and the same number again of irregular fighters, bolstered by Iranian-provided artillery and antitank missiles. Iraqi forces numbered 90,000 men, 1,200 tanks and armoured cars, and 200 aircraft.[11] More than 100,000 refugees fled to camps across the border with Iran. By now Barzani was aware that he was too reliant on Tehran's support and he was fearful that should an agreement be reached between Iran and Iraq it would be disastrous for the Kurds. Barzani lobbied Washington repeatedly for assistance and for further reassurance that he would not be let down. Washington, however, was not forthcoming. The Algiers Agreement proved either Barzani's naivety or his overestimation of Washington's influence over Tehran.

THE ALGIERS AGREEMENT OF 1975 AND ITS AFTERMATH

During this time, a full-scale conflict between Iran and Iraq directly over border and water rights was only averted by negotiations culminating, in early 1975, in a peace agreement signed at a meeting of the Organization of Petroleum Exporting Countries (OPEC) in Algiers. In return for dropping support for the Kurds, the Shah was to gain sovereignty over half of the disputed waterway. In addition Iraq would abandon its claim to Khuzistan, one of Iran's oil-rich regions. Within 48 hours, Iran withdrew its military support of the Kurds. A two-week ceasefire negotiated by the Iranians on behalf of the Kurds was not adhered to and Kurds fled across the border in groups of tens of thousands. The Iraqi military began a vicious campaign of reprisal; killing thousands, not only *peshmerga* but also civilians. The Iraqi army created a security zone in the border areas between the Kurdish region and Turkey, Syria and Iran, 600 miles long. This resulted in the destruction of an estimated 1,500 villages.

Barzani was defeated, both militarily and emotionally. The mantle of his leadership was passed to his son, Massoud Barzani.

The restored peace between the powers left the Kurds exposed and without a sponsor. Unable to continue armed conflict, Barzani's fighters were left with a battered infrastructure, in considerable disarray. The 'autonomous region' accounted for only half of the Kurdish-populated area and up to 300,000 Kurds were resettled, often to Arab provinces far from the north. Arabs occupied the destroyed Kurdish villages and boundaries were redrawn to ensure that previously Kurdish provinces now had Arab majorities.

In June 1975, a rival focus for Kurdish aspirations emerged, the Patriotic Union of Kurdistan (PUK), founded in Damascus, and headed then, as now, by Jalal Talabani.

The period following, up to and including the span of the Iran–Iraq War, was both confused and confusing. Initially, Saddam Hussein attempted to build up the Kurdish region economically, in part an attempt to fend off new calls for a separatist armed struggle. At the same time, however, he tried to impose his Executive and Regional Councils on the region. Both the KDP and PUK sought backing from outside regional players in rivalry. In 1980 the PUK gained some ground through an alliance with the Islamic Republic of Iran before attempting to negotiate autonomy with Baghdad.

By 1987, Saddam Hussein had decided to end the threat posed by Iranian collusion with the Kurds once and for all.[12]

4
The Anfal Campaigns

SPOILS OF WAR

The term 'Anfal' has its origin in one of the *sura*, or verses, of the Koran, and alludes to the 'spoils of [holy] war'.[1] It was used by the Ba'athist military machinery to refer to a series of eight military offensives that took place in Iraqi Kurdistan in the spring and summer of 1988. A distinction from other military campaigns by the Ba'athists against the Kurds, and the cause of its notoriety in the outside world, was the systematic use of chemical weapons against both military and civilian targets. Also key to the devastation caused by the Anfal campaigns was the physical destruction of an estimated 3,000 villages, the displacement of approximately 1.5 million people and the mass execution of civilians. While exact figures have yet to be established, it is believed that up to 180,000 people were killed as a result of the Anfal campaigns.

THE LOGIC OF DESTRUCTION

The rationale for the Anfal campaigns has its origin in the Iran–Iraq War (1983–88), which by 1987 had taken a significant toll on Iraqi military manpower, and reduced a hitherto healthy economy to a parlous condition. In 1986, when the Iranian government succeeded in brokering a truce between the PUK and the KDP,[2] Saddam Hussein feared the formidable prospect of an alliance between joint Kurdish forces and Iran. Iran, usually on the defensive throughout the conflict, was threatening to gain the upper hand. In response, Saddam Hussein issued Decree No. 160 of the Revolutionary Command Council on 29 March 1987, appointing his cousin 'Ali Hassan al-Majjid to command the Northern Bureau of the Ba'ath.[3] Decree 160 gave al-Majjid virtually unqualified power in the 'autonomous region' of Iraq. His decisions and directives were to be obeyed without question by all intelligence agencies, including military intelligence (the *Istikhbarat*), and by all domestic security forces, including the Popular Army Command (*Qiyadat al-Jaysh al-Sha'bi*) and the military commands in the northern region.[4] 'Ali Hassan al-Majjid was to be the supreme commander; the overlord, of all aspects of Anfal.[5]

Prior to the appointment of al-Majjid (subsequently known as 'Chemical Ali'), actions against the *peshmerga* were directed by the Iraqi army's First and Fifth Corps, based in Erbil and in Kirkuk. During Anfal the Ba'ath party took direct charge of the anti-Kurdish operation. Its modus operandi was to raze the villages of Iraqi Kurdistan so as to ensure that support for *peshmerga* forces was impossible.

In the first weeks and months after his appointment, Chemical Ali began a preliminary wave of village clearances and relocated the inhabitants of destroyed villages into *mujamma'at*, or government resettlement camps. This period also saw the first Ba'athist use of chemical weapons against the Kurds, notably in the villages of Balisan and Sheikh Wasan, in the Balisan valley. These attacks were precursors to a pattern that became ubiquitous over the course of the next year. Chemical weapons were delivered by bombs from aeroplanes and helicopters of the Iraqi air force, leading to burning, blindness, vomiting, and in some cases death, of Kurdish victims. Villages would be subsequently looted, then destroyed by troops and by *jash*;[6] the surviving villagers having fled for shelter and assistance.

In the wake of the first attacks villagers seeking help from the hospital at Erbil were divided into groups by age and sex, and detained in an *Amn* (General Security Directorate) detention centre. The men would be taken away in busloads, and never seen again. Surviving women and children were dumped in an open plain, on the banks of a river, and left to fend for themselves.[7] This procedure would become established as a common pattern throughout the course of the next year.

In total, 703 villages were destroyed by forces acting under Chemical Ali in the course of 1987. Villagers fled to *peshmerga*-controlled areas, moved in with family in other towns and villages, or were relocated to government complexes in the north and centre of Iraq.

THE SPRING OFFENSIVES OF 1988

The first time that the term 'Anfal' was routinely used by the Iraqi military and by the Ba'ath party was during the military campaigns that began in February 1988. The Ba'athist lexicon described the *peshmerga* as 'saboteurs'; Jalal Talabani, the leader of the PUK, as an 'agent of Iran'.[8]

The first 'Anfal' campaign consisted of an attack on the Jalafi valley villages of Bergalou and Sergalou, in the mountains of south-eastern Iraqi Kurdistan, which were important PUK strongholds. The villages were also close to the Dukan Dam and hydroelectric power station; a key military objective for the PUK. The region was already defined as a 'prohibited area' by the Iraqi government and its inhabitants were accustomed to regular bombardment both by troops and artillery. Previously, they had experienced chemical attacks during the operations of 1987, although without significant loss of life. In February 1988, the first shots of the Anfal campaign were heard, culminating in a month-long siege of the Jalafi valley. PUK troops held out for weeks, but were hopelessly outnumbered. The Ba'ath party employed ground troops, the air force, the Republican Guard, and chemical weapons to lay siege on the villages. They were later bulldozed and razed to the ground, precipitating the flight of refugees to the town of Sulaimaniya and to Iran. Hundreds of *peshmerga* and civilians died, either directly as a result of the military action or indirectly by exposure when attempting to cross into Iran. Men and teenage boys captured by the military simply 'disappeared'.

THE ATTACK ON HALABJA

Shortly afterwards Iraqi troops attacked the town of Halabja with chemical weapons. Halabja is a town close to the Iranian border, and had long been a stronghold of PUK *peshmerga*. It had been targeted by Iraqi troops in 1987, when parts of the town were bulldozed in retaliation for *peshmerga* support. Its strategic importance was based largely on its proximity to the Darbandikan Lake, which was a significant source of the water supply to Baghdad. In early March 1988, the Iranian army made a concerted thrust to take Halabja. They shelled the town heavily on 13 March, and took it two days later. The Iraqis counterattacked on 16 March, with conventional air strikes and artillery shelling. In wave after wave of bombing attacks the air force first delivered what appeared to be napalm or phosphorus. Later in the day, chemical weapons were used. Eyewitnesses have reported how

> Dead bodies – human and animal – littered the streets, huddled in doorways, slumped over the steering wheels of their cars. Survivors stumbled around, laughing hysterically, before collapsing. Iranian soldiers flitted through the darkened streets, dressed in protective

clothing, their faces concealed by gas masks. Those who fled could barely see, and felt a sensation like needles in the eyes. Their urine was streaked with blood.[9]

Survivors fled towards Iran, where they were treated with atropine injections, the only available antidote to the toxins used in the attacks. They were housed in refugee camps at Sanghour, near the Persian Gulf, and at Kamiaran, near the Kurdish city of Kermanshah. Halabja was left under the de facto control of the Iranians. When finally retaken by the Iraqis it was entirely levelled. Exact mortality figures have yet to be established. Human Rights Watch has the names of 3,200 victims, but estimates that between 4,000 and 7,000 people were killed.[10]

Human Rights Watch contends that the attack on Halabja, although the single most devastating chemical attack throughout the period of the Anfal campaigns, was not in fact part of Anfal.[11] Halabja was a city; the Anfal campaigns were designed to break the back of resistance among the rural Kurdish population. Unlike the Anfal attacks on villages, there was no rounding up of civilians for detention or execution. The Halabja attack, however, broke the morale of PUK fighters in Sergalou and Bergalou. The villages were swiftly taken, and the first Anfal campaign, which had involved input from 27 Iraqi army divisions, was concluded.

THE ATTACK ON SAYW SENAN

The second Anfal campaign began on 22 March 1988, the day after Kurdish New Year, with the chemical shelling of the village of Sayw Senan. The following day, the army attacked with ground troops. Over the course of the following week, the situation in the village was chaotic. Some fleeing villagers were put in temporary camps, some were detained, and some were never seen again. In contrast to the first Anfal, disappearances were not restricted to men and teenage boys; hundreds of women and children also vanished, notably those that fled Qara Dag towards the adjacent region of southern Germian. In one village, hundreds of men, women and children that surrendered to the Iraqi forces were never seen again.[12]

THE REMAINING ANFAL CAMPAIGNS

The third Anfal campaign was similar in numerous respects to the two preceding campaigns; heavy assaults from the air and ground troops; mass destruction of villages; and the creation of thousands of displaced Kurds. There had been disappearances of men, women and children in the first two campaigns, but the third chapter of Anfal saw a marked increase in the systemisation of the elimination of Kurdish civilians (although the full bureaucratic machinery would later be refined). Targeted at villages on the plain of Germian, the aim again was to destroy PUK support. Typically, both civilians and *peshmerga* alike were duped into surrendering to Iraqi forces by false promises of amnesty and taken to 'preliminary collection points' such as those at Leilan, Aliawa, Qader Karam and Chamchamal in the north, and Tuz Khurmatu and Qoratu further south.[13] Once detained, groups were separated according to age and sex. Many were moved repeatedly to different detention camps. In all, conditions were deplorable; food was practically non-existent, and there were few or no facilities for hygiene. The detained were repeatedly reassured that they were safe and that they would eventually be relocated to government complexes. Many were taken away by truck, and never seen again. Over 10,000 inhabitants of southern Germian alone are thought to have disappeared.[14]

Subsequent Anfal campaigns continued in this pattern. While the bulk of efforts were directed at PUK-controlled areas, the final Anfal campaign was targeted at strongholds of Barzani's KDP. Some camps have passed into Kurdish lore as bywords for unspeakable terrors, including those at Tikrit, Topzawa, Dibs (women's camp) and Nugra Salman (where the elderly were held). In all camps, prisoners of both sexes and all ages were regularly beaten and rations were pitiful to the extent that some, especially the elderly and the young, died of starvation. Mothers were separated from children. Many were taken away, blindfolded and handcuffed, never to be seen by their relatives again.[15]

Besides the total 'disappearance' of up to 100,000 Kurdish victims, ample evidence exists of the use of mass executions of men, women and children as a means of destroying Kurdish resistance. Typically, prisoners were taken from the camps in convoys of buses or other vehicles, handcuffed, blindfolded and driven to remote locations in south and central Iraq. Here, weakened by lack of food and water and by the stifling conditions inside the vehicles, they were pulled out and executed by machine gun alongside freshly-dug mass graves. One convoy was thought to consist of over 1,000 people, all executed in this way over the course of a few hours. It is thought that 12,000 were killed in one location alone. Only since the end of the Ba'athist regime have these graves begun to come to light.

The final Anfal commenced on 25 August 1988 with poison gas attacks on the village of Badinan, which was intended to crush what resistance remained in those areas of Iraqi Kurdistan controlled by the KDP. Like its predecessors, the campaign was marked by mass shootings of civilians and arbitrary detentions. The Iraqi military itself recorded the detention in custody of over 13,000 civilians.

AMNESTY

On 6 September 1988, a 'general and comprehensive amnesty' was announced, allowing the return of refugees from Turkey, and the dispersal of prisoners in camps.[16] Returning refugees were allotted to new complexes, optimistically described as 'new villages', despite the absence of housing and the presence of watchtowers.[17] Here, they were expected to build their own shelter without provision of materials. Return to their original villages was an impossibility for the refugees; not only did the villages not exist, but it was forbidden. Similarly, 'Anfalak'[18] were prohibited from leaving the complexes on pain of death. There were other repercussions for survivors:

> those who benefited from the Anfal decree … [were not to be] treated on an equal footing with other Iraqis in terms of rights and duties, unless they can effectively match good intentions with proper conduct and demonstrate that they have ended all collaboration with the saboteurs, and that they are more loyal to Iraq than their peers who have benefited from the above-mentioned amnesty decree.[19]

Nor were they permitted to buy state land or work as state employees, until a period of two years had elapsed.

Up until the summer of 1989, Saddam Hussein continued razing towns and villages, and resettling their inhabitants. Mass executions were reported as occurring well into the autumn and winter of 1988. Within a year of the conclusion of the campaigns, two-thirds of Iraqi Kurdistan was estimated to have been depopulated of Kurds. In addition to the tens of thousands of internally displaced people created by the Anfal campaigns, 60,000 people sought refuge in Turkey. Turkey was a reluctant host; anxious to defuse the possibility of attention being drawn to the plight of its own Kurdish population.

Thus, it refused refugee status to those that had crossed the border, and denied non-Turkish institutions and agencies access to the camps in which Anfalak were housed. A greater number of refugees – an estimated 100,000 – sought and received assistance in Iran.

INTERNATIONAL RESPONSES TO THE ANFAL CAMPAIGNS

Full details of Anfal and of the use of chemical weapons took some time to reach the outside world. US Secretary of State George Shultz declared on 8 September 1988 that the use of chemical weapons by Iraq was 'unjustified and abhorrent' and unacceptable to the civilised world.[20] Early attempts to investigate the use of chemical weapons were largely thwarted by the governments of both Iraq and Turkey. The UN was asked by 13 countries to investigate the allegations, but Turkey and Iraq's refusal to comply made it impossible for investigations to go ahead.[21]

Evidence of the use of chemical weapons was provided by a team of three doctors from the organisation Physicians for Human Rights (PHR). PHR visited a number of refugee camps, specifically to investigate claims that poison gas was used against civilians on 25 August 1988. It concluded that Iraqi aircraft attacked villages with bombs containing 'lethal poison gas', killing many and causing 'severe suffering' among survivors, both animal and human.[22]

> According to PHR, bombing runs were followed by the appearance of yellowish clouds at the site of the bomb bursts. Birds and domestic fowl near bomb bursts were killed within two to five minutes, followed closely by sheep, goats, cows, and mules. Larger mammals and people close to the point of detonation began to die soon afterwards. Their skin darkened and yellow, sometimes bloody, discharge drained from their noses and mouths.[23]

The medical findings indicated exposure to mustard gas, although the exact composition of the weapons remained unclear. Deaths within minutes of exposure, as witnessed during the attacks, suggested the use of at least one other chemical additive.[24]

Separate research was conducted into the gas attacks at Halabja by Dr Christine Gosden, Professor of Medical Genetics at Liverpool University. Gosden concluded that a number of chemical agents had been used, including mustard gas, and nerve agents SARIN, TABUN, and VX. Testifying to a Senate Judiciary Subcommittee in April 1998, she stated:

> Saddam Hussein clearly intended to complicate the task of treating the Halabja victims. At a minimum, he was using Halabja as part of the Iraqi [chemical weapons] test programme. Handbooks for doctors in the Iraqi military show sophisticated medical knowledge of the effects of chemical weapons.[25]

What, perhaps, was not apparent even to the authors of the chemical weapons attack was the legacy that the attacks would leave in their wake. Gosden found that ten years later the attacks had left a devastating inheritance both for direct survivors and for their descendants including respiratory problems, eye disorders, skin diseases, neuro-psychiatric problems, cancers, congenital abnormalities, infertility, miscarriages, stillbirths, and neonatal and infant deaths.[26]

In early 2003, the US and UK governments would tout the use of chemical weapons by Saddam Hussein as a proof of both the Iraqi government's possession of and willingness to use weapons of mass destruction. Yet in the immediate wake of their use in the Anfal and Halabja attacks, the reaction of both governments was discernibly guarded. Internal documents pointed to the US administration's reluctance to believe that Iraq had indeed used chemical weapons – arguing that there was no evidence to suggest that Iran was not either solely, or at least jointly responsible for the attacks.[27] In the UK, between 1986 and 1991, twelve Early Day Motions[28] were tabled calling for the abandonment of the supply of arms to Iraq and condemning what happened at Halabja. Not one was signed by now prominent figures including Tony Blair, Jack Straw, Robin Cook, Geoff Hoon or John Prescott. The historian Peter Sluglett describes the events as having 'occasioned little reaction on the part of Iraq's patrons in the West beyond some feelings of unease, a feeling, perhaps, that a headstrong and wayward child had gone a little too far'.[29] He adds, 'As time went on, it appears that US and British intelligence agencies did indeed have a fairly clear idea of what was happening [but] clearly realised that forthright public condemnation would be bad for business and kept silent.'[30]

The international community was not entirely mute. In response to Massoud Barzani's appeal to the UN to prevent further chemical assaults, the UN Security Council passed Resolution 620 on 26 August

1988, which condemned the use of chemical weapons.[31] This act was largely symbolic; the gassing of Kurds continued until the autumn. In the US, a bill was proposed which, if introduced, would have cut US$ 800 million worth of credit guarantees for exports to Iraq. The bill met opposition from the US administration, largely at the behest of powerful lobbyists acting on behalf of US food producers, who were major exporters of produce to Iraq, and thus failed to become law.

5
The First Gulf War:
From Uprising to Democracy

BACKGROUND

In 1988, the main Kurdish political parties formed the first National Front of Kurdistan, a political force in waiting.[1] The Front would not have too long to wait before an opportunity to become operational arose. In 1990, the government of Iraq annexed the territory of Kuwait, giving rise to a series of events that became the First Gulf War.

THE INTIFADA (UPRISING)

The constitution of Iraqi Kurdistan has its origins in the outcome of the 1990–92 Gulf War; the uprising or intifada against Saddam Hussein following the ceasefire signed with NATO troops; the resulting crackdown against the Kurdish rebels in the north and the Shi'ites in the south; and the subsequent refugee crisis.

Whether the US and its allies are responsible for encouraging the 1991 uprising, and hence for the appalling tragedy that followed, is a matter of continuing debate. In the minds of many Iraqis, the mistake of the US was to encourage a popular and spontaneous uprising, but to decline to support it with arms. Some have also accused the Iraqi opposition in exile of failing to capitalise on a key opportunity.[2]

The allegation of US incitement is most often seen to stem from ex-US President George Bush's statement that 'there's another way for the fighting to stop, and that is for the Iraqi military to take matters into their own hands to force Saddam Hussein, the dictator, to step aside'.[3] This, along with other statements carrying a similar sentiment, was broadcast to the Iraqis by the CIA-backed radio station Voice of America on and around 15 February 1991.[4] Their position in history is moot. Some have argued that responsibility for the rebellion lies in the hands of the Americans; others that the Kurds and Shi'ites would have rebelled in any event.

The human cost of the subsequent crackdown was extraordinary and devastating to the Kurdish region, coming as it did so soon in the wake of the Anfal campaigns. However, the resulting imposition of the no-fly zone above the 36th Parallel gave Iraqi Kurds some respite from the Baghdad regime.

The uprising began days before Saddam's ground-war defeat in late February and his surrender in early March 1991. It started in the south of the country, with revolts in the cities of Basra, Suq al-Shuyukh, Nasiriya, Najaf and Karbala.[5] In the north, the first cities to fall were Raniyya and Chawar Qurna, then Koi Sanjaq, Sulaimaniya, Halabja, Arabat, Erbil and eventually Kirkuk on 20 March 1991. The Iraqi writer Faleh 'Abd al-Jabbar describes how the pattern of the rebellions was remarkably similar:

> Masses would gather in the streets to denounce Saddam Husain and Ba'thist rule, then march to seize the mayor's office, the Ba'th Party headquarters, the secret police building, the prison and the city's garrison (if there was one). As they marched, people would shoot at posters or wall reliefs of the dictator. As the cities came under rebel control, the insurgents 'cleaned out Ba'thists and mukhabarat.' There was little or no regional coordination during the rebellion. It was often unclear in one town what was occurring in the other, or even, in one quarter of a town, what was happening in an adjacent district.[6]

In the north, events moved quickly. Facing the prospect of Saddam Hussein's defeat, many *jash* saw that an opportunity had arisen to turn against him. The forces and confidence of the *peshmerga* multiplied in consequence. Kurdish leaders have since proclaimed to have been taken by genuine surprise at the scale of the popular protest.

From a military perspective, the Kurds had notable successes. Over 50,000 members of the Iraqi armed forces are thought to have deserted in the north. In Sulaimaniya an estimated 900 members of the *mukhabarat* were killed in a day of fighting. Predictably there were revenge attacks on members of the Iraqi security services. The brunt of these were reportedly reserved for members of the security service apparatus and prominent Ba'athist apparatchiks. Journalist and film-maker Sheri Laizer describes visiting a *peshmerga* military camp during the rebellion.[7] Ordinary soldiers, she reported, were treated well. Known Ba'athists, torturers, and secret service agents, by contrast, were imprisoned in stifling conditions with little access to water or air.[8] Revenge killings almost certainly occurred, both in Iraqi Kurdistan and, especially, in the Shi'ite south of the country.[9]

Recent excavations of mass graves have raised the prospect that some contain the bodies of Ba'athists killed by rebels.

THE BA'ATHISTS RESPOND

The US did not back the rebellion, however. Numerous reasons have been put forward including fear of an Iranian-style Shi'ite revolution, a desire to preserve Iraq's territorial integrity or a vested interest in preserving Saddam Hussein's regime.[10] Despite the scale of the uprising, Saddam Hussein found it easy to crush. In the south of Iraq, the Republican Guard quickly retook Basra, Najaf and Karbala with unprecedented savagery, killing an estimated 300,000 people in the process. In the north, the Iraqi army began its counteroffensive operations in late March, using ground troops and helicopter gunships. Intense bombing of Kirkuk led to its being recaptured on 28 March. Sulaimaniya was taken by 3 April 1991, followed by the cities of Dohuk, Zakho, and Erbil.[11]

EXODUS FROM IRAQI KURDISTAN

More than 100,000 people are thought to have been taken into detention during the operations in 1991. Men were routinely rounded up, and as occurred during the Anfal campaigns, many were never seen again. In some towns in the north, hospital patients allegedly had their throats slit and were thrown from windows. In total at least 20,000 people are thought to have died in the crackdown on the northern rebellion. Within days an exodus of vast proportions began. Up to half a million people took refuge in Turkey, and one and a half million in Iran. Thousands died of cold, exposure and hunger in their flight. Others were killed by continuing attacks from Iraqi forces, including the use of phosphorous bombs from helicopters.[12]

Prior to the outbreak of hostilities between Allied forces and the government of Iraq, the UN had pre-positioned supplies and facilities in all four of Iraq's neighbouring countries, to accommodate the projected 300,000 refugees it estimated would or could have been created during the war. In the event, only 65,000 fled during the coalition bombing; the adequacy of the pre-positioned supplies was dwarfed by the crisis created after the fighting had ended between Iraq and the allies.

The High Commissioner described the crisis as representing the 'highest rate of influx'[13] in the 40-year history of the UN

High Commissioner for Refugees (UNHCR). Within days of the crackdown, the refugees' situation had become desperate. The half million attempting to reach Turkey, and those displaced within Iraqi Kurdistan were stranded in mountain passes; inaccessible areas with little shelter, water or cover. In addition, the lack of roads made the provision of supplies almost impossible.

TURKEY, IRAN AND THE IRAQI KURDS

While Turkey was praised by its NATO allies for its efforts to help the displaced, in reality its treatment of the refugees left a great deal to be desired. The movement of Kurds into Turkey created a dilemma for Ankara. Anxious not to do anything that would inflame, or in any sense highlight its own 'Kurdish problem', or to add to the 30,000-plus Iraqi Kurds still in Turkey as a result of the Anfal campaigns, it initially refused to let the Kurds down from the mountains into more hospitable terrain on the Turkish side of the border, despite most of the refugees being hopelessly under-prepared for the wintry conditions of the mountains.[14] The press reported nursing mothers with babies and young children being beaten back by Turkish soldiers with rifle butts.[15] Initially, Turkey called for refugee camps to be established in Iraq. Turkish President Özal decided to let the Kurds cross the border only on 16 April, almost three weeks after many of the Kurds had begun their flight from the towns and villages of Kurdish Iraq.[16] Furthermore, though a signatory to the 1951 Convention Relating to the Status of Refugees, Turkey did not and continues not to recognise non-European asylum seekers as refugees.[17]

By far the greatest number of refugees crossed into Iran, where in comparative terms they enjoyed a better welcome. Around a million Iraqis crossed the border, and approximately 150,000 camped on the border. Ninety-four camps and reception areas were established, many within towns destroyed during the Iran–Iraq War.[18]

RESOLUTION 688[19]

At the instigation of France, Turkey and Iran, the UN Security Council called a meeting on 5 April 1991 to discuss the adoption of a resolution that would condemn the repression by the Iraqi government of its own people. The adoption of Resolution 688 did not go unchallenged: Cuba, Yemen and Zimbabwe voted against it; China and India abstained; and Iraq lodged a formal protest.[20] Some observers noted with dissatisfaction that the resolution was not tied in with Resolution 687, passed two days before, laying down the terms of the ceasefire with Iraq.[21]

Among other measures, Resolution 688 stated that the Security Council:

1. [Condemned] the repression of the Iraqi civilian population in many parts of Iraq, including most recently in Kurdish populated areas, the consequences of which threaten international peace and security in the region;
2. Demands that Iraq, as a contribution to removing the threat to international peace and security in the region, immediately end this repression and expresses the hope in the same context that an open dialogue will take place to ensure that the human and political rights of all Iraqi citizens are respected;
3. Insists that Iraq allow immediate access by international humanitarian organisations to all those in need of assistance in all parts of Iraq and to make available all necessary facilities for their operations.

This resolution coincided with the first appeal of the UN Disaster Relief Office (UNDRO) to cope with the Kurdish refugees. Five days later, Prince Sadr al-Din Aga Khan was appointed by the UN Secretary-General to be Executive Delegate of the Secretary-General in the context of a UN Inter-Agency Humanitarian Programme for Iraq, Kuwait, and the Iraq/Iran and Iraq/Turkey border areas. The role encompassed coordinating and overseeing humanitarian assistance and negotiating on behalf of the UN with the government of Iraq. On 18 April 1991 a deal was struck between the UN and the Iraqi government to provide humanitarian assistance by the UN to displaced Iraqi Kurds and Iraqi Kurdish refugees. Iraq agreed to ensure safe passage of relief supplies and provide forms of logistical support.[22]

Resolution 688 raised a number of important issues in international law. Internal acts of repression by the Iraqi government were included in the resolution's definition of international peace and security, where they had the consequence of generating an outflow of refugees towards and across international borders. This gave the Security Council a mandate to act even where action amounted to interference with domestic affairs. This seemed to contradict Article 2(7) of the UN Charter,[23] which prohibits intervention in matters within a state's domestic jurisdiction. Nonetheless, the adoption of the resolution appeared to establish that such internal repression was within the Security Council's sphere of confidence.

The severe emergency situation was exacerbated by a number of difficult factors. As previously discussed, Turkey was reluctant and initially refused to admit Kurdish refugees from Iraq. Furthermore, Turkey's opposition to relief operations being performed on Turkish territory was such that it placed obstacles in the path of the Office of the UN High Commissioner for Refugees performing standard protective functions.[24] In any event, the magnitude of assistance required, appalling weather conditions and the impassability of mountain roads would have hindered relief operations even were Turkey willing to provide them.

No attempt was made in Iran to prevent refugees from crossing the border, and in some instances there was remarkable generosity; one town with a population of 25,000 played host to 75,000 fleeing Iraqi Kurds.[25] Nonetheless, the Iranian side also came with complications. Sour relations between Iran and the west made negotiation difficult.[26] Camps, though in some conditions well provided, were remote, and heavily guarded. It was also alleged that good quality relief supplies from international humanitarian organisations were substituted by Iranian officials for second-rate replacements in some camps. The Lawyers' Committee for Human Rights concluded that refugees were left with the unenviable choice between the uncertainty of returning to Iraqi Kurdistan and extreme isolation in remote, heavily guarded but well provisioned camps of Iran.[27]

'OPERATION PROVIDE COMFORT'

On 13 April 1991, the US in agreement with the Turkish government commenced a relief operation for refugees caught in the border area as a stop-gap measure, up to and until the UN was able to meet the humanitarian need. 'Operation Provide Comfort' involved the provision by land but mostly by air, of 15,500 tons of relief supplies, administered by over 20,000 personnel from 13 nations.[28] However, the operation did not meet the needs of the refugees, and it was clear that they would have to be persuaded to return to Iraq if aid was to be adequately supplied.

'OPERATION SAFE HAVEN'

Momentum for the creation of a safe haven within Iraq gathered in the first two weeks of April 1991. The idea was suggested by Turkish

Prime Minister Özal to UK Prime Minister John Major, who called for the establishment of UN-protected enclaves within Iraqi Kurdistan at an EC summit on 8 April 1991. On 16 April 1991, President George Bush announced that US military forces would move into Iraqi Kurdistan and establish refugee camps to shelter and feed the refugees massed in the border areas between Iraq and Turkey, declaring,

> The approach is quite simple: if we cannot get adequate food, medicine, clothing and shelter to the Kurds living in the mountains along the Turkish-Iraq border, we must encourage the Kurds to move to areas in northern Iraq where the geography facilitates, rather than frustrates, such a large-scale relief effort.
>
> Consistent with UNSC Resolution 688 and working closely with the United Nations and other international organisations and with our European partners, I have directed the US military to begin immediately to establish several encampments in northern Iraq where relief supplies for these refugees will be made available in large quantities and distributed in an orderly manner ... adequate security will be provided at these temporary sites by US, British and French air and ground forces, again consistent with United Nations Security Council Resolution 688 ... all we are doing is motivated by humanitarian concerns ...[29]

A first camp was established at the border town of Zakho, financed by the European Community and by the Dutch government. Gradually the safe haven increased in size to stretch as far as Amadiyya in the east and Dohuk in the south, as Iraqi troops and police were rolled back at the insistence of the Allies. Unsurprisingly, the Baghdad government protested in a letter to the UN Secretary-General that 'Operation Safe Haven' constituted 'a serious, unjustifiable and unfounded attack on the sovereignty and territorial integrity of Iraq'.[30] Nonetheless, the UK and US governments warned that Iraqi aircraft were prohibited from flying north of the 36th Parallel, and that armed forces were not to be sent into the 36-by-63-mile zone created by the operation for the safety of its Kurdish inhabitants.

From the beginning of the Allied forces' relief operation there was tension between the military powers and the UN. The UN Secretary-General did not wish to grant coalition troops official status as a UN peace-keeping force and refused to do so. Administration of the Zakho camp was handed over to the UN authorities on 13 May. On 23 May 1991, the UN representative in Iraq announced an agreement to station up to 500 UN security guards, carrying only side-arms, in four Kurdish provinces. They were tasked with patrolling UN relief centres in both the north and the south of Iraq.[31] On 7 June 1991, humanitarian relief efforts were taken over by UNHCR. By September, almost all of the Iraqi Kurdish refugees had been persuaded to return.

That so many had been persuaded to return so quickly is attributable to a number of factors; Turkey's obvious discomfort at accommodating refugees and its refusal to grant asylum put pressure on those that had crossed the border to return; while refugees remained for some time in a number of camps in Iran, virulent attacks of food poisoning, thought to have been the responsibility of Iraqi agents, caused large numbers to re-cross the border. 'Operation Provide Comfort' was probably the main inducement. Routes of return were clearly mapped out, and relief and medical supplies provided along the way. It was often possible for community leaders to travel ahead to ensure that conditions would be suitable for the return of their people.

There were some setbacks, however, as refugees refused to return to areas outside of the protected zone below the 36th Parallel. Sporadic attacks by Iraqi troops displaced upwards of 200,000 people from Sulaimaniya and Erbil in October and December 1991 respectively, and a further 40,000 from Erbil the following March,[32] by which time almost half a million people remained internally displaced within Iraq.

The refugees' return was premised on the assurance that once within Iraq, they would be safe from further attacks by Iraqi forces. Not only did a moral obligation lie with the UN/coalition to ensure this would and could be honoured but it is prohibited to return refugees to a country where they may face persecution under the principle of *non-refoulement* in customary international law.[33] The challenge that lay ahead for the international community was to find a long-term method of ensuring the safety of the returnees without a major military presence. The UK Foreign Secretary Douglas Hurd had stated on 17 June 1991 that they 'went into northern Iraq in order to persuade the Kurds to come down from the mountains – to save lives. We don't want the operation to end in a way that will merely recreate the same problem.'[34] To this end measures included a 5,000-strong rapid reaction force within Turkey, backed by air support. This did not last the summer, and was entirely withdrawn in September 1991. Thus, the sole security force within Iraqi Kurdistan consisted of the contingent of lightly armed UN guards, numbering at most 500, but often as few as 100.[35]

NEGOTIATING AUTONOMY WITH SADDAM HUSSEIN

Faced with renewed insecurity, and justifiably cynical about the security afforded by the 'safe haven', Kurdish political parties realised the need to consider the impossible and negotiate with Saddam Hussein for an autonomy agreement. The idea was backed with support from within the coalition, notably the UK and the European Community, who declared on 29 July that 'it would be appropriate for the international community to give its support to a [satisfactory autonomy] agreement on the basis of Resolution 688 of the Security Council'.[36]

Nevertheless, ensuing negotiations were marked by short-lived triumph and enduring disaster. Mas'ud Barzani and Jalal Talabani haggled with Baghdad in parallel. Their joint goal was for Baghdad to offer 'expanded autonomy within the federated structure of Iraq promising democracy, pluralism and constitutional rule in Baghdad'.[37] Early on in the talks, Talabani claimed that he wrested from Saddam Hussein an agreement to dismantle the Revolutionary Command Council (the inner sanctum of the Ba'ath party) and hold free elections. In May 1991, Massoud Barzani announced that he had won from Baghdad the designation of Kirkuk as the administrative capital of the autonomous region.

As the sceptics suspected from the start, Saddam proved a fickle deal-maker. Negotiations broke down in June as the Iraqi government moved the goalposts several times and made conditions that the Kurdish leaders could not meet. These included the stipulation that the Kurds join the Ba'athist government in Baghdad. By the autumn, fighting had broken out between Iraqi troops and the Kurds. On 20 October 1991, Iraqi forces were withdrawn from the three northern governorates of Erbil, Dohuk and Sulaimaniya and the Kurdish region was placed under economic siege. Salaries to civil servants were cut off, and an embargo imposed (oftentimes referred to as 'internal supply restrictions' to distinguish from the UN embargo against Iraq)[38] preventing foodstuffs and fuel from crossing the front line that now separated the 'autonomous' north from the rest of the country. This crippled the economy, and paralysed the political parties that constituted the Kurdistan Front. Iraqi shelling of towns such as Kifri, Kalar and Maydan, displacement of Kurds in Kirkuk and the surrounding region, and the stepping up of the 'Arabisation' process demonstrated the international community's 'security measures' for the Kurdish region had their limitations.

6
Democracy in Iraqi Kurdistan

A RAINBOW ALLIANCE

The origins of the Kurdistan Regional Government (KRG) lie in the Kurdistan Front, a rainbow alliance of Kurdish parties formed in the aftermath of the Anfal campaigns in 1989. It included the KDP, the PUK, the Kurdistan People's Democratic Party (KDPD), the Kurdistan Socialist Party (PASOK), the Kurdistan Branch of the Iraqi Communist Party, the Assyrian Democratic Movement and the Kurdistan Toilers' Party.[1] Opportunity for the Front to constitute a de facto government came with the withdrawal of the Iraqi government's administration of the area in October 1991. The lack of formal structure of the KRG necessitated the holding of elections in May 1992. It must be noted that the Kurdish-administered region, under the de facto jurisdiction of the Kurdish political parties, did not extend to all those areas of Iraq in which the Kurds were in a majority.

INTERNATIONAL AMBIVALENCE

Even at its inception, the KRG was regarded ambivalently by the outside world. The US, ideologically supportive of the democratic process, tentatively welcomed the election. However, its longstanding commitment to the territorial integrity of Iraq also made it circumspect. On 15 May 1992, the US government declared its hope that the elections would 'help lead to a better life for all the people of northern Iraq ... [it] welcome[d] public and private assurances by the Iraqi Kurdish leadership [that the elections would deal] only with local administrative issues [and did not] represent a move towards separatism'.[2] The UK government likewise declared that it was happy with the elections as long as they did not represent a move towards the creation of 'Kurdistan'.[3] The European Parliament on the other hand passed a resolution expressing approval, and encouraging pursuit of the path towards autonomy.[4] The international community had already demonstrated, in its response to the refugee crisis in the wake of the uprising, its confusion on policy with regard to Iraqi sovereignty and territorial integrity and it persisted.

AUTONOMY FROM A KURDISH PERSPECTIVE

Autonomy for the Kurdish region in Iraq was not a novel concept. It had been negotiated several times between Kurds and the central government, usually faltering over the extent of the territory that should be included in any agreement, the means of determining the extent of the territory, and of course the Ba'ath party's reluctance to honour agreements. However, the 1970 March Manifesto remained a valuable legislative tool for the Kurds. Among its provisions it was determined that Kurdish should be taught alongside Arabic in all areas with a Kurdish majority, that Kurds would participate fully in government (including the cabinet and the armed forces), and that the Constitution should be amended to declare that 'the Iraqi people is made up of two nationalities, the Arab nationality and the Kurdish nationality'.

In order to prevent further atrocities by Saddam, the political bodies resulting from the election insisted that the Kurdish region would remain a part of Iraq.

ELECTORAL PROCEDURE

Despite the Kurds' desire for a legitimate election in the eyes of the UN, the UN declined to offer its assistance or recognition. Nonetheless, international monitoring (by, among others, Pax Christi,[5] and the International Human Rights Law Group) did take place. In addition, the Kurdistan Front passed legislation to prove it was taking pains to ensure the highest standards of probity and fairness. Two elections were to be held. The first would decide membership of the 105-person National Assembly. The second would be a presidential election, to decide the holder of the post of Leader of the Kurdistan Liberation Movement.

Both elections were held on 19 May 1992 using a proportional representation electoral mechanism under which any party gaining 7 per cent or more of the vote would win a place in the assembly.[6] In the event, the two main parties, the KDP and the PUK, dominated the outcome almost equally. None of the other parties were able to meet the 7 per cent threshold, so their remaining votes were divided between the KDP and the PUK. In the assembly, the votes ultimately translated as 50 seats each for the main parties, five extra seats being provided for minority groups (four for the Assyrian Democratic Movement, and one to the Kurdish Christian Unity party). None of the four candidates running in the leadership election (Massoud Barzani of the KDP, Jalal Talabani of the PUK, 'Uthman 'Abd al-'Aziz Muhammad of the Islamic Movement, and Mahmud 'Ali 'Uthman of PASOK) were able to muster an absolute majority, and further elections were ultimately postponed.

By July 1992 ministries had been established. In effect, these were divided between the two main parties with each minister being deputised by a counterpart from the other party. Prime Minister Dr Fu'ad Masum of the PUK was deputised by Rosch Shawais of the KDP; Amin Mawlud of the KDP, Minister for Industry and Electricity, deputised by the PUK's Ameen 'Abd al-Rahman, and so on.[7] Talabani and Barzani did not participate in the elections for the assembly, weakening its credibility in the opinion of some. In his statement to parliament Prime Minister Dr Fu'ad Masum declared:

> The election of the Kurdish parliament was a great victory for our people. Our enemies anticipated that we would drown in a sea of blood. The Iraqi regime hoped that the people would side with it so that Saddam Hussein could claim a victory to cover his defeat. But as we expected, the people stayed true to their traditions and the national liberation movement rose to the occasion.[8]

The result was regarded as a triumph for Kurdish democracy, but the equal split between the two main parties augured badly. The initial difficulty was not conflict but paralysis, with the two factions operating not so much in league with each other, but in parallel.

A NEW KIND OF POLITICAL SPACE?

Since Iraqi Kurdistan's self-declared election in 1992, it has become difficult to define it as a political space.

The 1992 elections were held in order to fill the political vacuum created by the withdrawal of the Iraqi central government's presence in the north. Baghdad considered the KRG 'illegal', and yet offered nothing in its place. The holding of elections within a part of one nation, in the absence of the consent of that nation's central government raised the question as to what kind of political space was created, and whether the elections jeopardised Iraq's territorial sovereignty. This question remains unanswered in a number of respects.

As mentioned, the international community took an ambivalent stance towards the territory under the governance of the KRG. It lauded the attempt at establishing a democracy under the nose of a despot, but tempered its enthusiasm with a concern that Iraq should stay intact. Resolution 688 of 1991 reaffirmed 'the commitment of all Member States to the sovereignty, territorial integrity and political independence of Iraq and of all states in the area'.

The Kurdish Front assured that the elections did not in any sense represent a move toward separatism. From the start, the Front declared itself to be doing little more than meeting a need, but the Elections Act of April 1992 observed that

> the Iraqi government has recently carried out an unprecedented measure, namely the withdrawal of its administrative units and personnel from Kurdistan, thereby creating a unique administrative and legislative vacuum. The Iraqi Kurdish Front, which was conducting negotiations with the central government, has thus been thrown into a very complicated and challenging situation … the [IKF] is determined to take up this challenge … It is taking the first step to catch the train of the civilized world. It intends to reconstruct Kurdish society on the basis of democracy and respect for human rights in accordance with international norms and agreements.[9]

It proceeded to describe the Front as a 'de facto' ruling power that would, 'demonstrate to the world that the people of Iraqi Kurdistan are capable of … self-government'.[10] However, a position on the Kurdish region's relationship with the rest of the country was not forthcoming until later in the year when, in a special communiqué, the Kurdish parliament declared a federal union with the rest of Iraq.

The communiqué noted that statehood had been an ambition of Kurds since before the 1919 Treaty of Sèvres, which promised some form of state-like self-determination. However, its own proclamation fell far short of the creation of a state:

> the parliament, in exercising its duties and its right to decide the destiny of Iraqi Kurdistan in accordance with international commitments and conventions, has agreed unanimously to specify the legal relationship with the central government of Iraq as one of federal union within a parliamentary, democratic Iraq based on a multi-party system and respect for human rights.[11]

Some have pointed out the threat of a breakaway Kurdish state would not have arisen as and when it did had it not been for the creation of the safe haven by Allied forces.[12]

Iraqi Kurdistan has been treated as a de facto 'state' by agencies of governments, which do not otherwise recognise it as such. UK immigration authorities have, for example, sought to return asylum seekers to Iraqi Kurdistan in the face of evidence of continued harassment by Ba'athist security services in the rest of Iraq.

RELATIONS BETWEEN THE PUK AND KDP

A rift broke out between the two main Kurdish parties after the elections. Underlying tensions were clearly exacerbated by the double embargo imposed on the region, Saddam Hussein's economic siege and the UN sanctions against Iraq.

Both sides accused the other of letting themselves be manipulated by regional players Iraq, Iran and Turkey. Certainly, the challenges facing an emerging democracy in a hostile environment, lacking the full blessing of the international community, were substantial, if not insurmountable. Danielle Mitterrand noted in a speech to the Chatham House Institute in 1994,

> One wonders how a democracy can flourish in a country abandoned to the bombing of their Iranian and Turkish neighbours and to the destructive intrusions of the Iraqi army with all the exactions, the withdrawal of the currency,[13] power cuts, deportation of the population living in the unprotected part of Kurdistan, the double embargo imposed by the Iraqi government, a complete lack of energy supplies, the burning of the crops, and the daily tragedy of anti-personnel mines.[14]

Much of the animosity between the two parties originates within the history of Kurdish politics and the rift between factions of the KDP, leading to Jalal Talabani's announcement of the creation of the PUK in 1975. But events started to snowball in May 1994 regarding a land dispute north-east of Sulaimaniya. By the time a lasting agreement was found, Iran, Turkey, Ireland, France, the US and even Iraq had hosted, or had offered to host, mediation talks.[15] An operations room was established on 21 May 1994 to oversee the restoration of normality. This was largely administered by Ahmad Chalabi and other members of the Iraqi National Congress (INC).[16]

Between 16 and 22 July 1994, the parties met in Paris, and with the assistance of the French government and observers from the UK and US embassies, produced a new draft constitution for the KRG. The Turkish government was concerned that the agreement constituted a roadmap for Kurdish quasi-nationhood and refused to grant exit visas to the two politicians required to sign it in Paris, in the presence of French president François Mitterrand. Thus, the Paris Agreement failed.

A new strategic agreement, signed on 21 November 1994, amounted to nothing. The parties again disagreed over the collection of border tariffs and land ownership of Erbil which was the seat of the KRG.[17]

During talks in Ireland in 1995, the KDP and PUK representatives agreed on the demilitarisation of Erbil, the turnover by the KDP of customs revenues to a joint bank account, reconvening of the KRG, and to reassure outside interests of their respect for Iraq's territorial integrity and Turkey's 'legitimate security interests'. There were widespread hopes on all sides that these Drogheda talks would succeed where others had failed.[18] However, the rift materialised again in 1996 when in August, the KDP allied itself with Baghdad to retake first Erbil and then the eastern city of Sulaimaniya. Barzani's justification for such an unholy alliance was that perceived PUK/Iranian joint forces posed a threat to Iraqi territorial integrity.[19]

Though seemingly routed, the PUK was able to recover most of the territory it had lost including Sulaimaniya with support from the Iranian military. By this time, resurgence in violence between Iran and Iraq began to look like a real possibility. In October 1996, US-sponsored talks were held in Ankara. Conferences were held sporadically throughout the following year all of which appeared to be making progress until October 1997, when there were renewed disagreements between the KDP and PUK over land ownership.

Beginning with an overture made by Jalal Talabani, the KDP and PUK again agreed to forge a long-lasting peace and by July 1998, US President Bill Clinton was able to declare that both leaders had

made positive, forward-looking statements on political reconciliation. We will continue our efforts to reach a permanent reconciliation through mediation in order to help the people of northern Iraq find the permanent, stable settlement which they deserve, and to minimize the opportunities for Baghdad and

Tehran to insert themselves into the conflict and threaten Iraqi citizens in this region.[20]

Barzani and Talabani met in Washington in September 1998. In what was termed the 'Final Statement of the Leaders Meeting', they informed the world that they had reached a number of significant agreements. They condemned internal fighting, pledged to refrain from resorting to violence or seeking outside intervention against each other as a means for settling differences, agreed to comply with the human rights provisions of Resolution 688, agreed to facilitate the free movement of citizens, and vowed to refrain from negative press statements. Other provisions were made for revenue sharing, the status of the key cities of Erbil, Dohuk and Sulaimaniya, and for the organisation of free elections. A timetable was set for establishing milestones on the continuing road to peace.

Any lack of confidence in prospects for unity between the two Kurdish parties were subsequently proven wrong. The peace, so elusive during the early 1990s, continued to be maintained.

7
Human Rights in Iraqi Kurdistan

BACKGROUND

Even the most cursory glance at the history of the Iraqi Kurds illustrates the appalling extent to which they have been subjected to human rights violations on a systematic basis which has been effectively unchecked by the international community for several decades. Human rights abuses did not begin with the advent of the Saddam Hussein regime in 1979, or with the Ba'athists. They have been a feature of relations between the central governments and the Kurds since the creation of Iraq. The involuntary displacement of civilians, disappearances and destruction of property have all been a hallmark of this abuse.

Kurds have not been the sole victims of the Iraqi state. The Shi'ites and Marsh Arabs have also suffered, as have Turcomans, Chaldaneans and Assyrians inhabiting the predominantly Kurdish three northern governorates. Nor has the Iraqi government been the sole perpetrator of abuses against the Kurds in the region. Successive regimes in Iran and Turkey have likewise committed atrocities against Kurds and manipulated them with little respect for international borders.

The creation of a quasi-Kurdish 'state' provided some protection against the abuse of human rights, but nonetheless it continued. Almost half of the Kurdish population of Iraq lived outside of the three governorates, many in and around Kirkuk, and were perhaps subjected to some of the worst rights abuses – including torture, detention without charge, eviction, and denial of citizenship and language rights – to have occurred since the crackdown on the uprising in 1991. On several occasions throughout the 1990s, Turkish interventions in Iraqi Kurdistan, ostensibly operations to counter the activities of the Kurdistan Workers Party (PKK), have resulted in destruction of property and the deaths of substantial numbers of civilians.

For many Kurds, the very fact of their oppression is inseparable from larger issues relating to Kurdish autonomy or self-determination.

CRIMES OF THE BA'ATH REGIME

At the risk of some repetition, it is useful here to describe some of the human rights abuses perpetrated by the Ba'athist regime against the Kurds before moving to the sphere of international law.

A key theme of the Iraqi state's oppression of the Kurds was its suspicion of Kurdish demands for autonomy. Even as Saddam Hussein negotiated the March Manifesto in 1970 with Mullah Mustafa Barzani, he employed terror tactics against the Kurds as a means of weakening support and political structures, and to bring the Kurds into line with central government authority. At no stage did the Iraqi military shy from extending its offensives to civilian areas; throughout the 1970s civilians lost their lives or livelihood as a consequence of Iraqi military attacks. Amnesty International documented political oppression during this period and noted the detention of an estimated 60,000 men with links to the KDP in the south of Iraq in 1976.[1]

One of the consequences of the Algiers Agreement with Iran in 1975 was the creation of a 'security belt' along the borders with Iran and Turkey, between five and 30 kilometres wide. In the process up to 1,400 villages are thought to have been destroyed and 600,000 victims resettled into collective townships.[2] At the same time, the Iraqi government attempted to shift the demographic makeup of the oil-rich Kurdish regions. The administrative map of Iraq was redrawn in what amounted to gerrymandering on a massive scale, ensuring that an Arab majority existed in key oil provinces. Tens of thousands of Kurdish residents were evicted from the regions of Kirkuk, Khaniqin, Mandali, Shaikhan, Sinjar and Zakho. Many were dumped in the southern desert regions and others in camps effectively under military control. Arab families were brought in to Kurdish regions induced with financial and land ownership rewards.

The 1980s saw the pace of atrocities against the Kurds accelerated with little scrutiny by the outside world. One of the most infamous events in recent Kurdish history is the disappearance of up to 8,000 male members of the Barzani clan in 1983, in retaliation for Massoud Barzani allying the Kurds with Iran at the beginning of the Iran–Iraq War.

Amnesty International reports describe a catalogue of abuses.[3] Where it proved difficult to detain suspects, government forces would instead detain their relatives, including youths, children and pregnant women. It has been reported by Amnesty that in 1985,

Iraqi forces arrested 300 children and teenagers in Sulaimaniya in retaliation for acts by the *peshmerga*, and that they were tortured and 29 were executed without trial. Other allegations include further retaliatory killings in the same year, both by firing squad and burial alive. This pattern of summary executions, either following unfair trial proceedings or in the absence of any trial proceedings at all, continued in 1987 when reportedly 360 people – including 14- and 17-year-old children – were executed in the space of two months.

The Iran–Iraq War was a difficult time for the Kurds and for the protection of human rights and lives. While most of the heaviest fighting took place further south, the Kurds' position on both sides of the border exposed them to the war both politically and militarily. In its report on Iraq, published in 1991, UNHCR estimated that Iraqi Kurdistan had the dubious distinction of being one of the most heavily mined regions of the world, with 20 million mines thought to have been laid during the 1980s, largely during the Iran–Iraq War but also in response to uprisings by the *peshmerga*.[4] In the early 1990s, it was not uncommon for over 2,000 deaths or injuries to be caused by landmines in a single year.[5] The use of different types of mines including lightweight plastic explosives, and careless and unmapped distribution often in civilian and/or agricultural areas, increased the likelihood of casualties and made detection particularly difficult.

But it was the Anfal campaigns of 1988 that finally began to alert the outside world to the scale of Iraqi atrocities against the Kurds (although arguably, Anfal only drew the response it deserved some time after it occurred). The rationale of the campaigns was to crush the Kurdish collusion with Iranian forces. However, the response was so disproportionate as to suggest that the underlying motive was genocide. Anfal became synonymous with the use of chemical weapons at Halabja. However, by far the most casualties were caused by mass executions and other indiscriminate killings of both *peshmerga* and non-combatants. The hallmark characteristics of Anfal – mass executions, arrests and relocations – are believed to have carried on after the campaigns' end (marked by an amnesty granted to survivors and refugees in 1988).

The next chapter in Saddam's flagrant abuse of Kurdish rights was his response to the uprising following the end of the First Gulf War in March 1991. The brutality of the Iraqi government's reaction, including the use of tanks and other heavy armaments, helicopter gunships, and allegedly phosphorous bombs on fleeing civilians, provoked the flight of almost 2 million people, which ultimately prompted the adoption of Security Council Resolution 688, and the establishment of the safe haven.

The establishment of the safe haven by no means rendered Iraq's Kurds totally immune from human rights abuses. Many Kurds lived south of the 'green line' separating Kurdish control from that of the Iraqi military. In and around Kirkuk, the government stepped up its programme of Arabisation, expelling or coercing the departure of an estimated 120,000 Kurds, and members of other non-Arab ethnicities, between 1991 and 2001.[6]

BREACHES OF INTERNATIONAL LAW
BY THE GOVERNMENT OF IRAQ[7]

The Kurds, and the many other ethnic groups that make up Iraq, have been victims of atrocious human rights abuses and thus gross violations of international law. As a member of the UN, Iraq was obliged under Articles 55 and 56 of the UN Charter to promote 'universal respect for, and observance of, human rights and fundamental freedoms for all without distinction as to race, sex, language or religion'. In addition, Iraq was bound to implement numerous other human rights obligations by virtue of its voluntary ratification of key international treaties.[8] Both the Charter and the treaties required Saddam's regime to respect and safeguard a wide range of civil, political, economic social and cultural rights. Iraq was also required to comply with the various international supervisory procedures established under those treaties.

In particular Iraq made a unilateral declaration to comply with the terms of the 1975 UN Declaration on the Protection of All Persons from Being Subjected to Torture or Other Cruel, Inhuman or Degrading Treatment or Punishment and to implement its provisions. The General Assembly urged states in 1977 to demonstrate voluntary compliance with the Declaration in this way.

The evidence of Saddam's regime's actions against the Kurds, particularly in the course of the Anfal campaigns but not limited to events in 1988, certainly pointed to a prima facie case involving acts prohibited by the Convention on the Prevention and Punishment of the Crime of Genocide, to which Iraq was a state party. Article 1 of the Convention confirms that genocide is a crime under international law and, under Article 3, that conspiracy, direct or indirect incitement and attempt to commit genocide are all punishable, as is complicity in genocide.

A key element of the crime of genocide, and one which requires very strong and precise evidence to establish, is the requisite intent to destroy a group in whole or part. The Special Rapporteur on Iraq stated that 'it would seem beyond doubt that these policies, and the Anfal operations in particular, bear the marks of a genocide-type design' and that 'the Anfal Operations constituted genocide-type activities which did in fact result in the extermination of a part of this population and which continue to have an impact on the lives of the people as a whole'.[9]

In addition to the treaties to which Iraq was a signatory, the UN adopted numerous norms and standards in the forms of declarations, principles and guidelines.[10] Many of these are pertinent to Iraq's abuse of human rights.

HUMANITARIAN LAW

Iraq ratified and is legally bound by the terms of the four Geneva Conventions of 1949.[11] Iraq has not, however, ratified the two Additional Protocols to the Geneva Conventions dealing with the protection of victims of international and non-international armed conflicts respectively.

The Geneva Conventions are primarily applicable to situations involving conflict between states. The Kurdish political parties lack state status. Nonetheless, Article 3, common to all four conventions, requires states parties to respect minimum humanitarian standards in cases of armed conflict occurring in that state's territory and which is not of an international character. A state is required to ensure that persons taking no active part in the hostilities, such as civilians and members of armed forces placed *hors de combat* for any reason, are treated humanely and without discrimination, and that the wounded and sick are collected and cared for.[12]

Common Article 3 also states that the parties to the conflict should endeavour to bring into force by special agreements all or part of the other provisions of each Geneva Convention.

Acts prohibited by Common Article 3 represent breaches of international humanitarian law, and are a flagrant violation of Common Article 1 of all four Conventions, by which state parties, 'undertake to respect and to ensure respect for the [Geneva Conventions] in all circumstances'. In addition, such acts contravene the general enforcement provisions common to all four Conventions that oblige states to take the 'measures necessary for the suppression of all acts contrary to the [Geneva Conventions]'. It should be noted, however, that violations of Common Article 3 are not classified under the terms of the Geneva Conventions as 'grave breaches' and do not, therefore, fall within the special enforcement rules governing grave breaches.

It is also necessary for a conflict to reach a certain degree of severity before it can be considered to fall under Common Article 3. Riots and other civil disturbances, even if suppressed with lethal force, would not generally fall within its scope. There is no doubt, however, that much of the conflict waged between the Iraqi government and the Kurds was of a level to which Common Article 3 would have applied. Excessive and illegal use of force in quelling lesser disturbances would in any event be caught by the provisions of international human rights law which continue to apply in a state of emergency or other conflict.

Although Iraq is not party to the two Additional Protocols to the Geneva Conventions dealing with the protection of victims of armed conflict, attacks against civilians are widely condemned and prohibited by the customary laws of armed conflict. General Assembly Resolution 2444 (1968) reaffirms principles that must be observed by all parties in armed conflict, including the prohibition of attacks on the civilian population and the requirement to distinguish at all times between civilians and persons taking part in hostilities.[13] Similarly, the Declaration on the Protection of Women and Children in Emergency and Armed Conflict of 1974 prohibits and condemns 'attacks and bombings on the civilian population, inflicting incalculable suffering'.[14]

The Anfal campaigns were characterised by gross violations of human rights and humanitarian law committed on a massive scale and in the words of the UN Special Rapporteur, was 'accomplished in a clearly systematic fashion through the intentional use of obviously excessive force'.

The use of chemical weapons by Iraq in the Iran–Iraq War was in breach of the Geneva Protocol for the Prohibition of the Use in War of Asphyxiating, Poisonous or Other Gases, and of Bacteriological Methods of Warfare of 1925 to which Iraq was a party. Although this Protocol only applies to international conflicts, it reflects three important customary principles of international law: the right to adopt methods of warfare is not unlimited; methods and weapons that cause unnecessary suffering and superfluous injury, whether to civilians or combatants, are prohibited; and non-combatants must always be protected and, in particular, the indiscriminate targeting of civilians is outlawed.

In view of their international regulation, resort to chemical weapons in civilian areas may well amount to serious violations of the laws and customs of war, even in an internal conflict. The Statute of the International Tribunal for the former Yugoslavia for example expressly includes the 'the employment of poisonous weapons or other weapons calculated to cause unnecessary suffering' as a violation of the laws and customs of war.[15] The use of such weapons against non-combatants would certainly fall within the general prohibition of violence, murder and cruel treatment in Common Article 3 of the Geneva Conventions. The Declaration on the Protection of Women and Children in Emergency and Armed Conflict also strongly condemns the use of chemical and bacteriological weapons as 'one of the most flagrant violations' of the Geneva Conventions and the principles of humanitarian law.

The Ba'athist regime refused to inform the United Nations Office of Project Services (UNOPS) of the location of mines laid during the Iran–Iraq War or in its wars with the Kurds. In view of their international regulation, the indiscriminate laying of mines in civilian areas again may well amount to serious violations of the laws and customs of war, even in an internal conflict.

HUMAN RIGHTS STRUCTURES AND THE KURDISH AUTHORITIES

Both parts of the KRG dedicated resources to human rights observance and protection. During the KHRP visit to Iraq in 2003, the fact-finding mission visited the Office of Human Rights, Displaced Persons and Anfal Affairs, the Bureau of Human Rights in Sulaimaniya, and the Ministry of Human Rights in Erbil.[16] Each is charged with the investigation of human rights issues within their territories, including prison conditions, unfair detention, and detention without trial. However, neither the Erbil nor Sulaimaniya-based institutions are empowered to hold government authorities to account.

WOMEN'S RIGHTS IN IRAQI KURDISTAN

Iraqi legislation under the Ba'ath party adhered largely to Shari'a legal principles concerning the rights (or lack thereof) of women. The establishment of the safe haven enabled the nascent women's rights movement in Iraqi Kurdistan to lobby successfully for legislative change and also to establish the building blocks of new educational tools promoting women's rights and gender awareness within a broader context. Some aspects of Kurdish society however, remained heavily patriarchal and imbued with a strong belief in family 'honour'. This importance attached to honour is strongly embedded in the social cosmology of the Kurds, and honour killings have been known to occur.

One issue particularly pertinent to women in Iraqi Kurdistan has been the large proportion of women-headed households within the internally displaced persons (IDPs) population. This, a direct effect of the Anfal and similar campaigns, has caused untold suffering within a society in which matriarchal households are traditionally unknown, and are not easily reassimilated into the social fabric.

Ironically perhaps, Saddam's Iraq was once held by the west as a beacon of progressiveness in the Middle East with regards the rights of women. In 1993 a UN Children's Fund (UNICEF) report stated:

> Rarely do women in the Arab world enjoy as much power and support as they do in Iraq. Women in Iraq are granted the full rights of citizenship, and are also expected to fulfil their role in building the country ... Women pursue high political positions ... [t]hey pursue professional careers in labor and social services ... The 1970 Constitution affirmed the equality of all citizens before the law, and guaranteed equal opportunities without discrimination by sex ... In 1980, women were granted the right to vote and hold office. In 1974, education was made free at all levels, and in 1979/1980 it was made compulsory for girls and boys through the age of twelve. These legal bases provide a solid framework for the promotion of women and the enhancement of their role in society. They have had a direct bearing on women's education, health, labour, and social welfare.[17]

It is true that the secular nature of the Ba'athist regime contrasted distinctly with many others in the Middle East and that women's participation in the professions was encouraged as a matter of Ba'athist policy. However, the utopia of gender equality as described by the UNICEF report was heavily qualified by some significant factors, particularly that Saddam Hussein's regime was a brutal dictatorship and neither women nor children were exempt from its draconian laws or their enforcement. These included decrees that obliged citizens to inform the authorities of knowledge of any subversive behaviour, which was enormously destructive to family life. Later attempts by Saddam to bolster his authority by appealing to back-to-basics Islam contradicted the earlier secular agenda. Decrees of the Revolutionary Command Council (RCC) were issued which repeatedly enforced state control of women's lives and sanctioned archaic attitudes. Cynically perhaps, for a purportedly secular state, Decision 110 of the RCC 'exempted from punishment or legal questioning men who murdered their mothers, daughters, sisters, paternal aunts, brothers daughters or fathers brothers daughters, if they were deemed guilty of an honour crime'.[18] Perhaps as invidious were Saddam's Nazi-like attempts to increase the Iraqi birth rate during the Iran–Iraq war. Strategies employed by the state included financial incentives for men to marry war widows: '[F]or marrying a woman with a middle-school certificate a man received a grant of 200 dinars, for a high-school graduate 300 dinars, and for a university graduate 500 dinars.'[19] Contraception and abortion were made illegal, which consequently led to a rise in backstreet abortions.

Arguably, the creation of the safe haven raised the situation of Kurdish women (bar those living below the 'green line') considerably above the lot of Iraqi women in the rest of Iraq. However, prior to 1992, they were doubly disadvantaged by their gender and by their ethnicity. Neither women nor children were exempt from the mass executions of the Anfal campaigns; the remains of about 300 Kurdish women were recently found in a mass grave in a village south of Mosul, each one had been shot at close range.[20] Women were also among the tens of thousands of Kurds who 'disappeared' during this period. The Iraqi troops routinely separated Kurdish men, women and children in 'sorting centres' before being moved to towns or prison camps.[21] Thousands of young women were taken away by the army, often never to be seen or heard from again.[22]

A document confiscated from the Ba'ath party offices in Kirkuk in 2003 finally revealed what may have been the fate of some of these women. Written at the height of the Anfal campaign on 10 December 1989, the letter was addressed to the General Directory of Intelligence in Baghdad. It lists the names of 18 women, aged between 14 and 29, and details how 'according to your [General Directory of Intelligence in Bagdad] orders' these women were sold as slaves or transferred to nightclubs in Egypt.[23] The whereabouts of these women or whether they are still alive is not known. This does, though, give added credence to the suspicion that many Kurdish women were given as 'gifts' to men in Iraq under Saddam's regime.

Those women who survived the Anfal campaign to head households became impoverished and socially marginalised. In its 2002 report the UN Human Settlements Programme (HABITAT) reported that

> it is observed that there is a predominance of women and children IDPs that have been displaced: they are now living mainly in the collective towns in Erbil and Darbandikhan, in the urban centers of Dohuk and Sulaimaniya and in the rural areas in Sulaimaniya. These groups exist in precarious housing conditions and their livelihoods are most uncertain.[24]

Furthermore, the report noted that women and children formed the majority of IDPs and 'the shortage of living space, access to education by only 50% of the children, high rates of illiteracy, shortage of health care and the lack of any regular employment, are factors that have serious implications'.[25]

In the euphoria accompanying the 1992 elections there was a bold attempt to unshackle Iraqi Kurdistan from some of the more oppressive aspects of Ba'athist family law. In the weeks before the elections in May, women parliamentarians and others from the main political parties (including the KDP, PUK, the Communist Party, the Democratic Independent Party of Kurdistan, and the People's Party of Kurdistan) established a women-only committee charged with the drafting of alternative family law legislation. Proposed reform related to three key areas of legislative concern, which were marriage, divorce and inheritance. It included, *inter alia*: reducing the number of wives a man can have from four to two; abolishing the *talaq* divorce, by which a man can divorce his wife by repeating thrice 'I divorce you'; and new provisions in the criminal code entailing equal treatment for men and women in adultery cases. The committee garnered significant public support for the measures, including 30,000 signatures in a petition taken around schools and hospitals. Despite initial momentum, the proposals failed to overcome reactionary forces within the Kurdish parliament and Saddam's laws remained on the statute books.

Those efforts initiated in 1992 subsequently bore some fruit. Successful lobbying of the Kurdish parliament in Erbil in 2002 resulted in a divorcing of family law from Shari'a diktats and closed the loophole that had previously made honour killings 'legal'.

The relatively stable conditions that have emerged in Iraqi Kurdistan since the signing of the Washington Agreement in 1998 have allowed the emergence of women's groups, NGOs and charities. These organisations remained localised and poorly funded, yet some, such as the Khatuzeen Centre for Social Action, one of the first local, non-politically-affiliated NGOs for women's issues to be established in Erbil, went from strength to strength. Run by local volunteers, the centre is occupied with a broad range of pursuits including the improvement of health, hygiene and of women's literacy; challenging the prevalence of child labour (especially in households headed by women, including Anfal widows); and penal reform. The organisation was instrumental in lobbying the KRG to pass legislation divorcing Shari'a law from the civil code relating to gender-oriented issues. This has resulted, *inter alia*, in changes to divorce, custody and inheritance laws, and increased the penalty for perpetrators of honour killings to 25 years, or death.

While the Kurdish parliament showed itself increasingly receptive to changes in legislation, attitudes in some parts of Kurdish society remained entrenched. In tribal areas especially, many of the challenges faced by women (and men, perhaps to a lesser degree), have been social. In a number of areas of Iraqi Kurdistan, the practices of betrothal at birth and sibling swap marriages are prevalent and continue and there are valleys in remote parts of the region in which every marriage was between close relations.[26] Sibling swap arrangements involved the marriage of sets of siblings, almost invariably without consent, and often arranged at birth. If one couple divorced, the other pair or pairs were also obliged to divorce. The practical effect of the arrangement was that the social pressures for the couple to remain intact were enormous. The psychological ramifications for many women are, according to Hardi, a high incidence of severe depression, and increasingly, suicide in the form of self-immolation. These practices while less commonplace today continue to occur.

Since the fall of Saddam's regime, there is a sense among Kurdish women that their freedom of choice and movement are still curtailed if they do not conform to the stereotype of the ideal Kurdish woman. Gender-based violence too remains a recurrent problem in Kurdish regions. Conjugal violence committed by a husband against his wife is widely accepted in Iraq and even explicitly condoned by legislation. According to Article 41(6) of the Iraqi Penal Code of 1969, no crime is committed in the punishment of a wife by her husband if it is seen as educational. Moreover, religious fundamentalist movements have risen in popularity, which have adversely affected women. Despite the introduction of legal reforms prohibiting 'honour killings' in northern

Iraq, Kurdish women's organisations fear that this practice is still prevalent and that the legislative developments are merely inciting the perpetrators of these crimes to go to more extreme lengths to conceal their crime. The concern is that the bodies of women have simply been hidden or mutilated to conceal their identities to prevent criminal prosecution. [27]

In spite of the current human rights vacuum left by the end of hostilities and the insurgent violence, there is some hope that if Iraq can progress further along the path to recovery and reconstruction, the post-Saddam era will herald a new recognition of and protection for the rights of women throughout all the regions. In the January 2005 elections, the quota system enabled women to win 31 per cent of seats in Iraq's new National Assembly, ensuring the participation of women in the highest echelons of Iraqi politics. The new Iraqi constitution marked a move towards more liberal, egalitarian values with respect for human rights. Equality before the law,[28] equal opportunities[29] and the right to participate in political life[30] for both men and women are guaranteed. The constitution explicitly outlaws all forms of violence and abuse in the family[31] and imposes an obligation on the state to ensure 'social and health security and the basic requirements for leading a free and dignified life' for all, but 'especially children and women'.

However, the Iraqi constitution still establishes Islam as a basic source of the legislation, leaving the door open for its provision to be interpreted along the lines of traditional tenets of Shari'a law. This could potentially have profound ramifications for the rights of women should religious fundamentalists gain power in Iraq. For women in Iraqi Kurdistan, protection of their rights is bolstered by the fact that the 1992 Kurdish regional constitution, while safeguarding the religious identity of all groups, does not specify one religion as a source of its provisions. There are discrepancies between the two texts, but the Iraqi constitution does state that the Kurdish regional constitution will take precedence in most areas of conflict.

Provided fundamentalism is kept at bay, the Iraqi constitution provides a framework which can serve to bolster the status of women in Iraqi society by providing legal guarantees of equality. However, this is still an Islamic text, and this means that its terms are still open to patriarchal and discriminatory interpretation should the political elite so wish.

The situation for women's rights remains, therefore, insecure. Women's groups in Kurdistan are aware of the limitations of the

legal guarantees of their rights and as such they have drafted a Bill
of Rights to be put before the Kurdistan constitutional committee in
2006.[32] The document mirrors similar international women's rights
documents and bans customary practices such as female genital
mutilation, polygamy and forced marriage. The drafters of the text
are conscious that it has little chance of becoming law but see that
the worth of the exercise is in providing a vehicle for women's issues
to be heard on the political level. However, if women's rights are to
be taken seriously within the new Iraq, then more stringent legal
obligations are needed than the present constitutional protection.

8
The Displacement
of Kurds in Iraq

A DISPLACED HISTORY

Ongoing conflict and serious human rights abuses have caused the displacement of more than 1 million people within Iraq. The majority were forcibly displaced from their homes under Saddam Hussein's regime. In Iraqi Kurdistan, large-scale displacement was employed as a tactic by Saddam, to gain control and consolidate power in areas perceived to be politically opposed to the state or particularly rich in resources. However, Turkish military incursions, PKK activity, internal conflict between the Kurdish political parties, and deportations of Kurds and Turcomans from government-controlled areas of Iraq have also contributed to the numbers of IDPs in the region.[1]

Following the rise of the Ba'ath party, internal displacement was provoked in the north and central Iraq as part of the Iraqi authority's campaign to neutralise Kurdish desires for independence and to strengthen control over some of Iraq's largest oil reserves. Human rights violations occurred during the campaign, including the systematic change of the ethnic composition of the region.[2]

The displacement which has occurred in and around Kirkuk has had political ramifications because of the vast oilfields in this area and the tensions between its ethnically diverse populations. In campaigns initiated in the 1960s and continuing until the 1990s, the Iraqi authorities displaced thousands of non-Arabs from Kirkuk and the surrounding areas. The majority of those displaced were Kurdish, but other ethnic groups were affected by the regime's campaign, such as Turcomans and Assyrians.

In 1963, the campaign's first year, the Ba'athist government destroyed villages around Kirkuk following Barzani's insistence that the Kirkuk oilfields be incorporated into the Kurdish autonomous region. Setting a pattern for subsequent incursions, villagers in the region were expelled from their homes and places of work, and replaced with Arabs brought from southern and central Iraq.

Following the imposition of the autonomy law in 1974, the Iraqi government sought to pressurise the Kurds living outside of the autonomous region. Restrictions were placed on the acquisition or retention of title deeds to property and on employment and the transfer of government employees to posts outside the Kurdish region. Place names were 'Arabised' and financial rewards were offered to Arabs who married Kurdish women in an attempt to expedite the process of ethnic assimilation. Kurds were also victims of arbitrary arrest, prolonged detention without trial, torture, or execution.[3]

Further attempts to alter the north's demographic balance accompanied the reprisals against the Kurds in the advent of the ceasefire agreement signed between Iran and Iraq in 1975. The Iraqi government endeavoured to alter in advance the result of any official census in favour of the Arab population at the expense of not only Kurds, but also Assyrians and Turcomans. The government continued its policy of village destruction to the extent that an estimated 600,000 victims were thought to be resettled in government complexes, or 'collective towns'. These uprooted Kurds, evicted from their homes in disputed or sensitive oil-rich areas (notably Kirkuk, Khaniqin, Mandali, Shaikhan, Sinjar and Zakho), were relocated in government-controlled camps near urban centres and along main highways with restrictions placed on their residence and employment. In addition, large numbers of Kurds were expelled from the northern area entirely, and dispatched to barren desert regions in the south. Even after their return some years later, they were banned from re-inhabiting their former villages and resettled either in urban areas or in government camps. This was accompanied by large-scale gerrymandering which redrew the administrative map of Iraq. For the next decade, the destruction of an estimated 4,500 villages continued apace, initially as the Iraqi government created a buffer zone between itself and the region controlled by Kurdish forces, but subsequently affecting villages within government-held territory. From 1987 to 1988, the number of villages in the Kirkuk region affected by forced relocation, destruction and Arabisation reached more than 779.[4]

Iraqi people were also forcibly displaced as a result of human right violations and intra-Kurdish fighting in the northern provinces of the country. In March 1988, around 7,000 Kurds were murdered with chemical weapons during the poison gas attack on the city of Halabja. The Anfal campaigns accelerated the destruction of preceding campaigns, displacing hundreds of thousands and forcing many into the government's 'settlement camps', in which the majority remain. Anfal victims remember all too clearly the confused and terrible circumstances of their flight from their villages. By the end of 1989, 3,839 villages, together with 1,957 schools, 2,457 mosques and 271 small clinics, in Kurdistan had been destroyed. In addition, 219,828 families had been expelled from their towns and villages.[5] The huge amount of destruction demonstrates the suffering faced by the Kurdish region and its people in recent decades, particularly during 1987 and 1988, the two years in which the Anfal operations were carried out.

DISPLACEMENT SINCE THE ESTABLISHMENT OF THE SAFE HAVEN

1991 marked the beginning of a new wave of displacement. Saddam Hussein's response to the Kurdish uprising created some 2 million refugees from Iran, Turkey and Iraq,[6] and the Ba'athists stepped up the forced displacement of Kurds in and around the Kirkuk region. The majority sought refuge above the 'green line' separating the autonomous region from territory under the control of the Iraqi government, placing a further economic and humanitarian burden on a region already under pressure.

It is estimated that in the past twelve years, around 120,000 Kurds, Turcomans and Assyrians have been expelled to the Kurdish-controlled northern provinces, with a smaller number expelled to central and southern regions of the country.[7] Expulsion was systematic, bureaucratic, and usually involved the issuance of formal documents. In the camps of Takiyeh and at Bazian, every family has a story testifying to the brutal and extreme pressure that the Ba'ath party resorted to in its efforts to alter the demography of Iraqi Kurdistan. Torture, imprisonment and constant visits from security services were widespread. Many families had to flee to other parts of Iraq to escape prison, torture or execution.

Forcing Kurds to spy on their own family members was another form of coercion. Ali, in his late thirties, living in the Takiyeh camp at Bazian with his wife, children and mother, described how,

If you were a Kurd, you were forced to join the Ba'athists, and to become an Arab [by officially changing your birth certificate]. Either you spied on your own people, or they arrested you, or made you leave. My brother couldn't stand it, so he left for the north. After that, the Ba'athists ordered me to either get my brother or to bring information from the north. I refused. So they threw me into prison. I paid 500,000 dinar for my release – but they didn't let me out. The cell was one metre long by one metre wide. That was where you had to eat, pee, and sleep. There was no room, even, to lie down. Sometimes there were up to three people in the cell.[8]

The last decade has seen accelerated attempts to change Kurdish citizenship to Arab and to deny Kurds their own cultural rights in other fundamental ways. Such tactics have included the forcible use of Arab names for historic sites, city or town districts, streets, public buildings such as schools and hospitals, and private property such as restaurants, shops and other businesses.[9]

Since 1994 displacement of Kurdish populations has, most commonly, been a side effect of conflict between the two main Kurdish parties, the KDP and the PUK. This has usually occurred along the border between their respective territories; in and around the city of Arbil and along a fluctuating front line from Arbil to the Iranian border.[10]

After the First Gulf War, there was a de facto autonomous Kurdish region. The Kurdish parties, the KDP and PUK, started fighting for the control of the three provinces, causing the displacement of hundreds of thousands of people in the early 1990s. The UN estimates that around 805,500 individuals were displaced in the north, the majority between 1974 and 1991.[11]

EFFECT OF THE TURKISH-PKK CONFLICT

The destabilising effect of the ongoing conflict between Turkey and the PKK has contributed to the high numbers of internally displaced within northern Iraq. The Turkish army signed an agreement with the KDP in May 1997 to use its forces as a border police. The 1998 ceasefire between the PUK and the KDP came under further strain when several thousand PKK fighters moved back into northern Iraq in 1999 after withdrawing from south-eastern Turkey, destabilising the political and military balance in the area. Throughout the 1990s, Turkey carried out raids into Iraqi Kurdistan in search of Kurdish rebels which in turn led Iran to search for Kurdish organisations in Northern Iraq to use as proxies. The intervention of Iraq's neighbours caused the displacement of many Kurds living in this area, intent on escaping the region's insecurity and volatility.

9
Economic/Humanitarian Affairs in Iraqi Kurdistan

BACKGROUND

Prior to the First Gulf War Iraq depended heavily on oil exports as a source of revenue, importing on average 70 per cent of its food needs every year. Iraqi Kurdistan, however, was traditionally self-sufficient with regard to food grains and even supplied its excesses to the rest of the country. Following the First Gulf War, both regions were degraded economically. Not all characteristics were shared. Iraqi Kurdistan in some respects suffered more than the rest of the country. In others it was able to regain a degree of self-sufficiency with the development of its own stratagems for economic survival. Agricultural regions had been hard hit by years of conflict but the porosity of the region's borders with Turkey, Syria, and Iran allowed for informal, though considerable, commerce and importation of goods with attendant revenues from border tariffs. As a result, small-scale business activities in towns and cities prospered from six or seven years of relative stability.

Even before 1991 the Kurdish region was already suffering from the effects of ongoing conflict and the Anfal campaigns. Anfal took a particular toll on rural communities; 25 per cent of the region's 3.7 million population were victims of displacement. It destroyed the agricultural economy, and forced many rural dwellers into towns in the Kurdish autonomous region or Saddam's 'settlements' largely situated in the lowlands of the Kurdish region but outside of Kurdish administration. Mass displacement, with its resulting effect on the economy, occurred again in 1991 in the wake of Baghdad's brutal response to the Kurdish and Shi'ite uprisings. UN sanctions and Saddam Hussein's embargo on the north whittled away at revenue, reducing government income to tariffs charged to traffic crossing the borders of Iraqi Kurdistan with Turkey, Iran and Syria.

Improved relations between the PUK and KDP from 1998 gave the Kurdish economy a chance to recuperate. While a significant proportion of households relied on assistance from government and multilateral sources, prices stabilised.

OIL IN IRAQ: A BRIEF OVERVIEW

Oil has been a powerful force in the shaping of Iraq's destiny since significant deposits were discovered early in the last century. Iraq's estimated 112 billion barrels' worth of reserves are the second largest proven reserves of oil in the world, second only to those of Saudi Arabia.[1] Geologists suggested that there may be 100 billion barrels' worth yet to be discovered, the combination of war and sanctions having hindered development of resources and halted large-scale exploration.

Prior to Iraq's invasion of Kuwait in 1991, Iraqi oil production was in the region of 3.5 million barrels per day (bpd), falling in the immediate wake of the imposition of the oil embargo to around 300,000 bpd. This increased significantly during the course of the next decade; in 2002, monthly production was in the region of 2 million bpd. In July 2002, the Iraqi Minister for Oil 'Amr Rashid claimed that Iraq could be producing up to 3.5 million bpd by the end of 2003. This is doubtless a substantially overoptimistic estimate: experts from within the oil industry suspected sustainable production capacity to be in the region of 2.8 million bpd.

Iraqi oil facilities were in a poor state of repair. Sanctions banning the use of dual-use goods and underinvestment turned some of the world's best-functioning production facilities into the shoddiest, which utilised technology regarded as outdated and questionable (over-pumping and water-flooding) so as to maintain production. Estimates of the sums needed to rehabilitate Iraq's oil facilities have been in the region of US$ 30–40 billion.[2]

The sanctions 'lid' on Iraqi oil exports was lifted in December 1999, with the Security Council voting to remove all limits on the volume of oil that Iraq could export. Nonetheless, all exports had to be made through Security Council-approved routes; exports by other means were to be regarded as smuggling.

UN Resolution 986 dictated that at least half of exported Iraqi oil was to be transited through Turkey in effect, through the Ceyhan oil terminal in Turkey and the Turkey–Iraq oil pipeline.[3] Oil was also exported from the Gulf port of Mina al-Bakr. Ceyhan served European markets, while Mina al-Bakr served the east. Between 60 and 70 per cent of Iraqi oil was bought by companies from countries including

China, Sudan, Pakistan, Vietnam, Egypt and Italy, prior to being sold on to end-users.[4] The remaining oil was sold to Russian firms such as Tatneft, Slavneft, Sidanco, Rosnefteimpex, Soyuzneftegaz and Zarubhezneft.[5] The US was a significant end-user of Iraqi oil; in January 2003, American imports of Iraqi oil were in the region of 1.2 million bpd, as compared to 430,000 bpd exported to Europe and 140,000 bpd to Asia.[6] In addition to official channels, Iraq is alleged to have illegally exported significant quantities of oil through means other than those permitted by Resolution 986, notably to Turkey, Syria, Jordan and Iran.[7]

OIL IN IRAQI KURDISTAN: A BRIEF OVERVIEW

Oil was first discovered around the city of Kirkuk in the early years of the twentieth century. By 1925, the first concessions were granted to Turkish Petroleum Company, in which British Petroleum was a partner, along with Royal Dutch/Shell, and a French company which was precursor to TotalFina Elf. From this point onwards, Kirkuk became pivotal in relations between Kurds and the rest of Iraq. It has been alleged that as early as the 1920s attempts were made to change the demography of the region, displacing Kurds, Turcomans and Assyrians, and moving in Arabs in their place.[8] The painfully apparent arguments prevalent today regarding ethnic makeup are not new. In 1963, when Mullah Mustafa Barzani was negotiating the creation of an autonomous region with the first Ba'ath party regime, his attempt to include Kirkuk as well as the oilfields of north-west Mosul scuppered the negotiations. The government pointed to the results of a 1947 census indicating that Kurds consisted of no more than 25 per cent of Kirkuk city, and 53 per cent of the province.[9]

Other, though less significant fields in Iraqi Kurdistan include Bai Hassan, Jambur, Khabbaz, Saddam, and Ain Zalah Butmaiah Sufaia. Under the regime of Saddam Hussein, production in the north was under the auspices of the Northern Oil Company (NOC). Sixty per cent of the company's facilities were damaged during the First Gulf War.

PIPELINES

The bulk of Iraq's pipeline that exported crude oil was transited through the 660-mile long, 40-inch diameter Kirkuk–Ceyhan pipe. This had a maximum capacity of 1.1 million bpd. A second parallel pipeline with a maximum capacity of 500,000 bpd was originally designed to carry exports of Basra regular oil. Damage to pumping stations and oil terminals during the First Gulf War stood in the way of the pipelines operating at full capacity.

In 1975, the Iraqi government built the reversible, north–south 'strategic pipeline' facilitating the transfer of Kirkuk oil for shipment out of Iraq's Gulf ports, and oil from the southern oilfields for transit via the Kirkuk pipelines. This was disabled during the First Gulf War, and despite affirmations from Iraqi government ministers in 2001 that the pipeline had been rehabilitated, a UN report concluded in 2002 that it suffered from 'serious leakage'.

A Memorandum of Understanding was signed between Iraq and Syria in August 1998 for the reopening of a 50-year-old pipeline in Kirkuk between the two countries. By 2000, there were allegations that this had been reopened in contravention of UN sanctions.[10]

SANCTIONS

On 2 August 1990, immediately subsequent to the Iraqi invasion of Kuwait, the UN Security Council passed Resolution 660 condemning the invasion and calling for the immediate and unconditional withdrawal of Iraq's forces to the positions that it occupied on 1 August.[11] Four days later, the Security Council passed a new resolution, ushering in the sanctions regime that endured until May 2003. Resolution 661 prevented states from importing 'all commodities and products originating in Iraq or Kuwait', and 'any activities ... to promote the export ... of any commodities and products originating in Iraq or Kuwait'.[12] It was intended that these sanctions would be repealed on condition that Iraq met the conditions of Resolution 660. After the ceasefire in February 1991 sanctions were modified. Resolution 687 welcomed 'the restoration to Kuwait of its sovereignty, independence and territorial integrity and the return of its legitimate Government', and dictated that while Iraq itself was prohibited from selling oil, sale or supply to Iraq of foodstuffs, and materials and supplies for essential civilian needs were no longer prohibited. All remaining restrictions would be lifted once Iraq had complied with the resolution's principal conditions: that Iraq identify and destroy remaining weapons of mass destruction, that it demarcate its frontier with Kuwait and accept Kuwaiti sovereignty, that Kuwaiti and other nationals be released, and that a compensation committee be established for the payment of reparations out of oil revenues.

In March 1991, Iraq was visited by an inter-agency mission which reported that '[T]he Iraqi people may soon face a further imminent catastrophe, which could include epidemic and famine, if massive life-supporting needs are not rapidly met.'[13] A succession of resolutions were passed by the Security Council subsequently (including Resolutions 706[14] and 712[15]) which, had they been agreed by the Iraqi regime, would have permitted the sale of a limited quantity of oil to meet the basic needs of the Iraqi people. Baghdad's refusal to agree to the original oil-for-food resolutions was due in part to the accompanying provisions for on-site monitoring of the programme by UN officials, and because they required the Iraqi government to accept the presence of the UN Special Commission (UNSCOM). Baghdad wanted comprehensive lifting of sanctions, something the UN refused to countenance, given its belief (fed largely by the revelations of high-level defectors from Iraq), that Saddam Hussein was still in possession of significant quantities of weapons of mass destruction.[16]

Iraq was offered another opportunity to sell its oil in April 1995 when the Security Council, acting under Chapter VII of the UN Charter, passed Resolution 986, establishing the 'Oil-for-Food' Programme (OFFP). This was intended as a 'temporary measure to provide for the humanitarian needs of the Iraqi people, until the fulfilment by Iraq of the relevant Security Council resolutions, including notably Resolution 687 (1991) of 3 April 1991'. However, there was significant lag between the passing of the resolution and its implementation. A Memorandum of Understanding was signed between Baghdad and the Security Council in May 1996; the first food arrived in Iraq under the programme in March 1997. The resolution initially permitted Iraq to sell up to US$ 2 billion worth of oil every six months, a figure raised to US$ 5.26 billion in 1998.[17]

Not all the revenues raised by the OFFP were for the sole use of funding humanitarian assistance. Of the total, 25 per cent went toward helping Iraq meet its war reparation payments, 2.2 per cent toward the UN's operational costs in Iraq, and 0.8 per cent for the weapons inspection programme. Of the remaining 72 per cent for humanitarian assistance, 13 per cent was earmarked for the three northern governments, implemented on behalf of the government of Iraq by the UN in a programme managed by ten UN agencies, including the UN Office of the Humanitarian Coordinator in Iraq (UNOHCI), the Food and Agricultural Organisation (FAO), HABITAT, the International Telecommunication Union (ITU), the UN

Development Programme (UNDP), the UN Educational, Scientific and Cultural Organisation (UNESCO), UNICEF, the UN Office of Project Services (UNOPS), the World Food Programme (WFP), and the World Health Organisation (WHO).

CRITICISM OF THE OIL-FOR-FOOD PROGRAMME

The OFFP provided a lifeline for many of the inhabitants of the Kurdish region of Iraq, as it did for countless people elsewhere in the country.[18] Nonetheless it has also drawn a number of criticisms from within the Kurdish community, NGOs operating in the region, and indeed other UN agencies. From the outset, the OFFP never made explicit mention of the de facto state of Iraqi Kurdistan or the KRG for fear of jeopardising relations with the government of Iraq (which, of course, refused to recognise the legitimacy of the KRG). Despite the programme's reliance on the cooperation of the administrative apparatus of the KRG in the north, the UN and the government of Iraq were at all times the sole parties privy to the Memorandum of Understanding in which the programme had its origin. In a 2002 report, the UN agency UNICEF admitted that 'all parties are affected and often frustrated by the complex legal and political framework of the OFFP'.[19]

Both of the major parties in Iraqi Kurdistan complained that the UN paid more attention to avoiding conflict with the government of Iraq than the proper administration of the programme.[20] To an extent this is concurred with by the UNICEF report which stated that the 'government of Iraq may perceive any major policy change ... as an attempt to detach the three northern governorates. The obstacles to negotiating major policy and administrative issues in northern Iraq will seriously hamper the impact of any programme.'[21] The report further observed that 'since the start of the OFFP there has been no far-reaching comprehensive policy framework for planning, resource allocation and implementation of most programmes', and that an 'ad hoc' approach was dominating planning and programme implementation.[22]

There has been a lack of data available on the programme and where it has been available it appeared that spending was extremely slow. As of August 2002, for example, only 29 per cent of allocated funds had been spent on medicine throughout the period of the programme. In many other sectors, including agriculture, clearance of minefields, electricity and education, accurate data simply could not be obtained from UN sources. The KRG believed that if the programme's rehousing scheme continued at the 2002 rate, the provision of adequate shelter for the 100,000 families that still required it would not be accomplished until 2028.[23]

It is conceded that Baghdad meddled significantly in the operation of the OFFP,[24] but that the UN's Memorandum of Understanding with the Iraqi government gave Baghdad too much leverage over its affairs in the north. One minister in Erbil remarked that

> the hostile attitude of Saddam and UN bureaucracy meant that a lot of money just wasn't spent on the needs of the region. We submitted a number of projects that Saddam just blocked if he didn't like – for example, we needed electricity generation, so we submitted proposals for hydropower projects but they were blocked [by the Iraqi government]. The same happened with a large hospital in Sulaimaniya … at the end of the day, the UN didn't leave a positive impact here.[25]

The same minister added that in his opinion the UN was too responsive to the fears of Iraq's regional neighbours – noting that Turkey was able to scupper KRG plans for the opening of a bank by making a complaint to the Security Council.

A perceived side-effect of the OFFP was the creation of a dependency culture. Centralised purchasing of food and medicine and the importing of foodstuffs from outside of Iraq removed the incentive for farmers to plant crops, enervating the local agricultural economy. The UN's expressed reason for not buying local crops was that it would upset the Baghdad regime. Desire to avoid confrontation with Baghdad meant that UN agencies did not officially 'recognise' the ministries of the KRG, despite the paradox of their close collaboration and the KRG's need to sign off on joint projects.

Numerous other charges have been laid at the doors of UN agencies, which in concert with Baghdad's efforts hindered economic development in the Kurdish autonomous region. UNDP made a serious of recommendations on how best to rehabilitate the region, few of which were ever implemented. In addition, some, notably the Kurdish administrations, pointed to the UN agencies' underestimation of food and fuel requirements and its failure to address the need for revival of the rural economy as shortcomings of the combined presence of the various organs of the UN.

However, while not immune to criticism, the programme did provide much-needed assistance. Some estimated that were the programme terminated and no satisfactory alternative installed, over 60 per cent of the population, relying on OFFP's distribution of nine kilos of wheat per month per person to all Iraqi citizens, would be unable to feed itself.

EMBARGO

In October 1991, Saddam Hussein began to put the Kurdish region of Iraq under economic siege, cutting off salaries to employees and making the transport of goods and commodities between the north and the rest of the country impossible.[26] By the end of the year, Baghdad had in effect begun the creation of a fortified line between the two regions. Saddam ensured that fuel and foodstuffs did not cross the line to go north. In July 1992, Saddam Hussein introduced a complete ban on the importation of fuel. Within a few months the embargo was total. This diminished household purchasing power dramatically, and increased the price of kerosene 200-fold and rice 80-fold. Other commodities increased in price by similarly astronomical factors.[27] Baghdad used every tactic at its disposal to impose economic hardship on the region, and under international pressure would only loosen the grip temporarily. Smuggling compounded difficulties; while the Kurdish region had substantial wheat-growing capacity, Baghdad offered a substantially higher price than did the KRG, a powerful incentive for Kurdish farmers to sell their crops across the border.

In addition to the embargo, elements within the Iraqi government ensured the disruption of the UN's humanitarian relief efforts through harassment and assault of both UN and other aid workers. These included bombings, shootings, threats, searches, extortion, attacks on and confiscation of property, including vehicles, physical assaults, grenade attacks, and even rocket-launched grenades.[28]

An underlying criticism of the UN's activities in the north, however, is that it was overanxious to treat the Kurdish region as one and the same as the rest of the country, so as to allay regional fears regarding threats to Iraq's territorial integrity. The Kurdish authorities were unable to win any exemption from the UN sanctions placed on Iraq as a whole – thus placing the region under a double embargo, from the international community and from Saddam Hussein.

CURRENCY

The three governorates in effect enjoyed their own currency after the First Gulf War. Swiss-printed dinar banknotes, also known as Old Iraqi Dinars (OIDs), fell out of circulation in the rest of Iraq in 1992. Partly because of the limited print run of Swiss dinars, the currency held its value over the currency of the rest of the country extremely well, maintaining a value in the region of ten to twelve to the US dollar.

EMPLOYMENT

Reliable employment statistics for the Kurdish-administered areas are elusive, but a study made in 2000 by the UNOHCI showed unemployment to be between 5 and 12 per cent. The government was found to be a substantial employer. Thirty per cent of the adult population were employed 'in government services'; 22 per cent in agriculture, 24 per cent in the transportation sector, 18 per cent in the services sector and only 5 per cent employed in the manufacturing/industrial sector. Many held down more than one job or sought temporary employment alongside more permanent jobs. Large-scale displacement, urbanisation and conflict resulted in the creation of an informal labour market as former agricultural workers sought day employment on a casual basis in towns and cities. Various ministries of the KRG initiated research programmes into reversing the pattern of migration from rural areas in an attempt to kickstart the much denuded agricultural economy.

NON-GOVERNMENTAL ORGANISATIONS

UN agencies apart, numerous non-governmental organisations have operated in Iraqi Kurdistan since 1992. Many of the first NGOs to arrive in Iraq did so at the behest of the UN to help in relief efforts in the aftermath of the 1991 war and subsequent uprising. NGOs with offices in Baghdad found it almost impossible to function, as the Iraqi regime micro-managed their activities to an extreme degree. In consequence, most transferred either the bulk or the entirety of their operations to Iraqi Kurdistan. Initially funding was provided by the UK Department for International Development (DFID), the European Union and US Agency for International Development (USAID). After the KDP's joint attack on Erbil with Saddam Hussein in 1996, most

NGOs reconsidered their positions and some, including Oxfam and Médicins Sans Frontières, decided to leave.[29]

NGOs reported that on the whole operational conditions were 'exemplarily good'; although there were reports of some restraints on their activities by the PUK and KDP, including attempts to tax staff on an individual basis instead of through their employers, and monitoring NGOs in an attempt to influence their activities.

Among the most prominent NGOs in Iraqi Kurdistan were the Save the Children Fund, Help the Aged, the Mines Advisory Group, and the Japanese organisation Winds of Peace. All these organisations have faced difficulties stemming from the constitutional uncertainties attached to Iraqi Kurdistan. Because Baghdad refused to recognise the legitimacy of the Kurdish administration, many of the NGOs operating in the area were working 'illegally', without recognition of the central government, reliant on countries bordering Iraqi Kurdistan for access. The Iraqi government was also effective in driving a wedge between NGOs and UN, using its power of veto over UN staff as leverage over UN agencies in an attempt to manipulate them into breaking off NGO ties and funding. NGO officials stated that they were removed from the minutes of any meetings and 'ignored' by UN staff, or only able to meet them in an unofficial capacity outside of working hours.[30] There have also been allegations that by using its power of veto Baghdad blocked the entrance of UN workers from all but Third World or Arab countries. This resulted in Saddam capitalising, either on the sympathy of these staff to the Baghdad regime, and/or concern regarding their job security, to manipulate and hinder their relationships with NGOs. Many NGOs faced the choice of working either in the south or the north of the country.

The UK-based Mines Advisory Group (MAG) employed over 700 local staff as well as a small contingent of expatriates in Iraq.[31] MAG established an operation in Iraqi Kurdistan in 1992 primarily with the aim of removing mines laid during the Iran–Iraq War, and in anti-Kurdish operations of the late 1980s. Since 1992 MAG claims to have destroyed half a million mines and pieces of unexploded ordnance (UXO) and cleared tens of millions of acres of land, returning it to domestic and agricultural use.[32] Other MAG programmes included demarcating minefields from 'safe zones', erecting fences that prevented the movement of mines, and collating data that could be utilised by the local administration, UN agencies, and other NGOs working to clear and destroy mines and UXO. MAG also managed to secure pledges from the KDP and PUK that they would abide by landmine conventions.

The Save the Children Fund established its Iraqi operation in the wake of the First Gulf War, assisting Kurdish refugees crossing the border from Iran and Turkey. Hostility from the Iraqi central government led to the organisation closing down its operations outside of the Kurdish region and continuing to work in Iraqi Kurdistan without the consent of the Iraqi government, accessing the region from Syria and Jordan. Save the Children's first remit was the provision of emergency assistance, primarily shelter materials and food, to IDPs and refugees; although throughout the 1990s the organisation participated in village reconstruction and road-building schemes, educational facility rehabilitation and agricultural assistance. From 1999 Save the Children established a 'long-term programme' focusing on 'social development, community mobilisation, and capacity building for local authorities and NGOs'.[33]

10
The Kurds Have no Friends but the Mountains

TURKEY: A DIFFICULT NEIGHBOUR

Before, throughout and since the 1990s the Turkish government has had a vested interest in maintaining a profile in Iraqi Kurdistan. Having waged a programme of oppression against its own Kurdish population (denying even limited self-government, language rights, political expression, and other tools of ethnic identity), Ankara has long been concerned that moves towards Kurdish separatism in Iraq might spill over into south-eastern Turkey. Moreover the PKK, a Marxist-Leninist guerrilla group against which Turkey has engaged in a bitter war for the best part of two decades, has used Iraqi Kurdistan as a base.[1] Turkey has the second largest army within NATO after the US. Its military might, interests and the extent of its border with Iraq made it a critical influence in the region.

The international community found the formulation of a clear-cut position regarding Turkey's regional involvements difficult. Turkey's reluctance to grant asylum to the hundreds of thousands of Kurdish refugees fleeing Iraqi reprisal was born out of its unwillingness to exacerbate what it has long described as its 'Kurdish problem'. Turkey's record of human rights abuses has elicited both condemnation and appeasement from the west, in the knowledge that as the model for secular Muslim democracy in the Middle East, a candidate for EU membership and a NATO member, alienating Ankara would be counter-productive. Turkey's initial refusal to admit refugees was deplored, but without the country's willingness to host coalition airbases, overseeing the no-fly zone would have been impossible. Knowledge of the coalition's reliance on the use of Turkish territory gave Ankara substantial leverage throughout the duration of the 'safe haven'.

Ironically perhaps, it could be argued that it was former US President George Bush's desire to assuage Turkish fears regarding the Iraqi Kurds that led to the establishment of the safe haven.[2] Saddam Hussein's crushing of the Kurdish rebellion in the weeks after the end of the Gulf War precipitated a refugee crisis of unprecedented proportions across the border in Turkey. 'Operation Provide Comfort' and the creation of the no-fly zone in Iraqi Kurdistan allowed for the resettlement of fleeing Kurds; and relieved Turkish President Turgut Özal of an obligation to provide humanitarian aid to over 500,000 people. However, Turkish suspicion of the autonomous region soon followed. By virtue of geography, the Turkish government was able to regulate closely the safe haven's contact with the outside world; border crossings could be closed, and the exit of Kurdish officials (and entry of aid workers) carefully monitored.

Ankara's relations with the main Iraqi Kurdish political parties has been complex, as have relations between those parties and the PKK. Turkey, alongside bordering Syria and Iran, opposed the establishment of the Kurdish federal 'state'. Yet by 1992 Jalal Talabani had forged ties with the Turkish government, reportedly mooting to then Prime Minister Demirel the idea that Turkey should annex Iraqi Kurdistan.[3] Not being able to afford to antagonise Ankara, the KRG assisted the Turkish military in its operations against the PKK. In autumn 1992, *peshmerga* of both parties took part in a joint operation with Turkish troops in which 5,000 guerrillas seeking shelter in the mountains of Iraqi Kurdistan were flushed out.

Three years later, Turkish forces were involved in a larger operation against the PKK. This drew the attention of both the US and Europe, underscoring the potential for regional conflict in the border areas of Iraq, as well as western discomfort at Turkey's increasingly violent counter-terrorist measures against the PKK. Iraqi Kurds had tolerated a PKK presence since the previous Turkish operation, but prevented it from launching cross-border operations. Fearing that the policing system had broken down, in late March 1995, Turkey sent 35,000 troops into Iraqi Kurdistan to 'neutralise' over 2,500 PKK guerrillas suspected to remain there.[4] Perceived KDP support for Turkey's occupation met a response in the form of a PKK offensive against the KDP (supported, allegedly, not only by the PUK but also by the Iranian government). Iran was alarmed at the designs that Turkey, a US ally and NATO member, had on the region, so close to its border.

Turkey's stated position was that the ongoing power struggle between the PUK and KDP had led the PKK to establish camps in the area from which terrorist attacks against Turkey were being planned. It is argued that its intervention was related to the protection of Turkish citizens. Turkey's actions in Iraq were perhaps only partly guided by its desire to wipe out PKK resistance. Another consideration put forward has been that the incursion was a threat to the Kurds in order to ensure that they would honour any further agreement to restrain the PKK. More likely it was a show of force demonstrating the possible repercussions of further moves towards autonomy or secession from Iraq.

In any event, the lives of numerous innocent people were not protected. While civilian casualties of the ensuing operations were widely reported to be less than anticipated, the UNHCR evacuated several thousand Iraqi Kurds from the conflict area. Human rights groups documented numerous violations of human rights and humanitarian law by invading troops, including torture, killing, and the destruction of up to 70 villages.[5] A KHRP case currently pending before the European Court of Human Rights concerns the killing and mutilation of seven Kurdish shepherds in Iraqi Kurdistan by Turkish troops during cross-border incursions in 1995.[6]

In Europe, the scale of the operation alarmed western leaders; France and Germany in particular condemned the invasion and described it as disproportionate. Germany went so far as to temporarily freeze a US$ 106 million subsidy intended to finance the construction of two Turkish naval frigates.[7] The Clinton administration vacillated in its position, first appearing to express understanding of the need to take cross-border counter-terrorism measures, and then warning Ankara that the operation should be limited in scope and duration. A number of Members of Congress voiced their displeasure, also drawing attention to the US role in supplying arms used in the invasion, including F-16 fighters, Cobra and Black Hawk helicopters, and M-60 tanks.[8]

This was not the last full-scale invasion to be seen in the 1990s. On 14 May 1997, the Turkish government sent an estimated 50,000 troops across the border, again with the assent and backing of the KDP. This latest invasion demonstrated in textbook fashion the complexity of regional antagonisms. Turkey's aim was, once again, supposedly to annihilate the perceived threat posed by the PKK. However, the Turkish military acted on its own initiative and reportedly did not inform the country's new pro-Islamist government until twelve hours after the operation had begun. The military later accused Ankara of starving funds in an effort to ensure that it failed. Also lying at the heart of the operation was a desire to ward off the influence of Tehran (wielded through its support of the PUK, which, in turn, Turkey believed to be assisting the PKK). However, Iran vehemently denied its involvement in Iraqi Kurdistan in any way. The Turkish military believed its interests to be best served by KDP dominance of the region.

Turkey's position regarding Iraq and the Kurds was not a unified stance. Nor can it be regarded in isolation from other issues that it confronted, such as membership of the Council of Europe, its role and position within NATO, Cyprus, the increasing influence of Islam in the secular state, and of course, the unresolved 'Kurdish problem'. Despite the abduction, arrest and trial of Abdullah Öcalan[9] in 1999, and Öcalan's subsequent calling of a ceasefire, guerrillas of the former PKK remained active, both in Turkey and in Iraqi Kurdistan.

Since 1997 the Turkish military maintained an estimated 5,000-strong military presence in its 15-kilometre 'security zone' within Iraqi Kurdistan, in part as a consequence of its war against the PKK. These concerns have, for the Turks, justified continuing military and political involvement in Iraqi Kurdistan.

BEYOND IRAQ: THE KURDS OF TURKEY, IRAN AND SYRIA

As this publication has previously noted, the Kurdish population is as heterogeneous as any other of a similar size. It has been described as the world's largest nation without a state. However, nations represent and contain enormous diversity in terms of religious, cultural and political identity while maintaining common threads. Certainly, there are similarities evident in the way the Kurds have been treated by the states in which they live. Throughout the Kurdish region, governments have adopted the same tactics to control and subjugate the population, deny autonomy and cultural rights, and ensure economic marginalisation. In some cases nations have colluded with each other in creating joint strategies with which to tackle the 'Kurdish problem', or they have manipulated Kurdish sympathies, setting Kurd against Kurd exploiting political and cultural schisms.

There is no single Kurdish identity, but there are Kurdish identities that defy or transcend borders. Pan-regional relations between the Kurds have always been complex and intimate. The mountain ranges that mark frontiers between nations do not mark breaks in linguistic, cultural or familial continuity. Many of the characteristics of Iraqi campaigns against the Kurds – destruction of villages, displacement of villagers, intimidation, arbitrary detention, unexplained disappearances and military operations against civilian populations – have all been employed by the other regional players. At various times, and to varying degrees, Kurds across the region have faced restrictions on the use of their own language. Governments have themselves often paid little regard for borders. A longstanding agreement between the governments of Turkey, Iraq, Iran and Syria, for example, allowed each to attack 'terrorists' in the territory of the other. On several occasions in the last decade Turkey has sent several tens of thousands of troops across the Turkish/Iraqi border, with little regard for the well-being of the local Kurdish inhabitants. This has resulted in the deaths of civilians and the destruction of villages.

Certainly, while the Kurds must endure the artificial national distinctions imposed upon them by the Treaty of Sèvres (Iraqi Kurd, Turkish Kurd, Syrian Kurd, and so on), they have often been united in their shared plight. In the course of the past two decades, the means employed by the governments and military apparatus of Turkey, Iran and Iraq, have at some point come to resemble each other. In Turkey perhaps more markedly than anywhere else in the region the scale of village destruction has echoed the experiences of the Iraqi Kurds. The KHRP estimates that several thousand villages have been destroyed or evacuated by the Turkish military resulting, along with the creation of large-scale infrastructure projects (notably the construction of dams), in the displacement of some 3 million Kurds since 1985. Turkey has a very different standing in the community of nations than did the despotic regime of Saddam Hussein and yet a quick glance at the recent experiences of the Turkish Kurds shows remarkable parallels with events across the border.

In 1923 Mustafa Kemal (Atatürk) created the modern Turkish Republic. Early in the Republic's existence Atatürk made assurances that Kurds would be guaranteed a degree of autonomy and cultural rights.[10] The new government embarked on a radical programme of secularisation, and the creation of a unified, indivisible state based on one language, and one people. By necessity, this required the conversion of an ethnically and linguistically diverse people into a homogeneous population of Turks.[11] The Kemalist project augured a concerted suppression of south-east Turkey's Kurdish population. Suppressing a revolt of Kurdish officers and intellectuals, the Turkish government began a mass exile of Kurds accompanied by the destruction of villages; a campaign of displacement that lasted for almost 20 years. In 1934, the government implemented its Law on Resettlement, setting out a scheme of resettlement dividing the region into three zones: mountainous areas in which all the inhabitants were to be resettled for security reasons, Turkish-majority inhabited districts in which Kurdish migrants would be relocated, and a third consisting of areas in which the Kurdish population was to be diluted by an influx of Turkish immigrants.[12] The displacement campaign was discontinued in 1946. During the 1950s, the Turkish government began to allow Kurds to return to their traditional areas. But the respite was brief. The conflict with the PKK precipitated a violent renewal of the abandoned relocation strategy.

A military coup of the Turkish government in 1980 had the effect of intensifying the suppression of Kurdish identity, to the extent that the use of the Kurdish language, even in private conversation, was forbidden. The coup had prompted Öcalan and his PKK supporters to leave Turkey for Syria and Iraq. On the 21 March 1984 (Kurdish New Year, or *Newroz)* the PKK began a guerrilla campaign, targeting first Turkish military, later 'village guards', Kurdish villagers paid and armed by the Turkish state.[13] Turkey's response would echo of the Iraqi government's creation of a security zone in the 1970s, and foreshadow the Anfal campaigns later in the decade. It ushered in a new and deadly conflict, between a radical, politicised Kurdish force with considerable popular support among the Kurds, and a military regime determined to impose cultural homogeneity on south-east Turkey. The ensuing conflict divided loyalties in the region.

A number of rationales have been put forward as to why, since 1985, the Turkish government embraced village destruction with such zeal, and the factors that might dictate a village's fate at any point in time.[14] Certainly, the Kemalist principle of cultural assimilation played a large part. President Turgut Özal (himself half-Kurdish) believed that a cohesive Kurdish minority situated in the south-east of Turkey threatened the very fabric of the republic.[15] Controlling the region would only be possible if the Kurdish population was forced out of hamlets dispersed across a mountainous terrain, and concentrated within larger, centralised, managed settlements. This was a notion that continued to guide policy throughout the 1990s.

But the evacuations were significantly related to the conflict. In 1994 senior military staff also admitted that the village clearances were part of the government's strategy to defeat the PKK.[16] Village destructions were also conducted in reprisal if it was suspected that their inhabitants had given PKK fighters logistical support. Villages faced destruction if they were unwilling to join the village guard system (mirroring the *jash* system in northern Iraq). Villagers refusing to participate faced the prospect of security forces torching their homes and forcing them to abandon their villages. Often, villagers would be identified, photographed and numbered prior to being evacuated. From the early 1990s, notably beginning with the exodus of Kurds from Iraq in 1991, another motive for clearing villages was so as not to create an extension of the Iraqi autonomous region.

Further causes for Turkish displacements can be attributed to villagers fleeing violence between PKK fighters and Turkish security forces, and the systematic and widespread practices of extrajudicial killings, torture, and arbitrary detention that often accompanied the Turkish military machine, as well as the actions of village guards, sometimes used by the Turkish military to fight their battles by proxy.

The village evacuation policy and violations of international human rights law by the Turkish security forces have elicited widespread condemnation by international human rights organisations (notably the Kurdish Human Rights Project, and Human Rights Watch), and others institutions, both within Turkey and abroad. Its membership of the Council of Europe and desire for eventual EU accession has exposed its human rights record to the scrutiny of, amongst others, the European Court of Human Rights in Strasbourg and the Council of Europe. In 1998, the Council of Europe's Committee on Migration found that

> the evacuation of villages refusing to join the village guard system is carried out by the army with extreme brutality and no civilian supervision. It is frequently accompanied by the destruction of property and further violations of human rights such as sexual assault and humiliation, beatings and extrajudicial executions.[17]

Occurrences of village evacuations, torture, and other gross violations of human rights extended well beyond the arrest of Abdullah Öcalan in 1999, and despite the passage of reforms that appear to improve human rights on paper, the Turkish government's policy towards the Kurds remained of great concern.[18]

In some respects, the travails of Iranian Kurds is very different to those of the Turkish population. Relative to Turkey, Iran's Kurdish policy is tolerant with regard to Kurdish language rights and cultural expression including music, folklore and dance. But there are strong undercurrents of discontent with the Iranian government amongst the Kurdish population, which feels marginalised, politically, economically, and in religious matters, by the theocratic government of the Islamic Republic. Apparent stability in the Kurdish regions belies both a bloody recent history and strong support for a Kurdistan that enjoins the Kurdish regions of Iraq, Syria and Turkey with the Kurdish provinces of Iran. In at least two important historical respects Iran is seen as the crucible of Kurdish nationalist feeling: it was the birthplace of the PDKI, the Kurdish political party which would in turn spawn the KDP (out of which would emerge its own main rival, the PUK), and of the Mahabad Republic, in the northern Iranian city of Mahabad, which was, for a brief and ill-fated spell between January 1946 and December of the same year, the first self-declared Kurdish state ever to exist.

In Iran, there are an estimated 9 million Kurds representing around 12 per cent of the country's total population. The majority live in the provinces of Kermanshah, Kordestan and Azerbaijan which lie in the north-west tangent of the country bordering eastern Iraq, southern Turkey, and Azerbaijan. Prior to the overthrow of the Shah, relations between the Iranian state and the Kurds were difficult and often led to conflict. But the Shi'a, Islamic revolution of 1979 marked the beginning of a violent struggle between the Islamic Republic and the Kurds. The absence of any mention of the Kurds (or any other of Iran's minorities) within the Constitution, and the Islamic Republic's refusal to countenance any degree of Kurdish autonomy, fuelled the outbreak of conflict. Two political parties/factions, the PDKI (Kurdish Democratic Party of Iran) and Komala, acted as conductors for Kurdish sentiment in Iran. Differing ideologies drove internecine fighting between the two.

Armed resistance to the Islamic state carried on into the early 1990s, and by the time it had ended the death-toll, particularly on the Kurdish side, was considerable. The assassination of two major figures within the Kurdish political establishment effectively put paid to the PDKI operating in anything other than the utmost secrecy.[19] (PDKI Secretary General Abd al-Rahman Quassimlou was assassinated in a Vienna apartment in June 1989. His successor to the party leadership, Dr Sadiq Sharafkindi, was shot in Berlin in September 1992.) However, the cleric Muhammad Khatami received the support of 76 per cent of voters in Kurdistan province in the 1997 presidential election, ushering (a now perhaps expired) honeymoon period between the reformists and the Kurds. The PDKI and Komala both remain in operation underground in Iran; membership is punishable by imprisonment or death. There are, however, well established groups in exile in France, Canada, Australia and other nations.

While there are Kurdish representatives in the *Majlis* (Iranian parliament) no Kurdish political party or faction is permitted to exist, causing widespread dissatisfaction among the Kurds, and increasing the attraction of prohibited and underground political movements – including the PKK and Iraqi Kurdish political parties. In a 2001 report on the situation of human rights in Iran prepared by Maurice Danby Copithorne, Special Representative of the Commission on Human Rights,[20] the Special Representative notes that 'The [Iranian] Government has been reluctant to recognize the Sunnis as a distinct minority, particularly where they are also ethnic minorities. For example, for years, Sunni Kurds have complained of from officials in terms of permits for building or renovating mosques.' Copithorne also noted that in April 2001 a group of 30 Iranian parliamentarians had 'noted their dissatisfaction with the Ministries of Education and Foreign Affairs for failing to provide employment opportunities for Sunnis'. Economically, the Kurdish regions of Iran are depressed. Many of families inhabiting border towns rely on a smuggling economy and the presence of the Iranian security services is correspondingly high. Unemployment, drug use, and related social problems are all rife, exacerbating the Kurds' sense of discontent and marginalisation from the rest of Iran.

Estimated at being between 1.1 and 1.5 million,[21] the Kurdish population of Syria is substantially smaller than those of Iraq, Turkey or Iran. Nonetheless, Kurdish–Arab relations have played a significant role in Syria's history, and Syria has played a significant role in the history of the Kurds. Since Syria's independence in 1946, the Kurds of Syria have faced various forms and degrees of ethnic discrimination. These include the continued denial of Syrian citizenship to an estimated 200,000 Kurds following an exceptional census conducted in al-Hasakap province in 1962, the creation of an 'Arab Belt' (al-Hizam al-Arabic) along the Syrian border with Turkey and Iraq, the continued expropriation of Kurdish land, Arabisation, restrictions on Kurdish cultural expression and on the use of the Kurdish language. Periodically, even high-ranking Kurds have been expelled from the echelons of the military, government and other institutions. Kurdish is not recognised as an official language. Successive legislative instruments have attempted to expunge Kurdish from the public domain: in 1986, the use of Kurdish was banned from the workplace. Kurds cannot teach, write, study, or publish in their own language. Nonetheless, there is an active Kurdish political scene in Syria, currently represented by twelve Syrian-Kurdish political parties, all of which trace their origins to the establishment of the Kurdish Democratic Party of Syria (al-Party) in 1957.

Given its own discrimination against the Kurds, it is perhaps ironic that the Syrian government gave assistance, shelter and training to Abdullah Öcalan and the PKK following the Turkish military takeover in 1980. And yet do so it did. (The logic of Syrian support for Öcalan lies in grievances against Ankara held by the government in Damascus among which are disputes over the use of the Euphrates river as a water resource, and Turkey's alliance with Israel.)[22] This support created a number of tensions. Among other difficulties caused, the PKK allegedly levied a toll of goods, money and services against the Syrian Kurdish population.[23] It is also a paradigm example of a regional nation state manipulating Kurds' interests for its own geopolitical interests. Syrian sponsorship ended in October 1998, with Turkey's massing of troops against the Turkish/Syrian border and threatening to intervene militarily had Damascus not closed the PKK's training camps.

It is worth reiterating that the Treaty of Lausanne signed in 1923 imposed new definitions on Kurds that reflected no reality other than the cartographic calculations of the post-war powers. Relations between Kurds across the Middle East have been and continue to be characterised by a Byzantine complexity beneath which lies, if not a single united interest, at least a convergence of a number of interests. But all the landmark events in the history of the region (the Treaties of Sèvres and Lausanne, the establishment of the Mahabad Republic, the creation of the major parties, the PDKI and the KDP and the PUK, the Anfal campaigns, Turkish interventions in Iraq, the human rights violations against the Kurds in the south-east of Turkey, the arrest of Öcalan) have impacted upon the region's Kurds, if not always in the same way. At times, there has appeared to be near unanimity amongst the Kurds that has transcended borders.

Politically, there are close historical ties between many of the main Kurdish factions, even where they have come to define themselves by their areas of opposition. Virtually irrespective of borders, a large number have played a formative role in each other's development. Soon after the signing of the Treaty of Lausanne, Kurdish nationalist parties emerged which built cross-border ties. This accelerated with the establishment of the Mahabad Republic in 1946. Ephemeral though it proved, this bold attempt at independence saw Iranian and Iraqi Kurds brought together in a single administration.

The major political players in Iraq, the KDP and the PUK, both have their roots in the PDKI, formed in Iran in 1945. The Iraqi KDP in turn helped with the establishment of KDP in Syria in 1957.[24]

The PDKI is now outlawed in Iran, having been driven underground in the early 1990s. Filling the vacuum, Iranian Kurdish nationalist sentiment is largely drawn to the two rival Iraqi groups.

On occasion, a single event has brought a unanimous response among the Kurds. The impact of the Anfal campaigns is certainly one such: the chemical and gas attacks, mass executions, and use of prison camps so redolent of the Holocaust, mobilised Kurdish opinion perhaps as cohesively as any other tragedy in recent Kurdish history (even as it went largely unnoticed by the rest of the world). The kidnap and arrest of the PKK chairman Abdullah Öcalan in 1999 was similarly condemned across the Kurdish diasporas and beyond. Within much of the international community it was regarded somewhat cynically. The complexities of Kurdish realpolitik, however, dictated that the unanimity only went so far: in those areas of the Kurdish region of Iraq controlled by the KDP, pro-Öcalan demonstrations were forbidden.[25]

11
US Foreign Policy Towards Saddam: Pre-September 11

Following the First Gulf War, US policy towards Iraq was initially that of containment. This policy was built on the no-fly zones in both the north and south, and sanctions with the purpose of preventing Saddam from producing chemical and nuclear weapons, and launching any more attacks.

However, there were those who did not support this policy, namely Dick Cheney, the current Vice-President (at the time, Defense Secretary) and Paul Wolfowitz, the current Deputy Secretary for Defense (at the time, Under-Secretary for Defense). They both agreed that in the aftermath of the Cold War a new vision was required for US foreign relations.[1] Cheney and Wolfowitz submitted a draft for the Pentagon's 'Defense Planning Guidance' for 1994–99. The paper described a new vision for US policy and argued that America should have no rival on the planet, among neither friends nor enemies.[2] It called for use of force, if necessary, to implement this new world order.[3] The paper also referred to the doctrine of pre-emption, including the right and ability to strike first against any threat from chemical or biological weapons.[4] The document was extremely controversial politically and thus when it initially appeared in the public fora, it was dismissed as the work of a low-level employee.[5] However, the contents of this paper would eventually translate to US foreign policy in 2003.

Following President Clinton's election, in their final hours at the White House, Cheney and Wolfowitz released a final version of the report, acknowledging that the policy formulation had been theirs since its conception.

During the Clinton years the policy of 'containment' was adhered to with Clinton stating in 1998 that

the no-fly zones have been and will remain an important part of our containment policy ... because we effectively control the skies over much of Iraq, Saddam has been unable to use air power to repress his own people or to lash out again at his neighbours.[6]

In response, Cheney and others founded the Project for the New American Century (PNAC) in 1997. In open letters the following year, the 'hawks' urged the Clinton administration to recognise the provisional government of Iraq, headed by the opposition INC and remove Saddam from power. They also advocated unilateral action against Iraq because the US could 'no longer depend on our partners in the Gulf War coalition to enforce the inspections regime'.[7] The group consisted of at least ten members who would later act as advisors to Bush Jr's presidential campaign and/or take up positions within the next Bush administration.

During this period, US military forces had continued to see combat in Iraq. In weekly exchanges, allied aircraft fired missiles at Iraqi air defences that were perceived as a threat to the no-fly zone. US action did intensify on several occasions. In 1993 the US launched a missile attack against the Iraqi intelligence agency in retaliation for a foiled plot to kill the first President Bush after leaving office.[8] In 1996 Iraqi forces crossed a line of control in Iraqi Kurdistan and headed towards the safe haven. US forces responded by launching a heavy round of air strikes.[9] In 1998 following the removal of the UN weapons inspectors from Iraq, the US attacked through 'Operation Desert Fox' and struck suspected weapons facilities and targets throughout the whole country over a four-day period.[10] A stalemate persisted between the US and Iraq following the 1998 crisis.

The second President Bush entered the White House in 2000 determined to take decisive action against Saddam Hussein. During his election campaign, he stated that if it was discovered that Saddam was developing weapons of mass destruction he would 'take him out'.[11] On 16 February 2001, US F-16 strike aircraft and British Tornado GR1 bombers hit targets around Baghdad outside the no-fly zone boundaries. Bush hinted that the strikes were meant to send a warning to Saddam and degrade his ability to threaten pilots patrolling the no-fly zones.[12]

Bush demonstrated his desire to tackle Saddam early on in his administration, but had to wait until an appropriate time to act wholeheartedly.

Part II
The Present

12
The Road to War[1]

'EITHER YOU ARE WITH US,
OR YOU ARE WITH THE TERRORISTS'[2]

Post-September 11 saw the world's only remaining superpower, the US, announce this simplistic harsh criterion for determining allies and dividing the world stage. A state that is unrivalled in its political, military and economic power had experienced vulnerability; this could never be allowed to happen again.

On 29 January 2002, the international community was given the first indication of a historic global shift from the old Cold War doctrines of containment and deterrence to pre-emptive strikes for an unspecified threat when, in his State of the Union address, President Bush warned that the war on terror had just begun and labelled Iraq, Iran and North Korea as part of an 'axis of evil'.[3] Over the following year, when discussing Saddam Hussein, this policy would also be linked to the new doctrine of 'humanitarian intervention', which had been forged during the Kosovo conflict. Here President Clinton bypassed the UN Security Council, while claiming to act in accordance with customary international law as the US forcefully intervened to prevent human rights abuses.[4]

This accelerated, aggressive and proactive strategy, which would eventually culminate in the 2003 war in Iraq, found acceptability with the American public, given their sensitivities to any threat to national security, the revival of patriotism and the popularity of President Bush, following the events of 9/11. The seemingly swift defeat of the Taliban in Afghanistan, with minimal US casualties, lent further support to this policy.

The State of the Union address received wide media coverage throughout the world as a declaration of an inevitable war in Iraq. This created transatlantic tension, as European officials did not support this policy and complained that 'pre-emption' could not be reconciled with international law. Furthermore, China, a permanent member of the UN Security Council that had backed US military action in Afghanistan, condemned the speech, saying such words could 'damage the atmosphere for seeking solutions to relevant problems and it would not be conducive to world and regional peace and stability'.[5] Saddam Hussein did not respond to the State of the Union address officially, but the Iraqi Vice-President, Taha Yassin Ramadan, criticised the 'axis of evil' comment as 'stupid', and added that the US and Israel were the 'source of evil and aggression toward the whole world'.[6]

Over the next few months US–Iraq relations deteriorated rapidly, while the US and the UK drew even closer. Demands from the British Prime Minister, Tony Blair, to allow UN weapons inspectors to return to Iraq or risk military action, were rejected by Iraq. Speaking to German news magazine *Focus*, Iraq's Deputy Prime Minister, Tariq Aziz, said that Iraq was preparing itself for the consequences of disregarding the US and UK's demands.[7]

During this period a number of stories were leaked to the press. Most were accompanied by frequent confrontations with Iraq over relatively minor issues, with presumably the hope of having the cumulative effect of creating an atmosphere where all-out war with Iraq became necessary in the eyes of the US/UK public. Interviews regarding Iraq's weapons programme, such as an article in *Vanity Fair*, where an Iraqi defector claimed that Iraq was developing a long-range ballistic missile system, appeared regularly in the press.[8] US warplanes struck various targets in Iraq claiming retaliation for Iraqi attacks on British and American aircraft patrolling the no-fly zone. The US also expelled an Iraqi diplomat based at the UN headquarters in New York, after accusing him of activities incompatible with his diplomatic status.

Meanwhile, France and Germany adamantly reiterated their position that a war in Iraq without a UN mandate was unacceptable.[9] Britain and the US on the other hand adopted a different approach. When questioned regarding the necessity of a UN Security Council resolution, Tony Blair was deliberately vague and implied the contrary. He stated that an attack would be carried out within the confines of international law and that Iraq was already in violation of 23 UN resolutions.[10] President Bush clearly implied that as far as Washington was concerned a US attack on Iraq did not require a UN resolution.[11]

The UN adopted the role of mediator between the 'hawks' and the 'doves'. In early May 2002, for the first time since December 1998, the UN Monitoring, Verification and Inspection Commission (UNMOVIC) and Iraqi officials held initial technical talks about disarmament. In

July, however, further talks in Vienna ended without agreement. As a goodwill gesture in August, Iraq wrote a letter to the Secretary-General of the UN, inviting Hans Blix, the UN Chief Weapons Inspector, to Iraq for talks on disarmament issues. He refused, insisting that he would not travel to Iraq until Saddam Hussein approved the return of weapons inspectors.[12]

The stance of the US administration concerning the readmission of weapons inspectors into Iraq was clarified by Dick Cheney, the US Vice-President, who stated:

> Many of us are convinced that Saddam Hussein will acquire nuclear weapons fairly soon. A return of weapons inspectors would provide no assurance whatsoever of his compliance with UN resolutions. On the contrary, there is a great danger that it would provide false comfort that Saddam was somehow back in his box. Meanwhile he would continue to plot.[13]

Following this speech Tony Blair, under pressure from his own party, European leaders, and public opinion in the UK, held urgent talks with President Bush. It appeared that he had convinced him to try for a UN mandate for war rather than unilateral military action.[14]

However, on 8 September 2002, the *Observer* newspaper reported that the US had begun a military build-up for a war against Iraq, 'ordering the movement of tens of thousands of men and tonnes of material to the Gulf region'.[15]

President Bush addressed the UN General Assembly in mid-September 2002, and challenged the UN to confront the 'grave and gathering danger' of Iraq, or to stand aside as the US and like-minded nations acted together.[16] In response, Iraq announced that it accepted the 'unconditional' return of UN weapons inspectors.[17] The terms of the weapons inspections were then discussed, but 'unconditional' on the part of the Iraqis meant that eight presidential compounds continued to remain off limits.[18] This was unacceptable to the US and the UK.[19]

In Britain Tony Blair endeavoured to raise support for his strong US alliance by presenting a UK intelligence services dossier to Parliament. It claimed that Iraq had biological and chemical weapons, some of which could be deployed within 45 minutes. This assertion would eventually come back to haunt Tony Blair, and to a lesser extent President Bush.[20]

On 10 October 2002, the US Congress adopted a joint resolution authorising use of force against Iraq.[21] Six days later Iraq renewed its offer to readmit UN weapons inspectors. This coincided with an Iraqi referendum that gave Saddam Hussein a further seven-year term as president, with purportedly 100 per cent of the vote.[22]

8 November 2002 saw the UN Security Council unanimously adopt Resolution 1441, which outlined the inspection regime for Iraq's disarmament to be conducted by the International Atomic Energy Agency (IAEA).[23] Iraq's parliament condemned the UN resolution, and the head of Iraq's foreign relations committee advised MPs to follow the Iraqi leadership and reject the 'US'-drafted document.[24] The Bush administration responded by announcing that it would not wait for the UN Security Council to approve an attack on Iraq should this fail to comply with weapons inspections.[25] Although the Iraqi government initially voted unanimously to reject the UN resolution and called upon the US to disarm, the following day the Iraqi ambassador to the UN informed the Security Council that Iraq would in fact accept Resolution 1441.

On 18 November 2002, after a four-year absence, UN weapons inspectors arrived in Iraq to relaunch the search for weapons of mass destruction in laboratories, factories and Iraqi facilities.[26] In December they announced that Iraq had finally admitted to attempting to import aluminium tubing illegally for weapons purposes. Iraq claimed that it was for developing conventional weapons and not nuclear, as alleged by the US/UK.[27] This bad news was tempered with good. The inspectors were allowed to enter a presidential palace for the first time since they renewed disarmament inspections in Iraq, a bone of contention between the UN/Iraq when negotiating the terms of inspections. The situation from a UN perspective appeared to be improving.

On the other hand, from the end of November through to December, British and American planes fired on Iraqi air defences in what US Defense Secretary Donald Rumsfeld categorised as retaliations for Iraqi attacks, which were violations of Resolution 1441.[28] Iraq claimed that the missiles struck the offices coordinating the UN-sponsored OFFP, which was located at the premises of the Southern Oil Company in Basra. It wounded ten people and killed four.[29]

In Britain, Tony Blair initiated a shift in emphasis for the justifications of the war from weapons of mass destruction to combine it with human rights violations, using a report published by the British Foreign Office. It stated that Saddam Hussein had carried out 'systematic torture' on Iraqi opponents of the regime, and outlined other gross human rights violations on his part.[30] The change in tactics was partly to play on the public's sympathy for the victims of the violations and thereby lend support for the war, and also to invoke the doctrine of 'humanitarian intervention' as a legal basis for war.

On 8 December 2002, Iraq provided the UN weapons inspectors with a 12,000-page declaration of Iraq's chemical, biological and nuclear weapons programmes. Iraq stated that there were no weapons of mass destruction in Iraq.[31] In addition, Saddam Hussein apologised to the Kuwaiti people for invading their country in 1990, while simultaneously accusing the country's leadership of plotting with the Americans to invade Iraq.[32] Although President Bush had warned Iraq that the 8 December declaration had to be credible and complete, Hans Blix, having subsequently perused the documents, informed the Security Council that it was merely a reorganised version of the information Iraq had provided to UNSCOM in 1997.[33] The US reached a preliminary conclusion that the declaration of Iraq's weapons programmes failed to account for chemical and biological agents missing when inspectors left four years before, resulting in a material breach of Resolution 1441.[34] The head of the IAEA, however, requested a few months to reach a conclusion about Iraq's declaration on its weapons programme.

President Bush appeared to ignore this plea and continued to prepare for a war. He gave his formal approval to the deployment of a further 50,000 US soldiers to the Gulf.[35] Shortly afterwards, US military officials accused Iraq of shooting down an unmanned surveillance drone over southern Iraq.[36] The surest sign that war was imminent emerged when the US sent forces to Israel to strengthen their defences against possible missile attacks from Iraq. The US also announced that the Saudi Arabian government had agreed to allow American planes to use their bases in the event of a war with Iraq.[37]

The New Year saw US Defense Secretary Donald Rumsfeld signing a directive authorising the deployment of thousands more troops to the Persian Gulf. Britain entered into the military fray on 7 January 2003, when it announced that it would also mobilise 1,500 reserve forces and dispatch a naval taskforce of 3,000 Royal Marines and 2,000 members of the Royal Navy to the Gulf.[38] In Iraq, whilst celebrating the 82nd anniversary of the establishment of the Iraqi army, Saddam Hussein accused the UN inspectors of being spies and called his enemies the 'friends and helpers of Satan', in a pre-recorded announcement.[39] He also declared that Iraq was fully prepared for war.[40] Consequently, further troops were deployed by the US and the heaviest day of bombing in the southern no-fly zone in at least a year followed on 13 January 2003. Iraq reiterated its claims that many of these attacks were aimed at civilians.

In response to this growing military manoeuvring by the US, UK and Iraq, the French President put French forces on alert for possible action in Iraq, while Russia placed three warships on standby to go to the Persian Gulf to protect its own 'national interests' relating to oil.[41]

The US/UK continued to build up their troops in the region, while the weapons inspectors intensified their investigations in Iraq, visiting a record number of sites. On 9 January 2003, Hans Blix and Mohammed el-Baradei delivered an interim report to the Security Council. Mr Blix stated that 'We have now been there for some two months and have been covering the country in ever wider sweeps and we haven't found any smoking guns.'[42]

Despite this statement, a week later, the *Washington Post* reported that the UN weapons inspectors had discovered a cache of eleven empty chemical warheads not listed in Iraq's final declaration.[43] These were later found to have no traces of chemicals. The head of Iraq's weapons-monitoring directorate argued that the weapons were overlooked, as they were stored in boxes similar to those for conventional 122 mm rocket warheads. Nevertheless this discovery led to a US appeal to NATO for military support in the event of an Iraqi war. NATO, however, played no role in the campaign against Iraq.[44]

Anti-war demonstrators took to the streets of cities around the world on 18 January, to protest against the build-up of US/British forces in the Gulf. In response to this growing public display against the war, the US offered Saddam Hussein immunity from prosecution if he left Iraq.

With the situation deteriorating rapidly, Hans Blix instigated high-level talks with the Iraqi administration, and an agreement was reached for better cooperation under a ten-point plan.[45] Iraq agreed to allow the questioning of scientists and officials by the inspectors without a minder present. Although this had been the chief complaint of the weapons inspectors, Iraq's attempts to compromise appeared to have no effect on the US/UK who sent further troops to the region.

Indeed, by this stage, Britain's military contribution was larger than at the start of the First Gulf War.

The end of January saw anti-war political manoeuvring on all sides of the globe; Germany declared that it would not back a UN resolution authorising war against Iraq; representatives of Egypt, Jordan, Saudi Arabia, Syria, Iran and Turkey met in Istanbul and urged Iraq to provide more information on its weapons programmes; China and Russia joined forces with France and Germany in calling for the US/UK to work with the UN; the Iranian Supreme Council for National Security argued that military intervention was unjustified; and Iraq refuted Colin Powell's statement that Saddam had clear links with the al-Qaida network and advised the Iraqi people to be prepared for martyrdom in the event of an invasion.

On 28 January, Hans Blix gave a more detailed report to the UN Security Council on the progress of the weapons inspections. This report stated that although Iraq had been quite cooperative, there was an absence of full transparency, including the deliberate concealment of documents.[46] More importantly, the report found evidence that Iraq had produced anthrax in the 1990s and that it might still exist. It also indicated that Iraq may have lied about the amount of VX nerve gas it produced and noted its failure to account for more than 6,000 chemical bombs.[47]

The initial response to this report was varied. Iraq denied the allegations and insisted that they had complied with all their obligations. The head of the IAEA reiterated his plea for more time to complete inspections and stated that no evidence had been found to indicate that Iraq had 'revived its nuclear weapon programme since the elimination of the programme in the 1990s'.[48] The UN Secretary-General also recommended that the inspectors be given more time. However, the US administration rejected these calls, arguing that 'the more time they get the more time they're getting the run-around'.[49] Similarly, the Australian Prime Minister called on the Security Council to act and said that it was time for UN 'rhetoric' to be backed with action.[50]

A year after his controversial State of the Union address, President Bush delivered his second and stated that he would produce fresh evidence to the UN of Saddam's illegal weapons.[51] He continued, 'if Saddam Hussein does not fully disarm for the safety of our people, and for the peace of the world, we will lead a coalition to disarm him'.[52] The leaders of Britain, Spain, Italy, Portugal, Hungary, Poland, Denmark and the Czech Republic called on Europe to stand united with America to disarm Iraq, in a joint letter published in newspapers worldwide on the morning following President Bush's State of the Union address.[53]

On 6 February 2003, US Secretary of State Colin Powell presented tape recordings, satellite imagery and informants' statements to the UN, which he claimed constituted 'irrefutable and undeniable' evidence of concealment of weapons of mass destruction by Saddam Hussein.[54] Newspapers the following day reported that France, China and Russia rejected the argument by Colin Powell that urgent action needed to be taken against Iraq, and that the case for war had not been strengthened by his address to the UN Security Council.[55]

France, Germany and Belgium blocked a NATO plan to improve defences for Turkey, which responded by becoming the first country in NATO's history to invoke publicly Article 4 of the mutual defence treaty which binds the allies to talks when one perceives a threat to its 'territorial integrity, political independence or security'.[56] Subsequently, NATO dropped objections to Turkey's defence being strengthened in case of a war in Iraq, on the basis of US guarantees that sending surveillance planes and missile batteries to Turkey did not necessarily mean war.

Iraq in the meantime had furnished weapons inspectors with more documents endeavouring to clarify the questions regarding chemical and biological weapons and agreed to the use of surveillance planes by inspectors over its territory. France and Germany, backed by Russia, used this opportunity to put forward plans to boost weapons inspections as an alternative to war.

On 14 February 2003, Hans Blix delivered his verdict on Iraq's compliance, informing the UN Security Council that Iraq had not fully complied, but on the other hand no weapons of mass destruction had been uncovered.[57] The report did not alter France, Germany, Russia or China's firm stance against military action. In response, Saddam Hussein issued a presidential decree banning weapons of mass destruction and all materials used to create weapons of mass destruction.

On 24 February 2003, the US, Britain and Spain proposed a new UN resolution declaring that Iraq had 'failed to take the final opportunity' to disarm itself of weapons of mass destruction.[58] Plans for presenting such a resolution had previously been shelved when the French President, Jacques Chirac, publicly announced that France would veto a second resolution authorising military action. Furthermore, the Australian Prime Minister backed the resolution, on the basis that if it was not carried out then the credibility of the UN Security Council would be weakened. In response, Germany, France and Russia, presented a rival initiative stating that 'the military option should be the last resort'.[59]

The following day, Tony Blair, in an address to the House of Commons, announced that a vote on the proposed UN Security Council resolution would be delayed to give Iraq a last opportunity to disarm.

On 26 February 2003, in a televised interview with CBS News, Saddam Hussein rejected the offer of asylum and denied links with al-Qaida.[60] He also refused to destroy al-Samoud 2[61] missiles, which the US/UK had claimed were illegal. A swift turnaround ensued two days later when the office of the chief weapons inspector received a letter from Iraq agreeing in principle to destroy its al-Samoud 2 missiles and other items.[62] Weapons inspectors then destroyed four missiles.

On 8 March 2003, the US and Britain proposed a 17 March deadline for Iraq to disarm or face war, even though China, France, Germany and Russia stood firm in opposing a second resolution authorising war. The UN Secretary-General warned the US that it would be in breach of the UN Charter if it attacked Iraq without Security Council approval. In a report to the UN Security Council, Hans Blix stated that he suspected that Iraq was trying to produce new missiles, and that it would take months to disarm Iraq.[63] The head of the IAEA countered this by stating that there was no evidence of nuclear weapons development programmes in Iraq.

Saddam began pulling elite troops away from Iraq's northern border with Turkey, and moving Iraqi Republican Guard units south from Mosul to Tikrit. Other units moved into residential areas of Baghdad. US/UK warplanes continued to patrol the no-fly zone and attack various targets in retaliation for alleged Iraqi fire. Soldiers from the six-nation Gulf Cooperation Council (GCC) also took up positions for the defence of Kuwait.

The British government, under increasing domestic and international pressure, put forward six tests that the Iraqi president would have to pass to avoid war.[64] These included a televised statement by Saddam Hussein consenting to give up Iraq's weapons of mass destruction, permission for Iraqi scientists to be interviewed abroad, and the complete destruction of all al-Samoud 2 missiles. In response, the UN Security Council held a meeting to discuss this six-test plan but France rejected the proposal, saying that the new ideas did not address the key issue of seeking a peaceful solution to the crisis. Iraq also refuted the proposal, labelling it a previously rejected aggressive policy.

By mid-March, the British Foreign Secretary, Jack Straw, told BBC radio that 'the prospect of military action is now much more probable, and I greatly regret that, but it is not inevitable'.[65] The following day, George Bush, Tony Blair and Spanish Prime Minister, Jose Maria Aznar, held an emergency summit and gave the UN 24 hours to enforce 'the immediate and unconditional disarmament' of Saddam Hussein.[66] In retaliation, France, Russia and Germany issued a joint declaration, saying that there was no justification for a war and that the inspections were working.[67] Belgium announced that it would refuse transit rights to US forces if a war was waged without the authorisation of the UN.[68] The Pope issued a statement asking Saddam to avoid giving the west a reason to attack and warned that the conflict could trigger an explosion of terrorism. Iraq, on the other hand, issued a decree dividing the country into four military districts; a tactical manoeuvre for imminent battle.

Colin Powell then urged inspectors and journalists to leave Iraq *in case* of military action.[69] As a result of this Kofi Annan resigned himself to inevitable war and ordered that all weapons inspectors, their support staff and humanitarian personnel be evacuated.

The US/UK and Spain finally withdrew their draft resolution seeking UN Security Council authority for military action in Iraq on 18 March 2003, as they realised it would never be passed. This move was followed by a televised speech by President Bush in which he stated: 'Saddam Hussein and his sons must leave Iraq within 48 hours. Their refusal to do so will result in military conflict commenced at a time of our choosing.'[70] Saddam's eldest son rejected the ultimatum and warned that any US forces would face a bloody battle if they invaded Iraq.

Although President Bush's speech received support from his limited allies, in particular the UK, Spain, Australia and Poland, there was considerable condemnation from the rest of the world; the French President said that the unilateral decision was contrary to the wishes of the UN Security Council and the international community; the Russian President declared that it was a mistake; the German Chancellor said that there was no justification for a war in Iraq; China's Prime Minister said that every effort should be made to avoid war; the New Zealand Prime Minister stated that unilateral war was setting a dangerous precedent; and the acting

Malaysian Prime Minister asserted that unilateral action was an illegal act of aggression.

The day before the start of the war, Saddam Hussein appeared on Iraqi national television and rejected the US ultimatum to leave the country, as did the Iraqi parliament. Accepting the inevitable, Hans Blix declared his sadness that his work had not brought about the assurances required regarding the absence of weapons of mass destruction.

Air raid sirens announcing the beginning of war sounded for the first time in Baghdad on 20 March 2003. After much anticipation, coalition forces, led by the US, had launched a war on Iraq. There were two prevailing justifications for launching it: the belief of a threat from weapons of mass destruction; and to protect the Iraqi people from the gross human rights violations of Saddam Hussein.

THE KURDS' PATH TO WAR

There are two reasons why the Kurds had an important role for the US in the run-up to the war: one was military, as the Kurds had a large force of *peshmergas* available in a strategic position; and the second related to the US war against terrorism as they believed that an al-Qaida cell was located within Iraqi Kurdistan.

Early on the road to war, the US realised that the PUK and KDP could perhaps assemble as many as 80,000 *peshmerga* between them, to fight against Saddam. The Kurds, learning from their past experiences with the US, were in no hurry to become Iraq's equivalent of the Afghan Northern Alliance. The leaders of both the KDP and PUK were aware that the Kurdish self-rule in Iraqi Kurdistan could fall depending on the US implementation of a post-Saddam administration. They were therefore adamant not to assist unless they received guarantees for their safety and for Kurdish future status in a post-Saddam Iraq.

The 'war on terror' had also penetrated Iraqi Kurdistan. A small but powerful Islamist group, the Ansar al-Islam, with links to al-Qaida had allegedly taken control of a series of villages in the remote mountainous area of eastern Kurdistan on the border with Iran. Kurdish officials claimed that the group provided refuge and training to over 100 al-Qaida fighters who had fled from Afghanistan.[71] There were also reports that the group was testing the effect of toxic agents, such as cyanide gas and ricin, on farm animals.[72] The Kurds, however, were fearful that the Ansar al-Islam would intensify their activities and weaken the Kurds either during a war or in the post-war nation building that would follow. The call to war by the US strengthened the bonds between the two largest Kurdish parties in Northern Iraq and they adopted 'a united stand on Iraq'.[73]

In assessing Kurdish–US relations in the run-up to the war, it is necessary to look to Turkey, as a triangular relationship existed between the three.

US interests in Turkey had steadily expanded after the end of the Cold War due to the policy of containment. Turkey's proximity to countries such as Iran and Iraq, who were seen as threats to the US, and its status as the only Muslim country in NATO provided a useful tool in implementing this US policy. Turkey acted as a mediator between these states and was also a strategic point for gathering intelligence. Moreover, in the aftermath of the First Gulf War, Turkey became essential to sustain UN sanctions by preventing smuggling across the border with Iraq. The US also used military facilities in Turkey to launch patrols to the no-fly zone in Iraqi Kurdistan.

Although Turkey was a non-combatant during the First Gulf War, it had allowed the US/UK to use its airbases. Turkey had also cooperated in the Bosnia, Kosovo and Afghanistan conflicts. Consequently, when it came to planning the 2003 war in Iraq, the US were confident of Turkey's cooperation in relation to airbases. In addition, in order to launch an effective ground-force attack in the north of Iraq, the US needed to cross over 60,000 troops at the Turkish–Iraqi border. The military planned a serious thrust from the north to match and then meet up with its troops in the south who would enter from Kuwait. Thus, the US sought permission not only to use airbases for combat purposes but also to send troops across the Turkish border. However, the US/UK failed to take into account Kurdish–Turkish relations and the effects these would have on their military agenda.

The US entered into negotiations with Ankara to strike a deal on these military requests in 2002. As war was not imminent at this time, the US had no urgency to speed up the negotiations and thought that any stalling on Turkey's part related to bartering for a better financial compensation package. The US did not realise that foremost among Turkey's concerns was that a war against Saddam could lead to a fully independent Iraqi Kurdistan, which would have devastating effects for Turkey domestically. They feared that it would encourage Turkey's Kurdish population, estimated at over 15 million, to revive separatist movements. They were also worried about the Kurds gaining control of the oil-rich cities of Kirkuk and Mosul, as controlling such wealth would subsequently increase the Kurds' political power.

Slowly, rumours began to emerge from Ankara that the Turkish military would enter Iraqi Kurdistan once the fighting began to prevent the establishment of a Kurdish state and ensure that the Turcomans were given their own regional government controlling Kirkuk and Mosul. These rumours were later backed up by a *Guardian* article on 1 August 2002 when, in an interview, General Arman Kuloglo, an ex-military commander in Turkey, stated that he believed that Turkey would occupy Iraqi Kurdistan in the event of war because it 'doesn't want the towns of Kirkuk and Mosul to fall to the Kurds'.[74]

In July 2002, Paul Wolfowitz, the US Deputy Secretary for Defense, visited Turkey to continue to negotiate a deal for the war. It is believed that he had informally requested permission for American ground forces to be stationed in Turkey and use its airbases. It was also reported that Turkey was demanding and receiving assurances from the US that an independent Kurdish state in Iraqi Kurdistan would be prevented. The Turkish Prime Minister, however, announced that he was endeavouring to dissuade the US from taking military action against Iraq and made no mention of the context of the negotiations.

During this period, although the Kurdish parties did not officially lend their support for a war in Iraq, they attended meetings with opposition groups and US/UK officials. The purpose of these meetings was to decide on a post-war administration for Iraq. In this regard the KDP drew up a draft constitution in July 2002, which outlined a federal system for Iraq following Saddam's fall.[75] The opposition groups also announced plans that the provisional government would be established in Iraq immediately after the start of the war. These meetings served a dual purpose for the US/UK: to gain support from the Kurds in a war against Saddam; and to show unity, which would hopefully exert pressure on the Iraqi President to go into exile.

After months of negotiations, Jalal Talabani, the leader of the PUK, publicly issued an invitation on 15 August 2002 for the US/UK to invade Iraq from the PUK's territory. In an interview with CNN, Mr Talabani stated: 'I explained to the United States officials here that the Iraqi opposition, Kurds included ... have tens of thousands of armed people. These forces can liberate Iraq with the support of the US, with cooperation and coordination with American forces.'[76]

Turkey found itself in a difficult position. Although it valued its alliance with the US, it was still reeling from an economic crisis. More importantly, it was worried that the US had made secret agreements with the Kurds, leaving Turkey out in the cold. However, Ankara truly believed that the US valued its military support far more than any alliance with the Kurds. In October 2002, the Prime Minister declared: 'We know that the United States cannot carry out this operation without us.'[77]

In November the Kurds and the Turks fell out because of the speeches made by the Turkish Prime Minister during his election campaign, in which he threatened to seize the oil-rich cities of Kirkuk and Mosul in the event of a war. The Kurds responded by warning that such an occupation would turn into a Cyprus-style crisis and they would not accept intervention by Turkey. Two of America's most crucial allies had fallen out, with the US playing piggy-in-the-middle.

The beginning of December saw a flurry of diplomatic activity in Turkey. On 3 December 2002, US/UK diplomats met with Turkey's political and military leaders in meetings conducted by Paul Wolfowitz, the US Deputy Secretary of Defense. Following these, Turkey announced that it *would* allow the US/UK to use its airbases and airspace in a war against Iraq on the condition that a second UN resolution authorising the military campaign was obtained.[78] This announcement did not address the Turkish demands relating to Iraqi Kurdistan. It appeared that some sort of agreement had been reached but Mr Wolfowitz dodged all related questions.

The situation remained static until February 2003, when Turkish and US officials met in Ankara to finalise the agreement on the war. At this point the UN precondition appeared to be of less importance but instead Turkey issued a further ultimatum; either Turkish troops were allowed into Iraqi Kurdistan or Turkey would say no to the US. The US accepted this demand along with an agreement on behalf of the Kurds that their forces would not be allowed to enter Kirkuk and Mosul.[79] In concession Turkey agreed that its troops would steer clear of all Kurdish towns and cities, and stay out of Mosul and Kirkuk unless the *peshmerga* moved in. To that end, the Turkish foreign ministry issued a statement saying:

> The Turkish army will enter the region to prevent an exodus, to prevent the Kurds from establishing a free Kurdistan, to prevent them entering Kirkuk and Mosul, and to protect the Turcomans. We don't want a clash between Turkey and the Kurds, and for that reason we are sending lots of troops to the region as a warning.[80]

US officials offered assurances to the Kurds that the deployment of Turkish troops would be limited; purely for humanitarian purposes, under the control of the US-led coalition.

The Kurds, however, adamantly refused such a deal. They believed that if Turkish troops crossed the border they would pursue Ankara's own agenda and never leave Iraqi Kurdistan, particularly given Turkey's belief in its historical claims over Kirkuk and Mosul. Furthermore, even if Turkey only controlled some areas of Iraqi Kurdistan, it would cut the Kurds off from land access not only to Turkey but also to Iran and Syria. In response to the Turkish Foreign Ministry's statement, the Kurdish parties informed Turkey and the US that if a security problem arose or a mass exodus occurred beyond their ability to cope, then they would ask for help. The Turkish justifications for entering Iraqi Kurdistan were logically rejected.

Both sides believed that the US was favouring the other, while Washington tried to find a solution to the impasse. In the end Turkey would make the decision for them.

Prior to the meetings in Ankara, a formal request was lodged for permission to deploy British troops to Turkey, with the purpose of supporting the Americans in preparing for a northern front attack against Iraq. Turkey stalled in answering this request because of an irrational fear that the British were trying to influence the Kurds to distrust Turkey. Moreover, it was understood by the US during the Ankara meetings that any deployment of Turkish troops would be under the auspices of the US-led coalition. Turkey adamantly refused this condition and believed that the US would back down, as they appeared desperate to get rid of Saddam at any cost.

On 27 February the Turkish parliament voted to delay its debate on the agreement with the US.[81] The country's new government, led by a party with Islamist roots, paused to consider their voters' opinion, who were overwhelmingly opposed to any participation in the war. In conjunction with these issues, Turkey had also been endeavouring to join the European Union for a number of years. By supporting a US-led attack on Iraq, which France and Germany were adamantly against, they worried that it would adversely affect their application for EU membership.

On 1 March 2003 the Turkish parliament narrowly defeated a government motion that would have allowed up to 62,000 US soldiers to be based on Turkish soil for combat operations against Iraq. The loss of the northern front shocked Washington. No one in the Bush administration had expected Turkey to refuse the US request, primarily because it was understood that Turkey would never leave its most powerful ally out in the cold; in the long term they would have too much to lose. Turkey had proved itself unreliable; the US stopped trying to placate Turkey and instead focused its negotiations on the Kurds.

For the Kurds the most important battle had been won before the combat had even begun.

13
The Second Gulf War: 'Operation Iraqi Freedom'

'THEY WERE RECEIVED WITH BOMBS, SHOES AND BULLETS'[1]

On 20 March 2003, at 0315 GMT, President Bush addressed the US nation and announced that 'at this hour, American and coalition forces are in the early stages of military operations to disarm Iraq, to free its people and to defend the world from grave danger'.[2]

The first day of the war saw limited air strikes on Baghdad by the US-led coalition forces. Saddam Hussein responded with a televised address to the Iraqi people, calling the attack 'criminal' and vowed to win the war.[3] On the other side of the border, the Turkish parliament finally approved the use of Turkey's airspace by coalition aircraft, but remained insistent on sending its own troops unilaterally to Iraqi Kurdistan, as a price for coalition ground-force access.[4]

China, France and Russia, permanent members of the UN Security Council, denounced the US-led invasion.[5]

The war began relatively slowly, as military chiefs were obliged to revise their tactics due to the inability to use Turkish territory to stage a northern front. In addition, the coalition tried to persuade Iraqi forces to lay down their arms by dropping leaflets into Iraq in Arabic instructing soldiers on how to surrender.[6] Fewer civilian casualties would curtail the extent of the criticism for the war, both domestically and internationally. Iraq fired a number of missiles at Kuwait, and although they did not have a great military impact, the US/UK claimed that they were in all probability scud missiles.[7] This served to cast doubt on the truthfulness of Saddam's claims that he had not been developing a weapons programme; adding further to the justifications for military combat with Iraq.

The world waited for the 'shock and awe' tactics that had been promised by the US.[8] They did not come until the end of the first week and even then they were rather muted. Instead, American and British bombing targeted Iraqi command and control facilities, intending to break up the Iraqi military, so that no one knew who was in charge. Initially, concentrating on the south of the country, the US/UK forces advanced into Umm Qasr, before moving towards Baghdad. They met little resistance on the way, but were hampered by sandstorms.

In the south of Iraq it took 21 days of often ferocious fighting to destroy Saddam's regime. There were still plenty of battles to come aimed at flushing out pockets of resistance, but Saddam had lost his overall control.

THE KURDISH JERUSALEM[9]

On the northern front a further crisis began brewing on 21–22 March when Turkey announced that it had sent troops across the border unilaterally to Iraqi Kurdistan.[10] This caused the US to fear a 'war within a war' scenario between the Kurds and the Turks. However, Turkey later retracted this statement,[11] although it did amass thousands of troops on the border with Iraqi Kurdistan and the threat that they would unilaterally cross into Kurdish territories remained.

At a final round of talks with Turkey on 25 March, the US admitted failure at reaching an agreement with Turkey, and turned in earnest to working openly with Iraqi Kurds.[12] The northern front had been opened, making the estimated 80,000 *peshmergas* the second largest coalition troop contribution.

On the night of 26 March more than 1,000 members of the US 173rd Airborne Brigade arrived in Iraqi Kurdistan by means of a well publicised airdrop over the Kurdish airfield at Harir. The first ground battles in the north were not against Iraqi troops but against the Ansar al-Islam, who were cited as being strategically a more dangerous enemy, located at the rear of the Kurdish/US forces. *Peshmergas* and US Special Forces moved into the mountainous terrain held by the Ansar al-Islam, identifying targets and calling in air strikes from US jets. These tactics appeared to prove effective militarily as within days the Ansar al-Islam allegedly retreated to Iran.[13]

After ten days of war in Iraq there was still no sign of a major US troop build-up in the north. Kirkuk remained under Iraqi government control, and although there had been some bombing along the front line, the *peshmerga* busily fighting to their rear had not fired a single shot at them. When the Kurds finally turned their attentions to their front line, they adopted the same tactics as those against the Ansar al-Islam; operating behind Iraqi lines indicating targets for jets to bomb. There were some skirmishes with Iraqi troops in the areas near

Chamchamal, but they quickly gave up and the *peshmerga* pushed into Iraqi government territory north of Kirkuk.

The fall of Baghdad on 9 April affected the Iraqi resistance in the north. Government troops fled allowing the *peshmerga* to enter Kirkuk virtually unresisted the next morning.[14] They were given a hero's welcome.

Seeing Kirkuk fall so easily, the Iraqi forces in Mosul decided to surrender the city. The KDP acted as an intermediary and negotiated that the US stop bombing Mosul.[15] On 9 April the Iraqi forces laid down their arms and the city waited for the US forces to come. They did not.

Although scenes of joyful celebrations in Kirkuk and Mosul were broadcast all over the world, things quickly got out of hand as looting began. The US had been unprepared for such a speedy capitulation by Saddam's forces in the north and consequently there were not enough coalition troops on the ground to maintain order. The US tried to blame the PUK/KDP for taking Kirkuk and Mosul too fast. Others blamed the US, such as the Human Rights Watch, London director of the Middle East and North Africa division who stated that 'They had a long time to plan for issues such as this, but it seems nothing was done.'[16]

With a lack of US forces on the ground, it was up to the Kurdish security forces to restore order and prevent further looting. At a meeting in the Ba'ath party headquarters in Kirkuk, the leaders of the PUK and KDP stated that they were trying to stop the looting 'but the local people are very angry. They have been so oppressed and tortured ... It's going to take a couple of days to sort out.'[17]

Initially the PUK sent police and engineers from Iraqi Kurdistan to enforce security and reinstall basic services in Kirkuk, and they set up committees to return looted property to its owners.

There were other negative aspects to looting, however, mostly relating to land. Arab villagers complained that Kurds were reversing Saddam's 'Arabisation' process of ethnic cleansing by expelling them from land that had originally been owned by Kurds. Hundreds died in these interethnic clashes, causing thousands of Arabs to flee the areas for fear of reprisals. The Arabisation process had deeply scarred Iraq. The leader of the KDP, Massoud Barzani, issued a statement condemning the looting and attacks on Arabs, saying 'No Kurd is allowed to attack the property, life or integrity of any Arab citizen in any village, district or in the centre of main cities.'[18] Furthermore, he stated that 'the Arabs have full right to self-defence in such incidents'.[19] PUK officials also denied that, contrary to reports, expulsion did not represent their official policy, but conceded that some Kurds could have pretended to be PUK officials in order to 'pursue criminal activities'.[20]

There were also occurrences of Arabs killing Kurds. One such incident arose when Arab villagers occupied an abandoned army checkpoint and fired randomly at several Kurdish cars. They claimed that some Kurdish looters had tried to appropriate their petrol station and that this was their defence strategy.[21]

There were further tensions between the Kurds and Turcomans. These were provoked and worsened by Turkey's actions during this time. Turkey announced that there were more than 70,000 troops along the border ready to enter Iraq, having seen the *peshmerga* pour into the cities of Kirkuk and Mosul.[22] Their justifications were that they needed to protect the Turcomans. However, the US knew that the Kurds would not accept an invasion by Turkey and in order to prevent another war tried to assure Turkey that the Kurds were ultimately under their control. To that end the Kurds made it clear that the *peshmerga* would leave Kirkuk and Mosul as soon as sufficient US troops had arrived to control the cities.[23]

The US, in concession, also agreed to allow Turkish military observers to assess the situation in Iraqi Kurdistan[24] and pledged US$ 1 billion in aid to bolster Turkey's troubled economy.[25] In return, General Hilmi Ozkok promised that Turkish troops would not move into Iraqi Kurdistan before consulting the US. Tensions heightened, however, amid accusations that Turkish troops had deliberately fired shells on villages in Iraqi Kurdistan.[26] On 27 April US forces announced that they had intercepted attempts by Turkish military intelligence to smuggle arms in aid consignments to the Turcomans in Kirkuk.[27] This did not come as a great surprise to the Kurds as Turkey had regularly intervened surreptitiously on the border for a number of years.

Despite all of these issues, Kirkuk returned to normal within a very short period of time under the PUK's control. Businesses were open as usual and rubbish was even being collected a few days after its fall. In Mosul, however, some areas remained under control of Ba'ath loyalists and fedayeen militias, allowing a cycle of revenge killings to be established.

Ultimately, the situation in Iraqi Kurdistan was not as bad as that in the south despite a much smaller US military presence. The PUK and KDP were credited with managing a difficult situation particularly well, in light of the state of affairs in the rest of Iraq. There was no mass exodus and no massacre of Turcomans. Moreover, the Kurds did not rise to Turkish provocation and let the US coalition place Kirkuk and Mosul under their auspices.

The Kurds had made promises to the US; they had proved themselves to be reliable.

WAR OVER?

Commentators give different dates for the day the war in Iraq ended. Some refer to dates in mid-April while others refer to 1 May 2003.

KHRP contacted US Central Command and asked them for the official date the war ended. KHRP was informed that 'major combat operations' ended on 1 May 2003 as announced by President Bush on board the USS *Abraham Lincoln*.[28] However, when asked if this meant that the war ended on that date, US Central Command would not answer the question directly and reiterated that major combat ended on 1 May. KHRP then contacted the press desk at the Coalition Press Information Centre (CPIC), who replied by email that 'the official end of "Major Combat Operation" Pres Bush declared was 01 MAY 03. But please do not confuse, we are still at war.'[29]

THE CURRENT SECURITY SITUATION

The security situation in Iraq has been tense since the declaration of the end of 'major combat' on 1 May 2003. Individual factions have been targeting both military and civilian personnel, particularly in road convoys. It is believed that these attacks are being carried out not only by Iraqis, but also by foreigners who have flooded into Iraq to offer their support.[30] To that end no non-Iraqi males between the ages of 18 and 45 are allowed to travel to Iraq unless they can justify their reasons for being there. However, this policy has not prevented the unrest.

At the time of writing, the number of US forces killed in Iraq since the outbreak of the war is over 400. On the Iraqi side, there are no accurate figures as to the total loss of citizens' lives through combat or civilian casualties.

There have been a number of particularly shocking attacks, such as the bombing of the International Red Cross headquarters in Baghdad on 27 October 2003 that killed twelve people. In addition, on 19 August 2003, a huge truck bomb struck the UN headquarters in Baghdad, killing over 20 people including the UN Special Representative of the Secretary-General to Iraq, Sergio Vieira de Mello. Mr de Mello was also the UN High Commissioner for Human Rights. These types of attacks carried on throughout November/December 2003, and a number of casualties amongst foreign nationals in Iraq, including reconstruction workers, diplomats and intelligence officers, have been reported. Missiles are also being used to target planes at Baghdad International Airport and even a DHL cargo aircraft was struck.[31] Iraqi casualties have resulted from these incidences; for example when a bomb exploded outside the Italian police headquarters in Nasiriya, 27 people were killed and 79 wounded, including Iraqi nationals.

Such attacks have caused increased social tensions leading to a number of demonstrations, which in turn have added to the security problem.

Just one day after the announcement of the capture of Saddam Hussein, street battles and demonstrations against the coalition erupted in west Baghdad as well as other cities in the Sunni area. Since the capture of Saddam there have been a series of suicide bomb attacks, explosions and drive-by shootings raising insurgency to a new intensity.[32] Attacks have shifted emphasis from coalition forces to local Iraqi police working with the coalition. Tony Blair cautioned that 'the terrorists and Saddam's sympathisers will continue and, though small in number and in support, their terrorist tactics will still require vigilance, dedication and determination'.[33] However, the US claimed that capturing Saddam had provided them with some details to combat underground cells through documentation found in his briefcase.[34] Geoff Hoon, the Secretary of State for Defence, stated that 'Although in recent weeks there has been a decline in the number of security incidents in Iraq, following a peak in November, the security situation remains challenging.'[35]

Iraqi Kurdistan has remained relatively tranquil in comparison to the south of the country, as observed in an article from Erbil on 14 November 2003 which stated that 'there were no concrete barriers outside the hotel or US soldiers with weapons poised. Not even a local armed guard was visible.'[36] This is mainly due to the strong Kurdish establishment in Iraqi Kurdistan and the history of maintaining a civil society over the past twelve years. The worst attack to date was in November 2003 when at least four people were killed and 40 injured in a suicide bomb attack outside the offices of the PUK in Kirkuk. Such attacks have been rare in the north but a surge in roadside ambushes and assassination attempts is occurring, allegedly caused by the Ansar al-Islam returning to the north from Iran and joining forces with members of Saddam's regime.[37] A statement that purportedly came from Osama bin Laden, threatened increased terrorist activity in Iraq, named Kurds as legitimate targets and praised the Ansar al-Islam for their current activities.[38] Following the capture of Saddam, a volley of incidences have occurred in Mosul, which included the killing of Iraqi policemen, although not to the same extent as in the south of Iraq.

SECURITY STRATEGY

According to President Bush,

> Saddam loyalists and foreign terrorists may have different long-term goals, but they share a near-term strategy: to terrorize Iraqis and to intimidate America and our allies. In the last few months, the adversary has changed its composition and method, and our coalition is adapting accordingly.[39]

The strategy that the coalition has recently employed to deal with the current security situation is to announce the establishment of an indigenous counterinsurgency force comprising up to 850 troops from five political factions, including the KDP and the PUK.[40] They are going to be deployed in and around Baghdad and will work under the auspices of US Special Forces. This is the first step towards an eventual coalition handover of national security to the Iraqis along with the announcement by the UK that it was sending 500 fresh troops to Iraq suggesting that it was for the purposes of training Iraqi policemen.

The effectiveness of the initial 850-man force will allow the coalition to gauge the viability of a larger multiethnic force in the future. As most of the resistance is coming from the Sunni population, the majority of the force is Kurdish and Shi'ite. However, there has been some criticism by independent Governing Council members that 'this is a very big blunder … We should be dissolving militias, not finding ways to legitimise them. This sends the wrong message to the Iraqi people.'[41]

Kurdish *peshmergas* have been assisting US forces in the towns of Mosul and Kirkuk with local security measures. This new plan, however, will catapult the Kurds from being regional, ethnic entities with separate militias into national political entities, and may enhance their standing and status on a broader national scale.

14
Current Executive Structure in Iraq

SADDAM'S IRAQI OPPOSITION

Following the First Gulf War, the Iraqi National Congress (INC), an umbrella organisation for the main Iraqi opposition groups to Saddam's regime, was established. It was formally constituted when the PUK and KDP attended a meeting in Vienna in conjunction with dozens of opposition groups in June 1992. In October of the same year, major Shi'ite Islamist groups joined the coalition when the INC met in Iraqi Kurdistan. The Kurds played a valuable role in the INC, as they were the only member group with armed forces and a presence on Iraqi territory. Moreover, the members of the INC's first executive committee included the KDP leader, Massoud Barzani. In relation to Kurdish politics, the INC has been committed to the concept of a federal Iraq from the outset,[1] which assured the Kurds of their autonomy within a post-war Iraq.

In 1995 the INC attempted to launch an offensive against Saddam but it ended in failure although the CIA backed it. A year later, the Iraqi army destroyed its base in Erbil, Iraqi Kurdistan,[2] and the INC would remain quiet on the political scene until the run-up to the 2003 war in Iraq.

In its preparations for military action against Iraq in 2002, the US enlarged the scope of the INC and built up its capabilities. To that end, the KDP and PUK were two of six major opposition groups invited to Washington for meetings with senior State and Defense Department officials in August 2002. As military action approached, President Bush authorised US$ 92 million to be split between these different groups, including the PUK and KDP, to train and assist with their activities.[3]

The opposition began to plan their role in post-war Iraq by holding a conference with major opposition groups attending in London in December 2002. The meeting ended with an agreement to form a 65-member follow-up committee, which met in February in Iraqi Kurdistan. There they formed a six-seat committee, which included the PUK and KDP's leaders, to prepare for a transition regime.

On 15 April 2003, the US began the process of establishing a post-Saddam successor. They organised a conference in Nasiriya of approximately 100 Iraqis from various groups. Several Shi'ite clerics, however, boycotted the meetings and called for the establishment of an Islamic state. On 26 April another meeting was held in Baghdad, which ended with an agreement to hold a broader meeting within a month, to determine an Iraqi interim administration.

THE NEW IRAQI GOVERNMENT

The Coalition Provisional Authority

The Coalition Provisional Authority (CPA) was a US-run body created in May 2003 to govern Iraq after the collapse of Saddam Hussein's regime. The goal of the CPA, as stated by head administrator Paul Bremer, was to prepare Iraq for full sovereignty through the development of four pillars: governance, security, essential services and economy.[4] UN Security Council Resolution 1483 recognised the CPA, calling upon it to work 'towards the restoration of conditions of security and stability and the creation of conditions in which the Iraqi people can freely determine their own political future'.[5] In October 2003, the UN Security Council passed Resolution 1511, which affirmed that the CPA's responsibilities, authorities and obligations would be passed on to a sovereign 'internationally recognized, representative government established by the people of Iraq'.[6] The CPA was formally dissolved when power was handed over to the Interim Iraqi Government (IIG) on 28 June 2004, ahead of the dissolution date set out in UN Security Council Resolution 1546.

The CPA established the Iraqi Governing Council (IGC) on 13 July 2003, which was recognised by UN Security Council Resolution 1500 as 'an important step towards the formation by the people of Iraq of an internationally recognized, representative government that will exercise the sovereignty of Iraq'.[7] As the main body of Iraqi administration during the occupation, the IGC adopted the Transitional Administrative Law (TAL) in March 2004, which was to be the Law of the Administration of the State of Iraq for the Transitional Period.[8]

In order to establish effective representative government and make democratic elections possible, the CPA set out to produce an interim constitution which respected international law and human rights. The CPA deemed it essential to create a fair and effective justice system as well as open and transparent political institutions and processes.

Effective elected officials, strengthened local government systems and an empowered civil society were all considered to be important to the development of governance in Iraq. With respect to governance, the CPA has been criticiced for dismissing most Ba'ath government officials, losing the benefit of their expertise, notwithstanding that many of them were Ba'ath party members in name only, rather than ideology. The de-Ba'athification of the Iraqi security forces was a controversial move which later met with discord and criticism. CPA administrator Paul Bremer has been criticised for not calling back the nearly 400,000 troops that were put out of work when the Iraqi army was dissolved shortly after the war. This decision arguably led to the involvement of many former troops in the insurgency out of anger, resentment and dim prospects. Some of them sold weapons to insurgents, while others actively participated in the insurgency. In a June 2006 interview, Bremer admitted that the CPA had under-estimated the resiliency of the insurgency and that a new strategy would be required to defeat it.[9] There is a belief that today much of the Iraqi armed forces are made up of former Iraqi army officers and Ba'ath party officials who have been reincorporated into the new Iraqi security structure.

The fight against the insurgency, terrorism, ethnic conflict and all kinds of violent extremism present the greatest challenge to stability in Iraq. Therefore one of the main goals of the CPA was to assist the IGC in managing internal and external security. Moreover, the CPA helped the IGC to create its own defence and police forces, including a new army, air force and coastal defence force. The Iraqi National Intelligence Agency (INIS) was created to track narcotics production and trafficking, espionage, weapons of mass destruction and serious organised crime. The foundation of relations between Iraq and other states in the region, as well as the international community, was considered to be important to the development of security.

The CPA attempted to restore essential services to the Iraqi people by assisting the IGC in rebuilding Iraq's infrastructure, maintaining oil production, ensuring food security, and improving water and sanitation systems. The CPA also focused on education, health care, access to housing and the rehabilitation of key infrastructures such as transportation and communications.[10]

To facilitate the development of a market-based economy for Iraq, the CPA aimed to modernise the central bank, strengthen the commercial banking sector and re-establish the stock and securities market. Accountability was advocated by the CPA and IGC through the promotion of transparent financial arrangements and a sound resource allocation framework. To encourage private business, the banking sector was built up, and to further aid the economy, a scheme was devised for the oil industry.[11]

Despite these goals, the CPA was criticised for neglecting the unemployment problem that occurred after the war. Most of the funds designated for rebuilding Iraq were spent on rebuilding Iraq's infrastructure (such as water and electricity systems). Although this provision was crucial, funds may have been better directed towards implementing a comprehensive programme that would have provided the Iraqi people with immediate employment. Projects that had some short-term benefits would have provided a source of income and may have engendered a climate of hope in Iraq.

The CPA was praised by many Iraqis for promoting new organisations such as those aimed at the protection of women's rights; it provided funding for women's centres throughout the country which offered vocational training and educational opportunities to women. However, despite its intentions, the crucial error in the CPA's strategy was not consulting effectively with Iraqi people to determine their vision of the future of Iraq. Furthermore, the CPA's work has been marred by allegations of financial irregularities, contracts awarded to American firms under dubious circumstances, and general corruption. The origin of the CPA is not clear, with the US Army Legal Services Agency claiming that it was not a federal agency but rather a 'multinational coalition' and other government documents stating that it was a US government entity.[12] This ambiguity implies that it might be difficult to hold CPA officials, many of whom have been described as inexperienced,[13] responsible for the consequence of their activities, decisions and spending. That is to say, it is unclear whether the CPA met its goals of consultation, transparency and accountability in administrating Iraq during the interim period.

The Iraqi Governing Council and the Interim Iraqi Government

On 13 July 2003, the Iraqi Governing Council (IGC) was formed, signifying a step towards the formation of a democratic government in Iraq. The 25-member body comprised leaders from Iraq's principal religious and ethnic groups: thirteen Shi'ite Arabs, five Sunni Arabs and five Kurds, one Assyrian and one Turcoman. The members were chosen by the US-led coalition in conjunction with a number of Iraqi figures. The presidency of the Governing Council rotated between nine members, each term lasting a month. On 30 July 2003 Ibrahim

Jaafari, a Shi'ite politician and spokesman of the Da'wa party, became the first president of the Governing Council. Other council members who held the position of IGC president include Abdul Azis al-Hakim of the Supreme Council for the Islamic Revolution in Iraq (SCIRI), Kurdish leaders Jalal Talabani and Massoud Barzani, Iyad Allawi of the Iraqi National Accord, Muhsin Abdul Hameed of the Iraqi Islamic Party, Shi'ite scholar Muhammed Bahr al-Uloum, and former Foreign Minister Adnan Pachachi. The US-led coalition has been criticised for creating an Iraqi Governing Council based on ethnic and sectarian criteria, potentially setting a bad precedent for inter-Iraqi relations. However, realistically, Iraq was divided along tribal and sectarian lines long before coalition intervention and this was likely the only political system that would have been acceptable to Iraqi political leaders at the time of formation.

The priorities of the IGC included achieving stability and security, reviving the economy and delivering public services.[14] The IGC was also to play a key role in drafting a new Iraqi constitution. On 15 November 2003, the Coalition Provisional Authority and the Iraqi Governing Council agreed on a timetable for drafting a new constitution and holding of elections. Although no mention was made of a particular role for the United Nations, the IGC stressed its desire for UN participation in the implementation of the agreement. A Transitional National Assembly, which would elect an executive branch and appoint ministers, was to be established by 31 May 2004. This assembly (later known as the Interim Iraqi Government) was to take over governing responsibilities for Iraq by 30 June 2004. An interim constitution, known as the Transitional Administrative Law (TAL), was to be drafted and approved by February 2004. The TAL would specify the structure and scope of the transitional administration and allow for the dissolution of the CPA and the IGC after the handover of power. Furthermore, the agreement submitted a timetable for the drafting of a permanent Iraqi constitution by a democratically elected government. After elections which would take place by 31 January 2005, the democratically elected Transitional National Assembly would draft the Iraqi constitution. The TAL would expire and the new constitution would take effect once a democratically elected Iraqi government took office following elections to be held by 31 December 2005.

The TAL was drafted by a selected group of Sunni, Shi'ite, and Kurdish leaders along with other experts, under the supervision of the CPA. Signed in Baghdad on 8 March 2004, the TAL defined the foundations of Iraq as a liberal democratic, decentralised and pluralistic federal state. Power was to be shared among the central government and 18 provinces, as well as municipalities and local administrations. Although Islam was fixed as the official state religion, religious freedom and human rights protection were recognised by the document. Article 61(c) of the TAL stipulated that the constitution would not be ratified if two-thirds of voters in three provinces rejected it. Insisted on by the Kurds as a protection against majority rule, Article 61(c) has been criticised as a constitutional entrenchment of the tyranny of the minority. The TAL was opposed by many Shi'ite clerics, including Grand Ayatollah Ali al-Sistani, who believed that it virtually eliminated the options of future elected legislators. There was also concern about a provision that allowed for US-led forces to remain in Iraq indefinitely.

On 1 June 2004, shortly after the signing of the TAL, the IGC was dissolved and an Interim Iraqi Government (IIG) was introduced. The Interim Government consisted of a President with two deputy Presidents, a Council of Ministers including a Prime Minister, an Interim National Council and a Judicial Authority. The Council of Ministers was authorised to make laws that would remain valid unless they were modified or repealed by future Iraqi governments. However, the Interim Government was to 'refrain from taking any actions affecting Iraq's destiny beyond the limited interim period',[15] bringing into question the complete transfer of sovereignty to the Iraqi government. The role of the 100-member Interim National Council, which was to be chosen by a National Conference made up of representatives from the different governorates and regions of Iraq, was to liaise with the Interim Government on the creation of national consensus and promotion of reconciliation.[16] Iyad Allawi, a Shi'ite Muslim, was appointed Prime Minister of the IIG and Sheikh Ghazi al-Yawar, a Sunni Muslim, was appointed President.

UN Security Council Resolution 1546, adopted on 8 June 2004, affirmed the handover of power from the CPA to the IIG on 30 June and endorsed Transitional National Assembly elections to be held by 31 January 2005. The Iraqi Interim Government officially replaced the Coalition Provisional Authority on 28 June 2004.

The Iraqi Interim Government was viewed by many in the Arab world to be a puppet of the U.S. government. Furthermore, the policies of Iyad Allawi were widely criticised as overly harsh. In July 2004, Allawi announced the formation of a General Security

Directorate to fight the insurgency, promising to annihilate insurgent groups rather than granting amnesty to those insurgents who laid down their weapons. Former Ba'ath officials, however, were invited to join in the rebuilding effort, provided their hands were clean. The IIG announced tough new security measures in July that would allow the imposition of martial law and curfews. In response to criticism regarding the reinstatement of the death penalty in August, Associated Press reported that Iraqi Human Rights Minister Bakhtiar Amin asserted that it was necessary 'to fight the militants destabilizing the country with car bombings, kidnappings, sabotage and other violence'. The Higher Media Commission, created in July, was given the authority to impose sanctions on news outlets for crossing unspecified 'red lines'.[17] The shutdown of al-Jazeera by IIG in August prompted criticism from around the world that it was a serious infringement of freedom of expression. Although the Iraqi government defended its actions in the interest of state security, limiting the freedom of balanced media institutions to express their views ran the risk of limiting the involvement of the institutions and individual viewers in ongoing discussions about the future of the country. Such a restriction would only serve the insurgents in the end, leaving their propaganda as the only alternative news source to bigoted pro-government sources.

The Kurdish Regional Government

The Kurdish Regional Government (KRG), based in Erbil, is the executive body which controls the Kurdish provinces of Erbil, Dohuk and Sulaimaniya in northern Iraq. The KRG is made up of a coalition of parties, elected in May 1992 to the Kurdistan National Assembly. The coalition includes the Kurdistan Democratic Party (KDP), the Patriotic Union of Kurdistan (PUK), the Kurdistan Toilers' Party, the Kurdistan Socialist Democratic Party, the Kurdistan Islamic Union, the Kurdistan Communist Party, the Islamic Group and the Turcoman Brotherhood Party.[18] The Kurdish Regional Government is divided into a parliament, which forms the legislative branch, and a cabinet or Council of Ministers, which forms the executive branch. The current coalition government has a cabinet of 27 ministries and nine regional ministers without portfolios. The cabinet of the KRG, whose aim is to provide social services to the people and rebuild the region's infrastructure, administers the region by implementing laws passed by parliament that maintain law and order.

The development of a Kurdish Alliance

The First Gulf War in 1991, followed by an attempted uprising by the Kurds in Iraq, led to a refugee crisis which prompted the US and the UK to establish a safe haven in the Kurdish regions of Iraq. Protected by a no-fly zone north of the 36th Parallel, Kurds took control of the Kurdish provinces of Erbil, Dohuk and Sulaimaniya. The KRG was then developed as a coalition of Kurdish parties, the main two being the Kurdistan Democratic Party (KDP) under Massoud Barzani and the Patriotic Union of Kurdistan (PUK) under Jalal Talabani. The May 1992 elections split the Parliament almost evenly between the two parties and an ensuing power struggle led to the collapse of relations and eventually the outbreak of violence in 1994. After several failed attempts, a ceasefire was signed in 1997. The US brokered the signing of the Washington Peace Agreement in September 1998, which covered issues such as power-sharing, security arrangements and unifying the administration of the Kurdish region. Despite making a formal agreement to cooperate, the KDP and PUK maintained separate administrations in the zones they controlled after the ceasefire.

The KDP and PUK participated in a series of meetings in 2002, with the encouragement of the Bush administration, to consolidate peace and good relations, as well as implement the Peace Agreement.[19] The alliance of the two major Kurdish parties was seen as a necessary step in the governance of the Kurdish regions, as well as the development of democracy, human rights and civil society.

After the US-led invasion of Iraq in 2003, Kurdish authorities maintained control of the Kurdish regions and undertook to crystallise the unification process. The KDP and PUK reached an agreement over the joint administration of the KRG on 21 January 2006 in an effort to develop 'the democratic experience in the Kurdistan Region with further strengthening of stability and liberty'.[20] The Kurdistan Regional Government Unification Agreement stated that the positions of Prime Minister and Speaker of the House would be given to a KDP and PUK member, respectively, and that the posts would be alternated between the parties in subsequent elections. KDP members would be appointed Ministers of Finance, Peshmerga Affairs, Higher Education, Agriculture, Martyrs, Culture, Electricity, Natural Resources, Municipalities, Sports and Youth, while PUK members would oversee the Interior, Justice, Education, Health, Social Affairs,

Religious Affairs, Water Resources, Transportation, Reconstruction, Planning, and Human Rights ministries.[21]

However, according to the agreement, the sensitive Ministries of Finance, Peshmerga Affairs, Justice and the Interior will maintain Ministers from both parties, to control their respective regions, for the remainder of the year.[22] It has been speculated that the Peshmerga Affairs Ministry, responsible for about 160,000 fighters still loyal to their own party leaders, will be one of the most difficult to unite. There has been criticism of the size of the new united government, which will constitute 27 ministers representing a relatively small region with a population of about 5 million.

The unification of the KRG is crucial to the credibility of Kurdish authority in Iraq. A strong government and parliament are necessary in order to pursue one of the Kurds' key demands; the expansion of the Kurdish autonomous region, including the oil-rich city of Kirkuk and other towns and villages in northern Iraq. According to Article 136 of the new Iraqi constitution, the Iraqi government is obligated to conduct a census and, by December 2007, hold a referendum in Kirkuk and other disputed areas to determine the final status of these regions. Furthermore, the governance of the Kurdish autonomous region by the KRG will set an important precedent for Kurds elsewhere in the region. Ultimately, the KRG's management of Iraqi Kurdistan, if it is competent, could lend credibility to Kurdish aspirations of an independent state.

The Democratic Patriotic Alliance of Kurdistan

The Democratic Patriotic Alliance of Kurdistan (DPAK), renamed the Kurdistan Alliance (KA), was the electoral coalition presented as a united Kurdish list for the national election in January 2005. The Alliance comprised the two main Kurdish parties, the KDP and the PUK, and also included other smaller groups such as the Chaldean Democratic Union Party, the Kurdistan Islamic Union, the Kurdistan Communist Party, the Kurdistan Islamic Group/ Iraq, the Kurdistan Socialist Democratic Party, the Iraqi Turcoman Brotherhood Party and the Kurdistan Toilers' Party. The Alliance's joint list dominates the Kurdish parliament and is the second largest bloc in the Iraqi Council of Representatives. In the Iraqi legislative election in December 2005, however, the Kurdistan Islamic Union left the alliance because it claimed that the KDP and PUK were dominating the politics of Iraqi Kurdistan.

The Kurdistan Alliance ran in the December 2005 parliamentary elections on a platform of tolerance, justice and freedom in a federal, democratic Iraq. Promising to tackle corruption, promote equality and ensure freedom of expression, the Alliance campaigned under the slogan 'Our Vote, Our Future'.[23] Despite assurances that they would represent all Iraqi citizens irrespective of ethnic, political, or religious affiliations, the KA continued to push for control of Kirkuk, arguing that the oil-rich city, which was Arabised under Saddam Hussein, belongs to the Kurdish region.

The KRG was established by and for the people of Iraqi Kurdistan, devised as an authority to safeguard freedom. Through its own programme for economic and social development as well as full cooperation with the United Nations Oil-for-Food Programme, the KRG asserted its intention to provide the region and its inhabitants with a better quality of life. The KRG's stated aims also include maintaining the rule of law and providing a sense of security for its citizens, promising 'a democratic, federal and inclusive Iraq'.[24]

There has been evidence of continuing political rivalries between Erbil and Sulaimaniya, the respective headquarters of the KDP and PUK, despite unification efforts. It is clear that the conflict between the former rivals will not disappear. However, the new KRG is certainly making efforts to unite and build the confidence and trust of the Kurdish people. For true unification to take place, analysts have called for reforms to an overstaffed civil service, conflicting legislation and cultural practices in Erbil and Sulaimaniya, which embody a continuing climate of distrust between the KDP and PUK.[25]

In spite of the speculation about corruption and human rights abuses,[26] a representative for the United Nations Assistance Mission for Iraq (UNAMI) expressed its confidence in the Kurdish authorities' ability to respect the rule of law and human rights at the inaugural session of the Kurdish National Assembly in June 2006. In order to take advantage of the pledge of support from the UN and the current backing of the US, it is imperative that the KRG sincerely tackle head-on the issues of corruption, human rights abuses and residual political rivalry.

The first Iraqi election

The first elections in Iraq were stipulated in the interim Iraqi constitution, known as the Transitional Administrative Law (TAL).[27] According to the TAL, the elections, to be held on 30 January 2005, would determine the make-up of the 275-seat National Assembly, the provincial assemblies for each of Iraq's 18 provinces (41 seats each; 51 for Baghdad), and for the Kurdistan National Assembly (111 seats). No deadline was specified for the elected National Assembly to select an executive, the 'Presidency Council', which would consist of a President and two Deputy Presidents. The Presidency Council, elected by a two-thirds Assembly vote, would then have two weeks to choose a Prime Minister by consensus. The Prime Minister would have one month to secure approval of his nominations for cabinet, by a majority Assembly vote.

The TAL also stipulated that the National Assembly was to draft a constitution by 15 August 2005, which was to be put to national vote by 15 October 2005. If two-thirds of the voters in any three Iraqi provinces rejected the constitution, it would not be ratified. If the permanent constitution was approved, elections for a permanent government were planned to take place by 15 December 2005.[28] If the constitution was defeated, the 15 December elections would be for a new transitional National Assembly, which would redraft the constitution for a vote by 15 October 2006.[29] If necessary, the Assembly could, by 1 August 2005, request six additional months to complete the new draft of the constitution.[30]

On 31 May 2004, the Coalition Provisional Authority Order 92 established the central Independent Electoral Commission of Iraq (IECI) and empowered it 'to organize, oversee, conduct, and implement all elections set forth in the TAL'.[31] The current electoral system was chosen by an Electoral Committee of 18, appointed by the Iraqi Governing Council, in conjunction with the UN electoral mission and in consultation with a variety of Iraqis, including political groups, women's groups, academics and tribal leaders.[32] The Single Constituency Proportional Representation system, in which all of Iraq is treated as a single constituency, was endorsed by the Electoral Committee and adopted by the IGC. The closed-list system meant that political coalitions or alliances could submit lists of candidates, which would determine the order of appointment and could not be modified by voters. Under IECI rules, a female candidate occupied every third position on electoral lists in order to meet the TAL's goal for at least 25 per cent female membership in the new assembly. A total of approximately 18,900 candidates, 223 political entities and 34 coalitions took part in the January elections. The National Assembly ballot had a total of 7,785 candidates: nine multiparty coalitions, 75 single parties and 27 individuals. A further 463 candidates took part in the Kurdistan National Assembly elections.[33]

Pursuant to IECI Regulation 10/2004, eligible Iraqis living abroad were given the opportunity to vote in the January 2005 National Assembly election.[34] Eligibility requirements stipulated that voters must be at least 18 years of age and have Iraqi citizenship, or be eligible for Iraq citizenship. Out of an estimated 1.2 million eligible voters, around 275,000 registered and about 90 per cent of them voted.[35] The IECI ruled that up to 100,000 displaced Kurds from Kirkuk would be allowed to vote in the governorate for the provincial elections. The decision was condemned by Arab and Turcoman leaders, who claimed that it essentially gave control of Kirkuk to the Kurds, ahead of the planned referendum in 2007.[36]

Voter certification took place in Iraq from 1 November until 15 December 2004. Although formal registration was not required, registration centres operated to allow Iraqis to verify or correct personal information on file at over 458 registration centres around Iraq.[37] Unregistered voters needed only present valid identification to vote on election day. Each political entity was required to obtain 500 signatures from eligible voters to stand. Approximately 200,000 people were staffed at around 5,200 polling centres across the country.[38]

Insurgents' threats to target voters and polling stations reinforced widespread concern about voter security, leading US forces to conduct numerous counterinsurgency operations in the months prior to the election.

Questions about security as well as the legitimacy of the elections marred the planning process. While many Sunni Arab leaders called for the postponement of the elections until the security situation was improved, others asserted that holding free democratic elections would be impossible while US forces were still occupying Iraq.[39] Despite concerns, it was widely agreed that postponing the elections would have alienated the support of influential Shi'ite cleric Ayatollah al-Sistani. Furthermore, it was important to give Iraqi governing institutions credibility by making them more representative of the Iraqi people before the drafting of the constitution. However, Sunni boycotts threatened to skew the representation in the National Assembly in favour of the Shi'ites and Kurds. After a conference of Sunni political and religious groups at Baghdad's Um Al-Qora mosque in November, 2004, the headquarters of the Sunni Association of Muslim Scholars, 47 bodies had boycotted the January elections.[40] According to a poll conducted by the US State Department's Bureau of Intelligence and Research (INR) in December 2004, compared to

52 per cent of Arab Shi'ites, only 12 per cent of Sunni Arabs believed that the elections would be free and fair.[41]

The United Nations was involved in 'advising and supporting the IECI in its work to deliver credible and inclusive elections'.[42] The UN led an international coalition of electoral experts drawn from the Electoral Assistance Division, the European Union and the International Foundation for Electoral Systems, as well as individual donor nations.[43] Although the 'international team provided technical, logistical, financial and administrative assistance to the Independent Electoral Commission throughout the electoral process', it did not organise the vote itself.[44]

On 30 January 2005, approximately 8.45 million people, or 59 per cent of registered voters, cast their votes in the first multiparty Iraqi elections in over 50 years.[45] The candidates included the United Iraqi Alliance (UIA), which was comprised of 228 candidates and 22 parties, but largely dominated by two large Shi'ite Islamist parties, the Supreme Council for the Islamic Revolution in Iraq (SCIRI) and the Da'wa Party. The UIA won over 48 per cent of the votes for the new Iraqi National Assembly, taking 140 out of the 275 seats. The Kurdish Alliance (DPAK) took 75 seats, giving them just under 26 per cent of the vote and making them the major opposition party. Interim Prime Minister Iyad Allawi's 'Iraqi List' won the third largest share, taking 40 seats.

Sunni Arab groups were underrepresented in polls, prompting criticism of the vote. While Kurdish and Shi'ite groups boasted over 80 per cent voter turnout, the turnout in Sunni regions was as low as 2 per cent in the Sunni-dominated Anbar province.[46] Although many Sunni voters likely stayed away from the polls for fear of insurgent attacks, voter interest was low even in the most restive Sunni areas. Some groups, including the Iraqi Muslim Clerics' Association, had called for Sunnis to boycott the election, while others were intimidated by threats of violence against Sunnis who voted. Nevertheless, some Sunni groups who boycotted the National Assembly contest did participate in the provincial assembly elections. On election day, polling centres were guarded by over 100,000 members of Iraq's security forces, which were backed up by coalition forces. Increased security precautions were taken two days before the elections, limiting road traffic and closing the borders. Shops were closed on election day, and only cars with official permits were permitted to travel, in order to reduce the risk of car bombings.

According to Associated Press, suicide bombings and mortar attacks on polling stations resulted in about 35 deaths on election day.[47]

The announcement that voters must vote in the province where they were registered presented problems for internally displaced persons. However, approximately 100,000 former residents of Kirkuk were granted permission to vote in Kirkuk and about 200,000 Fallujah residents, who were evacuated during heavy fighting, were able to vote at polling stations set up in displacement camps and villages.[48]

The Kurds also elected the Kurdistan National Assembly on 30 January. The Kurdish Alliance received 1,570,663 votes, representing 90 per cent of the vote. The majority of Kurds saw voting for the coalition as a 'national duty'.[49] In provincial elections, the Kurds won about 60 per cent of the 41 seats in Kirkuk province with over 230,000 votes.[50] Turcoman won nine seats in Kirkuk, while Sunni Arabs won six. While Kurdistan Alliance's big win will likely strengthen the KRG's resolve in attempting to gain control of the oil-rich city of Kirkuk, it has also provoked boycotts and protests by Arab and Turcoman groups. [51]

According to the IECI, hundreds of organisations were registered to monitor the elections, most of whom were Iraqi, due to the security situation. Although it is impossible to say that the elections were totally free and fair, significant numbers of Iraqis participated in the voting, contributing their voice to the political process of choosing a representative government. However, the fact that many people were unable to vote or even to register due to security concerns, and that the political groups could not campaign freely, made the results of the election less than ideal. Despite these problems, the government was certainly more representative, leading the way for Iraqis to take control of their own affairs.

Drafting the constitution

With the designation of Iraq as a single constituency for the 30 January 2005 elections, each political entity required only 1/275 of the vote to obtain a seat in the Transitional National Assembly (TNA). This system permitted many more parties to run than a regional constituency system would have allowed. There was speculation that the TNA would not complete its ambitious agenda as many of the political entities on the ballot comprised coalitions of several parties, all with potentially disparate views. Over and above drafting the constitution and serving as an interim legislature, the objectives of the TNA included the election of a speaker and two deputies, the determination of a working procedure for parliament, the election of a presidency council and the approval of a cabinet.

On 3 April 2005, Sunni Arab Hajim al-Hassani was named NA speaker by a secret ballot vote of the TNA; his two deputies were also named, one a Kurd and the other a Shi'ite Muslim. The Presidency Council was approved on 6 April, with PUK leader Jalal Talabani as President and SCIRI members Ghazi al-Yawar and Adel Abdul Mehdi as his two deputies. The Presidency Council then nominated Ibrahim al-Jaafari for Prime Minister, and he received confirmation on 8 April.

On 28 April 2005, the TNA approved Prime Minister al-Jaafari's 32-minister, four-deputy cabinet. SCIRI members Bayan Jabor and Ali Allawi were named to two of the five major ministerial positions, the Interior and Finance ministries. Shi'ite independent Ibrahim Bahr al-Ulum was named interim Minister of Oil. Kurdistan Democratic Party (KDP) member Hoshyar Zebari was appointed Foreign Minister. The Defence Ministry went to a Sunni Arab and former security official in Saddam's government, Sadoun al-Dulaymi. Although Sunnis were given six ministerial posts, several Sunni politicians complained of the relative insignificance of posts awarded to Sunnis, such as the ministries for Culture and for Women's Affairs. While some decried the sectarian nature of the cabinet, claiming that posts should have been distributed on merit, others opined that it was a realistic representation of the ethnic and sectarian nature of division in Iraq and given the nature of the society and the elections, it was not expected by anyone that the distribution of ministers would be based on merit.

On 10 May, the National Assembly appointed a 55-member Constitutional Preparatory Committee (CPC), to begin drafting the permanent constitution. The CPC was originally comprised of 28 Shi'ite UIA members, 15 Kurdish Alliance members, eight members of Iyad Allawi's Iraqi list, one Turkman, one Christian, one Communist and one Sunni. The CPC was selected from among the members of the National Assembly, resulting in a poor showing for the disenfranchised Sunnis, many of whom boycotted the election. Concerns about the exclusion of a Sunni voice from the constitution drafting process led to negotiations which resulted in the agreement on 23 June 2005 to add 15 additional Sunni members to the CPC as well as ten Sunni Arab advisors to the drafting process. Iraqi leaders asserted that a draft of the constitution would be completed by the 15 August 2005 deadline.

While non-voting advisory groups assisted the panel in the drafting process, the constitutional decisions were to be made by consensus of the 55-member committee. The committee was chaired by Hummam Hammoudi, a SCIRI representative, and two deputy chiefs, the Sunni Arab legislator Adnan al-Janabi, and Kurdish lawmaker Fouad Massoum.[52] It was reported that Washington kept a low profile during the negotiations, so as not to compromise the appearance of independence and legitimacy of the new government.[53]

Constitutional challenges

The most controversial issues surrounding the new constitution, and the future of Iraq, Kurds and other minorities, were the purpose of the new constitution, the debate about federalism, the role of religion, security, the respect and protection of human rights and minority rights as well as the control of oil and water. The drafters were confronted with balancing the interests of the state, religious, tribal or ethnic communities, and the individual. Furthermore, the constitution had to address the growing ethnic and sectarian conflict and ideally offer steps towards a resolution.

Federalism, which can be seen as a compromise between Arabs and autonomy-seeking Kurds, was one of the most controversial and difficult constitutional issues in the debate. The Kurds suffered greatly at the hands of the centralised Iraqi state and wish to govern their own affairs; however, many majoritarian and centrist Arabs view federalism as a way of furthering Kurdish separatist agenda. The TAL recognised a three-level federal structure in Iraq, including central, provincial and regional governments. While the regional government structure was devised for the Kurds in particular, an article in the TAL allows for the creation of regional governments in any one or more provinces.[54] The Sunni Arabs generally rejected federalism, equating it with the break-up of the country and fearing it could cut them out of the country's oil wealth and leave them powerless.[55]

In the Kurdish push for federalism, the KRG was able to boast experience in the administration of the Kurdish region, as well as the strong support of its constituents, many of whom have strongly separatist views. For the Kurds, the principal of federalism was paramount in order for them to safeguard their hard-won northern autonomy, but still benefit from national wealth. Since 1991, in contrast to the rest of Iraq, Iraqi Kurdistan has flourished in many ways, with the building of hotels, offices, houses, airports and other businesses. Although basic services are still poor, the prosperity of

Kurdistan has led to the return of many Kurds from exile abroad.[56] According to an organisation called the Referendum Movement, the majority of Iraqi Kurds favour outright independence; the organisation obtained 1.7 million signatures on a petition circulated in 2004 which called for a referendum on independence.[57] However, the prospect of Kurdish independence is alarming to neighbouring Arab, Persian and Turkish states with their own Kurdish populations. Kurdish authorities, for now, have chosen to aim for the politically less risky goal of controlling all areas of Iraqi Kurdistan, including Kirkuk, but not the contentious province of Mosul, which was Arabised under Saddam's regime. Practical questions remained in the federalism discussions as to the proper distribution of power, including oil revenues and the drawing of regional boundaries.

Another point of contention in the drafting of the constitution was the status of religion. While it was recognised that Islam should remain the state religion, there was fierce debate about religious freedom guarantees and the precise role of Islam in the system of government. Arguments from Shi'ite leaders that Islam should be the main source of legislation met with criticism from women's groups, who claimed that it would compromise the rights of women, many of which were enshrined under existing laws. In general, the Kurds, who are largely secular, were against attempts at giving significant constitutional importance to Islamic law. The Kurdish opposition to a strong role for religion in the state led to the inclusion of safeguards against state-imposed religion. Regardless of the exact wording, however, the true effect of the provision would lie with its interpretation. Islamic law interpreted through a secular lens could result in the creation of a moderate Islamic state, whereas giving the power of interpretation to the clerics would result in a system more like Iran.

The lack of consensus on matters such as federalism and religious language, as well as the presence of sectarian tensions, led to the drafting period being extended four times. The Sunni Arabs felt increasingly marginalised from negotiations when these were moved from the Constitutional Committee to an informal forum of Shi'ite and Kurdish leaders. The Sunnis complained that they were excluded from backroom negotiations and refused to sign the various drafts they were shown. Other members of the Constitutional Committee also claimed that they were not participating enough in the negotiations on the new constitution. Sunni leaders urged the electorate to reject the constitution in the 15 October 2005 referendum. In the end, only three of the 15 Sunni members of the drafting committee attended the signing ceremony, none of whom signed.

Despite the absence of a consensus with Sunni Arab negotiators, on 28 August 2005, Shi'ite and Kurdish leaders presented the constitution to the TNA as the final draft. However, negotiations continued and on 13 September, the leaders of the Constitutional Committee, excluding the Sunni Arabs, presented a new draft to the TNA. On 18 September 2005, a few further amendments were made to the text in response to Sunni Arabs' concerns.[58] A compromise between Shi'ite and Kurdish leaders and the most prominent Sunni party, the Iraqi Islamic Party, led to additional amendments in the week leading up to the 15 October 2005 vote. It was speculated that the final amendments, which moderated de-Ba'athification provisions, reaffirmed Iraqi unity and created a panel in the parliament, empowered to propose large revisions to the constitution, saved the constitution from the so-called Sunni veto.[59]

It was widely thought that the drafting of the constitution would speed up the withdrawal of coalition forces, which was seen as necessary to achieving stability and ending the insurgency. The ethnic and sectarian divisions which marked the constitution drafting process were therefore ignored by the Committee in an effort to keep to the deadline. Consequently, the principle of consensus was sacrificed to some extent, with the promise that the first government elected under the new constitution would consider amendments to the constitution in the first four months. These amendments would have to be ratified by a similar referendum to the one that originally approved it. However, up to this point, neither the US nor the Iraqi authorities have been able to devise a clear plan to end the insurgency in Iraq and to give a new sense of direction to the constitutional structure in Iraq.

The new Iraqi constitution

The new constitution was endorsed on 15 October 2005. According to the Independent Electoral Commission of Iraq (IECI), the constitution was approved by 78 per cent of voters, with approximately 63 per cent voter turnout.[60] In the Kurdish provinces of Erbil and Dohuk, the constitution had over 99 per cent support, and over 98 per cent support in Sulaimaniya. The extremely high turnouts in those provinces were verified by UN and Iraqi officials.[61] IECI results state that there were 5,872 polling stations across Iraq, with 170,000 international and domestic observers accredited to monitor the vote.

Although it was largely rejected by Sunni Muslims in the referendum, only a two-thirds majority in three of Iraq's 18 provinces could have defeated it. In the province of Anbar, over 96 per cent rejected the constitution, while approximately 82 per cent voted 'no' in Salahadin province. In the province of Nineveh, which is populated by Kurds, Sunnis and Christians, 55 per cent voted 'no', 12 per cent short of the two-thirds majority requirement. The constitution barely passed in Diyala, with 51 per cent of the vote. Some critics charged that recent military actions of the coalition in predominantly Sunni areas prevented polling stations from being set up, leaving entire towns without any means of exercising their right to vote. The IECI reported that it received 135 complaints, but asserted that none of them were serious enough to have changed the outcome of the election. Despite allegations of irregularities, some Sunni leaders accepted the vote and looked ahead to the 15 December elections and the opportunity to amend the constitution. Fakhri al-Qaisi of the National Dialogue said that it was important to look to the December elections because 'a real presence for the nationalist forces in the next parliament [would] restore balance and serve the Iraqi people'.[62]

The Iraqi constitution, as it was adopted, recognises decentralisation, democratic governance and federalism, and contains several positive human and civil rights provisions. The new constitution describes the state as a 'democratic, federal, representative republic' (Article 1). While declaring Islam to be the official state religion, it guarantees full religious freedom of belief and practice (Article 2), and describes the national identity of Iraq as 'a country of many nationalities, religions and sects, and ... a part of the Islamic world' (Article 3). Under pressure from the Arab league, the 13 September draft was amended to say that Iraq is 'a founding and active member of the Arab league' (Article 3). However, Article 4 declares both Arabic and Kurdish as the official languages of Iraq.[63]

Article 1 of the new constitution contains a clear definition of federalism as a universal principle of the new Iraq. While the Transitional Administrative Law (TAL) recognized the principle of ethnic federalism for the *de facto* autonomous Kurdish region (Erbil, Dohuk and Sulaimaniya provinces), it did not define what this would constitute. Article 113 of the constitution reaffirms and acknowledges the region of Kurdistan, and its authorities. Article 115 stipulates that any one or more provinces of the 18 administrative provinces of Iraq have the right to form a region, although the executive procedures required to form these regions remains to be enacted by the Council of Representatives, according to Article 114. Although many Sunni groups have accepted ethnic federalism, many still oppose the wide-ranging powers conferred on regional governments in Articles 110 and 111. It has been speculated that Article 9(1), which sets out the fair distribution of oil revenues but adds that an additional amount of revenues will be distributed to 'damaged regions that were unjustly deprived by the former regime' will skew the distribution towards Kurdish and Shi'ite regions. Although it is stated that the system will assure 'balanced development in different areas of the country', the true effect of this provision will likely be seen in the interpretation by the Supreme Court and subsequent laws enacted by the Council of Representatives.

Islam was declared the official state religion by Article 2 and deemed to be 'a fundamental source of legislation'. Article 2 'guarantees the Islamic identity of the Iraqi people' but also guarantees 'full religious rights' to all individuals, including the freedom of belief and practice. Articles 2(a)–(c) state that no law may contradict 'the established provisions of Islam', the principles of democracy or 'the rights and basic freedoms' granted in the constitution. Although some have argued that these ideals are incongruent, the so-called established provisions of Islam are in fact widely debated among scholars and it will be up to the Supreme Court to unpack these provisions and give them meaning in an Iraqi context. Although the judicial authority is guaranteed to be independent by Article 84 and is granted the power to interpret the constitution, the make-up of the court, selection criteria for judges and the 'work of the court' are still to be determined by the Council of Representatives (Article 89).

Women's rights have been recognised by provisions throughout the constitution, and much of the language is gender-neutral. Article 14 states that all Iraqis are equal regardless of gender, race, ethnicity, religion or creed, protecting minority groups, including women, from discrimination and prejudice. Article 17 protects the individual's right to privacy, but only 'so long as it does not contradict ... public morals'. This vague provision could be used to restrict the freedom of women in their personal choices. Article 39 gives Iraqis the freedom to commit 'to their personal status according to their religions, sects, beliefs or choices', adding that it will be regulated by law. Personal status, or family, law has the potential to affect the rights of women significantly. This article leaves the mechanism of personal status law to the legislature, incensing women's advocates, who maintain that women should have the right to choose a civil court in matters of personal status constitutionally enshrined rather than subject to a simple majority vote by the Council of Representatives.[64]

Cultural, religious and political rights of ethnic and religious minorities have been stipulated in several articles. Article 3 recognises that Iraq is 'a country of many nationalities' and Article 4 grants Iraqis the right to 'educate their children in their mother tongue'. Article 121 guarantees 'the administrative, political, cultural and educational rights for the various nationalities' of Iraq. However, there has been some scepticism regarding Article 35(4), which states that the 'State will promote cultural activities and institutions in a way that is appropriate with Iraq's civilisational history and culture'. This provision could be used by the state to sanction the discrimination of funding of activities and organisations of minorities and it is recommended that the provision be amended to include the guarantee of non-discriminatory state support. Article 29(1)(A), which states that 'the family is the foundation of society; the State preserves its entity and its religious, moral and patriotic values', is vague and open to interpretation, potentially allowing the state to impose its own religious values on its citizens. It has been recommended that the provision be amended to remove the reference to religion, or alternatively to guarantee that the provision will not violate the equal rights of all Iraqis.

Although the constitution contains many positive human rights provisions, it lacks protective measures for many of the conferred norms and freedoms, as well as conflicting articles on civil society autonomy, minority and women's rights, and political freedoms.[65] Article 44, which was removed from the constitution before the final draft was submitted to United Nations Assistance Mission for Iraq (UNAMI), emphasised the rights of Iraqis to 'enjoy the rights stated in international human rights agreements and treaties endorsed by Iraq'. These treaties include the International Covenant on Civil and Political Rights (ICCPR, ratified in 1976), the International Covenant on Economic, Social and Cultural Rights (ICESCR, ratified in 1976), the International Convention on the Elimination of All Forms of Racial Discrimination (CERD, ratified in 1970), the Convention on the Elimination of All Forms of Discrimination against Women (CEDAW, ratified in 1986) and the Convention on the Rights of the Child (CRC, ratified in 1994).[66] Article 44 in the final draft constitution guarantees the rights and liberties granted in the constitution 'except by law ... insofar as that limitation or restriction does not violate the essence of the right or freedom'. This vague wording has the potential to be interpreted in such a way as to dilute the scope of the right, eroding the human rights protections entrenched in the constitution.[67]

The status of Kirkuk is addressed in Article 136. The article calls for a census and a referendum to 'determine the will of the citizens' upon normalisation of Kirkuk (in other words, 'de-Arabisation'). The deadline for the referendum is 31 December 2007. Article 137 states that the legislation enacted by the KRG since 1992 will remain in force, provided it does not contradict with the constitution. The moderate, secular Kurdish Alliance has the opportunity to play an important role in democratisation, setting an example for the rest of Iraq; however, it is imperative that the Kurds use their position of relative stability and power to mediate between disparate groups and implement the principle of consensus in all areas of the national legislative arena.

The second Iraqi elections

Following the ratification of the Iraqi constitution, a general election was held on 15 December 2005 to elect 275 permanent members of the Iraqi National Assembly. The electoral system used was prepared by the Transitional National Assembly, which modified the law that governed the 30 January 2005 elections. In the new system, 230 seats were apportioned among Iraq's 18 governorates, based on the number of registered voters in each region, including 59 seats for the Baghdad governorate. The seats within each governorate were allocated to lists through a system of proportional representation. The remaining 45 'compensatory' seats were given first to candidates whose votes reached a critical threshold level but who failed to gain a seat at the governorate level. The rest were then distributed proportionally to the seats gained at the governorate level. The compensatory seats were meant to award seats to smaller political entities with scattered support. Alternatively, seats could have been reserved for minorities; however, there would have been difficulty in identifying all the eligible political entities in a short period of time, and the legitimacy of those seats would have been questionable.[68] The presence of women in the National Assembly was ensured by the requirement that women occupy 25 per cent of the 275 seats.

The Shi'ite-dominated Unified Iraqi Alliance (UIA) came away with 128 of the 275 seats, while the Kurdish Alliance won 53 seats. The predominantly Sunni Tawafoq Iraqi Front won 44 seats, while Iyad Allawi's secular Iraqi List managed to win 25 seats. The Hewar National Iraqi Front, the Islamic Union of Kurdistan and Liberation and Reconciliation Gathering were among other groups that won multiple seats. The IECI reported that 11.9 million people, 76.4 per cent of registered voters, cast their ballots on election day in over 31,000 polling stations across Iraq.[69] The election was observed by 270,000 IECI-accredited political entity agents, 126,000 Iraqi observers and 949 international observers. A total of 307 political entities ran in the election, comprising 7,655 candidates. The IECI received 1,985 complaints about voting irregularities, 58 of which were determined to be capable of altering the results of the election; the complaints were adjudicated and the IECI decided to certify the December election results.[70] The final assessment of the December elections by the International Mission for Iraqi Elections (IMIE) reported that the investigations into complaints led to the cancellation of the results from 227 polling stations, which 'represented less than 1% of the total and had little or no impact on the final results' of the election.[71] It should be noted that the elections took place under extreme violence and therefore it is not possible to say for certain that the elections were completely free and fair. Moreover, the unbalanced results in some governorates were likely due in part to voter intimidation and localised fraud. However, the IMIE reported that, on balance, the results were credible overall.

In February 2006, the UIA nominated Ibrahim al-Jaafari as their candidate for Prime Minister, but persistent Sunni and Kurdish opposition led to his removal as a candidate in April 2006. Da'wa party deputy leader Nouri al-Maliki, known as a skilled negotiator and 'low-key political insider', became the Prime Minister designate on 22 April 2006.[72] He appeals to Kurds because of his noted independence from Iran, pro-federalist stance and cooperation with the coalition. However, al-Maliki has been called a 'tough Arab nationalist' who will likely push for the swift withdrawal of foreign forces from Iraq.[73] Realistically, however, the Iraqi authorities will not be in a position to call for a withdrawal of coalition troops until the security situation in Iraq stabilises to an appreciable extent.

On 20 May 2006, al-Maliki's choices for the 37-member cabinet were approved by a majority vote of the National Assembly. The national unity cabinet included members of all the major political parties and ethnic and religious minorities. While asking for a timetable for withdrawal of coalition forces, al-Maliki announced that his top priorities would be the restoration of stability and security.[74] Despite pledging the use of full force to subdue the insurgency, al-Maliki admitted that force alone would not be sufficient, stating 'We need other measures besides security. We need national reconciliation.'[75]

The sensitive posts of Defence, National Security and the Interior were not filled until June 2006. The Defence Ministry post was given to General Abdel Qader Jassim, a Sunni Muslim, who pledged: 'I do not carry any sectarian title. I'm here for all Iraqis...'[76] The Interior Minister, Jawad al-Bolani, himself a Shi'ite, expressed similar sentiments, promising neutrality and independence.

In the negotiations regarding the allocation of ministries, the US, threatening the withdrawal of military aid, insisted that the Interior and Defence Ministry posts be filled by inclusive, anti-sectarian candidates. US ambassador Zalmay Khalilzad's extensive involvement in cabinet negotiations represented a marked departure from the 'hands-off approach' taken during the Transitional Government's period in office. This provoked criticism from some Iraqi officials, who charged that the US involvement interfered too much with Iraqi politics. The Director of the Washington Institute for Near East Policy's Military and Security Studies Program asserted, however, that US influence over Iraq is decreasing and will continue to do so as U.S. forces pull out over the next few years.[77]

The National Assembly now has the difficult job of amending the constitution. The initial debate is likely to focus on the federal divisions of power, particularly policies surrounding oil and other natural resources. Other focus areas are likely to include decreasing the coalition presence in Iraq, quelling insurgent and sectarian violence, and giving power back to marginalised communities. It is clear, however, that US forces will not withdraw in the near future, as evidenced by the recent plan to send in more troops. US withdrawal at this crucial time could lead to an increase in violence, which would endanger the long-term US policy in Iraq and the Middle East. The continuation of the current policy, however, which lacks a clear objective or strategy, could allow for more violence and civil war. It seems that one of the biggest mistakes of the political leaders in Iraq and the administration of the coalition was the lack of effective consultation with the Iraqi people, particularly women and minorities. Any effective strategy to increase the security and stability of Iraq in the future must include effective dialogue and consultation.

In one of his first major moves, al-Maliki presented a national reconciliation package to parliament, aimed at defusing the insurgency and addressing ethnic and sectarian tensions. According to the 24-point plan, al-Maliki's government will endeavour to disband militias and integrate them into the Iraqi security forces wherever possible, and create a dialogue with insurgent rebels. Furthermore, the government has agreed to review the status of former Ba'ath party officials who were expelled from the Iraqi power structure and banned from the rebuilding process after the US-led invasion. There has been speculation that the plan will fail because al-Maliki refuses to engage in a dialogue or attempt to reconcile with the demands of radical Islamists. It is also unclear whether al-Maliki would even have the power to negotiate with radical Islamists, given the fragility of Iraq, the potential for civil war and the struggle for power among sectarian and tribal leaders. While it is important to benefit from the expertise and experience of former Ba'ath party officials, the Iraqi authorities must be sure that they are sensitive to the need to encourage accountability. Former Ba'athist officials, particularly those of whom were involved in torture, extrajudicial killing and the implementation of Saddam's brutal policies, should be held accountable for their actions, and their victims redressed, so as not to foster an atmosphere of impunity. However, al-Maliki's plan has been endorsed by Sunni Arab leader Adnan al-Dulaimi, who 'urged all Iraqis to join in the effort to rebuild their country,' while calling for the 'rapid release of detainees and a halt to raids and attacks on civilians' homes'.[78]

Relations between south Kurdistan and its neighbours

The development of federalism and the potential for Kurdish autonomy in Iraq has caught the attention of neighbours Iran, Syria and Turkey, who continue to repress their own sizeable Kurdish populations. The prospect of Kurdish prosperity and independence has serious implications for these countries, who have met privately for years to consolidate a common policy towards the Kurds. It is likely that these states will continue to repress their own Kurdish populations in the future, despite dealings with Iraqi Kurdistan, which are virtually inevitable and potentially very lucrative. Iraq's neighbouring states have a stake in the prevention of ethnic and sectarian divisions in Iraq, which could ultimately lead to the creation of an independent Kurdish state. The potential for an independent Kurdish state to fan the flames of rebellion in other Kurdish regions has led neighbouring states to favour a strong central government in Iraq, capable of bringing about political and economic stability.

Turkey has the potential to prosper from a stable Iraq, with which it can resume its lucrative trade relations; this includes the security of the two pipelines that carry oil from northern Iraqi oilfields to Turkish terminals at the Mediterranean port of Ceyhan. For Ankara, an additional consideration is whether a new government in Baghdad can successfully control its northern borders and put an end to the infiltration by the PKK, which the Turkish government has accused Kurdish authorities of supporting with arms, safe passage and other logistical help. Within a system of federalism under the new Iraqi government, Ankara would want the central government to minimize the autonomy of the federal regions, giving the Kurdish region a very limited capacity to act independently on matters of foreign policy and oil. Ankara has repeatedly declared that it would not tolerate full Kurdish independence in Iraq, stating that this would lead to the disintegration of the country and destabilisation of the region. Despite Turkey's interest in preventing Kurdish autonomy, the EU accession process has constrained Turkey's foreign policy options in Iraq. Ankara recognises that the EU would denounce any Turkish military intervention in Iraq aimed at preventing the Kurds from achieving independence or autonomy.

The Turkish government has maintained an interest in the status of Kirkuk, asserting that it seeks to protect the Turkish-speaking Turkman minority, who, along with the Kurds, lay claim to the oil-rich city of Kirkuk. Ankara has pushed for Turkman control of Kirkuk, claiming that Kirkuk is historically a Turkman city.[79] Turkey is vehemently opposed to the Kurdish control of Kirkuk, which would likely increase the stability and prosperity of the Kurdish region, bolstering any future bid for independence.

The US-led invasion of Iraq initiated a change in the landscape of Kurdish-Turkish relations. On 1 March 2003 Turkey's parliament failed to pass a resolution which would have permitted 62,000 US troops to be deployed and stationed in Turkey, even in the face of incentives and lucrative controlling stakes in the post-occupation of Iraq.[80] Consequently, Turkey changed the nature of its relationship to the KRG. The isolation and lack of US control in Baghdad compelled Ankara to deal directly with the KDP and PUK, as evidenced by the frequent visits of high-ranking Kurdish officials, including Massoud Barzani and Jalal Talabani, to Ankara. Currently, there are many Turkish contractors and companies working in the Kurdish region; the large potential for development in Iraqi Kurdistan and the Kurdish need for trade with and political support from Turkey demonstrate the mutual benefit of friendly Kurdish-Turkish relations. The pumping of oil from Kirkuk through Turkey's Ceyhan oil pipeline resumed in June, after being halted for nine months due to attacks. While the Turkish government has an interest in increasing oil export from the Iraqi Kurdistan through its Ceyhan oil pipeline, its foreign policy advisor was careful to point out that 'a regional authority is not a national one' and that any expansion requests would have to come from the central government of Iraq.[81] Apprehensive about increasing Kurdish economic and political sovereignty, he went on to say that Turkish foreign policy was concerned with ensuring 'the territorial integrity of Iraq along with the equitable distribution of its resources'.[82]

Turkey is aware that in the long term the existence of South Kurdistan will help the Kurds in Turkey realise their own aspirations for autonomy and self-government. Although Turkey has a common interest with Iran and Syria in suppressing their own Kurdish populations, alignment with extremist governments will only hurt Turkey's European Union accession goals. Alignment with the Kurds is a better long-term option for Turkey to maintain and develop healthy relations with the western bloc.

Syria shared a common ideology with Iraq for some time, as they were both ruled by Arab nationalist Ba'athist regimes since the 1960s. However, the regimes grew suspicious of each other over time and relations deteriorated further when Syria backed Iran in the Iran-Iraq War and opposed Saddam's invasion of Kuwait in 1991.[83]

Syrian-Kurdish relations were shaped in the 1980s and 1990s by the presence of Saddam Hussein as a common enemy. Dealings with both Jalal Talabani and Massoud Barzani during that period were used to create chaos for Saddam's regime.[84] However, Kurdish support from 1974 onwards of the US plan to topple Saddam's regime was met with suspicion by Syria's pan-Arab Ba'athist government.[85] Although Syria and Turkey have endured conflict in the past, which came to a head when Turkey threatened military action against Syria for its support of Turkish Kurdish rebels in the 1990s, the countries share the same views on the protection of Iraq's territorial integrity and of its national unity.

The decrease of oil exports from Iraq after the US-led invasion had a serious impact on the Syrian economy in 2003, contributing to the 2.5 per cent decrease in GNP and 22 per cent decrease in trade. Proclaiming interest in the safety, stability and unity of Iraq, the Syrian government pledged to restore diplomatic relations with Iraq in 2005. The Syrian Foreign Minister stated that Syria was interested in Iraq's ability to 'play its full role in the Arab and international arenas'.[86]

Despite a promising dialogue with the new Iraqi government, Syria's relations with the Iraqi Kurds have been tenuous. After a meeting with Syrian President Bashar al-Assad in March 2004, Iraqi Foreign Minister and KDP official Hoshyar Zebari commended Syria's position on the Iraqi people and asserted that Syria had 'an important role to play in helping the Iraqi build their state and restore sovereignty'.[87] However, the mood shifted when riots by Syrian Kurds in June 2004 were reported to be supported and organised by Kurdish leaders in Iraq. Both the KDP and the PUK reportedly allowed thousands of demonstrators to hold anti-Syrian protests in the regions under their control.[88] During his presidency, Assad has released dozens of political prisoners and has passed laws to liberalise the economy, while coming down hard on pro-democracy activists, leaving the status of Kurds in Syria unclear. What is clear, however, is that Syria and Turkey are in agreement that developments in Iraqi Kurdistan should be within a federal context, not giving rise to conditions which would facilitate Kurdish secession.

Iran's powerful influence over Iraqi Shi'ite politics can be traced back to 1979 when the religious regime in Iran provided support to Iraqi Shi'ites, persecuted by Saddam Hussein. The connection between ruling Iraqi Shi'ites and Iran have led to speculation about the influence that Iran has on the new Iraqi government. The Shah of Iran established a relationship with the Iraqi Kurds prior to 1979, when he assisted in the Kurdish struggle against Saddam Hussein. However, when Saddam agreed in 1975 to give Iran some control of the Shat al-Arab waterway, the Shah of Iran cut off all military support to Iraqi Kurds. This left the Kurds vulnerable, enabling Saddam to commence his military campaign against them in which many Iraqi Kurds lost their lives.

In 1979, Jalal Talabani and his newly established PUK backed the Iranian revolution of Ayatollah Khomeini in response to the Shah's betrayal of the Kurds. The military relationship that ensued between Talabani and Khomeini's religious government was based on the principle of a shared enemy in Saddam Hussein. Furthermore, Iran hoped that the PUK military presence in northern Iraq would keep the Turks out of Iraq. The supply of weapons from Iran was crucial for the PUK's fight against Saddam's regime, as well as the KDP, with whom the PUK was jockeying for power and territory.[89] In return, the PUK carried out special operations attacks with Iranian forces against sensitive positions inside Iraq and provided intelligence about Iraqi troop movements and locations.[90]

While relations between Talabani and Iran were maintained into the early 2000s, Iran viewed the growing US-PUK alliance as a threat to its interests. The relationship between the US and the PUK developed as the US looked for a reliable alliance in northern Iraq with which to open up a second front against Saddam; the PUK for its part looked to gain credibility by being recognised as the representative of the Iraqi Kurds in negotiations with the post-Saddam interim Iraqi government. At the same time, Talabani maintained good relations with the Iranian government by acting as a 'trusted mediator' between Washington and Tehran.[91]

With the toppling of the Iraqi regime in 2003, however, Iran feared 'that the new Iraqi regime, because of domestic factors and deep-rooted regional ambitions, would continue to pursue an anti-Iran policy'.[92] Despite these concerns, Iran has a powerful ally in Iraqi Shi'ite politicians, many of whom operated out of Iran during Saddam's rule.

The Kurds share with the Turks a similar secular view and could assist as a buffer against Islamic fundamentalism, cooperating to combat terrorism.[93] The historical relations between Kurds, Iran and Syria allow for the building of prosperous and mutually beneficial relations today. Acceptance of Kurdish autonomy in Iraq, and perhaps one day outright independence, will be a bitter pill to swallow for Iraq's neighbours. Rather than supporting rebellions in Syria, Turkey and Iran, the Kurds of Iraq should aim to establish good relations with their neighbours. So far, the KRG has called for support from Iran, Turkey, Syria and all Iraq's neighbours to work towards building unity and stability in Iraq.[94] Despite the fear that the developments in Iraqi Kurdistan would heighten feelings of Kurdish nationalism in its neighbouring regions of Turkey, Iran and Syria, it is now a fact that the new Iraqi constitution, which has been ratified by the Iraqi people, gives legal status to Kurdistan and allows for self-rule and self-administration. Long-term prosperity, progress and productivity demand that all parties work together cooperatively.

The future of south Kurdistan

The creation of an independent, democratic and stable Kurdistan is still a distant dream for Iraqi Kurds. The union of the Iraqi Kurdish nation through the unification of the KDP and PUK on 7 January 2006 established a joint administration in the Kurdistan Regional

Government. The agreement was presented to the Kurdistan National Assembly for ratification on 12 January.

In addition to increasing the credibility of Kurdish governance, the unification agreement aimed to secure and guarantee the historic achievements of the Kurdish people in Iraqi Kurdistan, as well as developing and cultivating the democratic experience, further strengthening stability and liberty.[95] The Kurds have worked determinedly to implement the process of democratisation in Iraq and have participated actively in all the elections, becoming an example of stability in Iraq.

Much of the constitutional debate in Baghdad was concerned with the demand for Kurdish independence, democracy and stability as well as for 'immediate action on broader territorial claims', in which Kurds endorsed a federal system that 'could provide the Kurdish people with a safe and secure system of self-governance'.[96] This demand is not a new one. For instance, when the Kurdish nation in Iraq was permitted to vote on a non-binding referendum for the creation of an independent Kurdistan, more then 92 per cent were in favour. Years of quasi-independence have increased the autonomy aspirations of the younger generations, some of whom perceive the new federal system to be a step backward toward Iraqi rule.[97] The strong sentiment in favour of independence has put nationalist pressure on Kurdish leaders. They have responded by pushing for a fair vote on the status of Kirkuk, without which many Kurds believe their liberation will not be complete.

Although Kurdish people maintain that the Kurds have the right to decide their own future, they also recognise that the international community will not allow for Kurdish independence in the near future, due to the current volatile situation in the Middle East. The neighbouring countries of Turkey, Syria and Iran worry that independence for Iraqi Kurdistan would encourage their own Kurdish populations to rise up. Arab and Islamic countries also reject Kurdish aspirations for independence, fearing the destabilisation of the region. This same fear led the US to endorse a weak federal structure that would keep the Kurds contained in Iraq.[98] If the Kurds were ever to attain independence, they would require the unconditional support of the US. In order to gain US backing the Kurdish leaders would have to persuade the US that an independent Kurdistan would lead to greater security in the Middle East and the wider region. The best way to do this is to continue to set an example and to be open, transparent and accountable to the Kurdish people, whom they have been democratically elected to represent. Kurdish leaders should tackle corruption and avoid the endemic atmosphere of impunity by holding their government accountable for any wrong-doing. To bolster a bid for independence, the Kurds would need to build up their infrastructure and strengthen their economy.[99] At present, the Kurdish leaders recognise that declaring Iraqi Kurdistan's independence would risk economic punishments such as sanctions or embargoes by its neighbours.[100]

If the Kurds are serious about creating a stable Kurdistan in the long term, the leaders must obtain the support of all Kurds in the region, including institutional and grassroots support from Kurds in Iran, Syria and Turkey. For the time being, the KRG has reaffirmed its commitment to a democratic, federal, inclusive and unified Iraq. The newly unified KRG should continue to work together towards a common policy and a national agenda that will demonstrate to the key international players that the Kurdish people are capable of, and ready for, independence and self-government.

15
Insurgency and Sectarianism

An insurgency occurs when the government 'fails to address social or regional polarisation, sectarianism, endemic corruption, crime, various forms of radicalism, or rising expectations'.[1] The insurgents are typically rebels or terrorists; the targets are usually government or military forces. Insurrection can weaken or undercut a government, hinder economic development and access to global capital, or at least force national leaders to alter key policies.

Far from offering a clear political alternative, the Iraqi insurgency is focused on weakening the existing governing regime and coalition forces (which are perceived to be occupying forces). What began as erratic and disorganised attacks against US troops and the Iraqi officials soon after the fall of Saddam's regime has grown considerably in scope and complexity. Attacks numbered approximately 25 per day at the beginning of 2004, and averaged 60 per day by the end of the year. In June 2006, coalition troops were reported facing 600 insurgent attacks per week.

As the insurgency has grown, its focus has changed from primarily US soldiers to anyone who is participating in the rebuilding and stabilisation of Iraq. Therefore, all other coalition forces, foreign nationals and Iraqis working with the coalition have become targets. Furthermore, insurgents have begun to target infrastructures, including oil and water pipelines or electricity pylons. Attacks have been coordinated during important periods such as elections and the holy month of Ramadan. On the day of the January 2005 elections, there were approximately 300 attacks, 'double the previous one day high of approximately 150 reached during Ramadan 2004'.[2]

The insurgents' aim is to weaken the coalition, break down the Iraqi people's tolerance of the occupation, weaken support for the Iraqi government, incite greater violence and ultimately to decrease the support of the world community.[3] Further, 'attacks against foreign nationals are intended to intimidate non-government organizations and contractors and inhibit reconstruction and economic recovery'.[4]

The methodology of the insurgents reflects the recognition that they are, in a traditional sense, at a disadvantage; rather than attempting to match coalition forces in military muscle, the insurgents focus on chipping away at the will of the coalition forces. The idea is to provoke coalition attacks on civilian targets, thereby increasing discord and decreasing popular support for the coalition. Therefore, the insurgency is more of a political battle than a military one. Since the declared end of the US-led operation on 1 May 2003, the insurgency has carried the total number of American military fatalities to over 2,000 as of June 2006.

DEVELOPING TACTICS OF THE INSURGENCY

Insurgent tactics vary widely between groups. While some insurgents target coalition forces and 'collaborators' without regard for collateral damage, including civilian casualties, others claim to focus on US forces and avoid civilian casualties. Generally, insurgent attacks are carried out in small groups (or cells) of five to ten men in order to maximise efficiency and retain mobility. Attacks are designed to allow insurgents to strike quickly and escape detection.

Assaults on convoys and patrols using improvised explosive devices (IEDs) are quite common. These explosive devices, made from former Iraqi military munitions and foreign-supplied explosive materials, are concealed or camouflaged along main roads and detonated when a convoy or patrol passes. Insurgents also carry out ambushes of military convoys and patrols swiftly and pull out before support can be called in. In hit-and-run mortar or rocket strikes on coalition bases, or locations associated with the Iraqi government or a foreign presence, insurgents fire a number of mortar rounds or rockets and quickly relocate before their position can be identified. Although less common, sniper tactics have been used by insurgents against private contractors, Iraqi forces and US soldiers. Since August 2003, suicide car bombs have emerged as one of the insurgency's most effective weapons, along with the roadside IEDs. The cars are driven by suicide bombers and often directed at Iraqi police stations, police or military recruiting centres, and US convoys.

Attacks on non-military and civilian targets have steadily increased since August 2003. Targets have included 'collaborators', or Iraqis perceived to be cooperating with the coalition; the United Nations headquarters; Shi'ite mosques and civilians; the International Red Cross and Christian churches. Foreign civilian contractors or aid workers have been the main targets of kidnappings and in some cases beheadings, the goal of which appears to be to drive foreign civilians out of Iraq and stall rebuilding and stabilisation efforts. Schools have not escaped attack by insurgents either; according to reports, at least 65 schools in Baghdad were attacked during school hours in the 2005–06 academic year.[5]

Apart from human targets, insurgents have attempted to destroy property and obstruct normal operations in Iraq. The oil industry has been a common target for such attacks. Insurgents, using either rocket-propelled grenades or explosives, regularly destroy oil pipelines in northern Iraq, and had expanded to southern Iraq by April 2004. There have also been allegations of insurgent attacks on water pipelines and the electricity grid.

THE COMPOSITION OF THE INSURGENCY

The exact composition of the Iraqi insurgency is difficult to determine, although it is often divided by analysts into several main ideological strands, some of which are believed to overlap. The Iraqi insurgency has grown from a disorganised assortment of groups, incited by resentment of occupation and anger at marginalisation, to a collection of fewer consolidated groups with increased coordination and confidence.

Former regime loyalists (FRLs) appear to have comprised the core of the nascent insurgency in the days following the fall of Baghdad. The FRLs, mostly Sunni Arabs operating out of central Iraq, included former Ba'ath party officials, the Fedayeen Saddam,[6] and some former agents of the Iraqi intelligence elements and security services, such as the Mukhabarat.[7]

It has been speculated that the dismantling of the Iraqi military by the Coalition Provisional Authority upon taking Iraq may have led to the involvement of thousands of marginalised former military officials in the insurgency.[8] These officers were ideal proto-insurgents, 'combining as they did idleness, relevant military and intelligence skills, and knowledge of the whereabouts of vast weapons stockpiles and relatively scarcer cash reserves'.[9] According to reports, in August 2003 there were estimated to be 100,000 former Iraqi security forces in the so-called Sunni Triangle. The British Prime Minister, Tony Blair, has recently expressed regret over the handling of Iraqi security officials, responding to criticism regarding the resulting 'security vacuum' which has encouraged former regime loyalists to take up arms against the newly installed government.[10] According to recent reports, however, most FRLs have splintered off into Islamist, political or other groups and therefore do not represent a relevant threat to the Iraqi government.[11]

Rather than depending on Ba'ath party ideology, from the start it appears that the insurgency relied upon nationalistic and religious ideas in their discourse.[12] It also appears to have grown in response to counterinsurgent tactics on the part of US forces. Although the vast majority of insurgents are thought to be Sunni Arab Iraqis, foreign fighters from countries including Syria, Saudi Arabia, Egypt, Jordan and Iran are thought to be responsible for the deadliest attacks.[13]

The *Mujahidin Shura Council*[14] (Majlis Shura Mujahideen fi al-Iraq) is one of the biggest threats to security and stability in Iraq. It is an umbrella organisation, formed in January 2006, made up of smaller Islamist insurgent groups; most notably, the Council includes the Iraq branch of al-Qaida, who was led by the Jordanian militant Abu Musab al-Zarqawi. This group has utilised 'bombs, small arms and mortar[s] against Iraqi and American soldiers'[15] and has two brigades exclusively assigned to suicide bombings. The aim of this group is the removal of coalition forces from Iraq (and in particular US forces) and seemingly the implementation of an Islamic government in Iraq.

The *Partisans of the Sunnah Army* (Ansar al-Sunnah) is a jihadist group with similar aims and tactics to the Mujahidin Shura Council. It is based in northern and central Iraq, and its members are largely Kurdish and Sunni Arab. Ansar al-Sunnah's members call for a withdrawal of US troops and a return to early Islamic practices.

The *Islamic Army in Iraq* (Al-Jaysh al-Islami fil-'Iraq) is a nationalistic insurgent group which aims to drive US forces out of Iraq. Widely seen as more nationalistic than religious, this group has utilised IEDs and kidnappings, targeted at US forces as well as foreign contractors.

The Islamic Front of the Iraqi Resistance (Al-Jabna al-Islamiya lil-Muqawama al-'Iraqiya) is a strongly nationalistic group which 'issues weekly updates of claimed attacks, has a comprehensive website and publishes a lengthy, monthly magazine, Jami''.[16] There has been some speculation that the *Islamic Front* is actually just a public relations tool for other insurgent organizations.

Smaller groups include the *First Four Caliphs Army* (Jaysh al-Rashidin), which operates as many as six brigades; the *Victorious Group's Army* (Jaysh al-Ta'ifa al-Mansoura), which operates a minimum of three brigades; the *Mujahidin's Army* (Jaysh al-Mujahidin), which has released dozens of videos of attacks on US forces; and *Muhammad's Army* (Jaysh Muhammad), a group best known for claiming the bombing of the UN headquarters in 2003.

Although there is little agreement on the number of insurgents, estimates have ranged from several thousands to over 200,000 (including part-time fighters and enablers). The director of the Iraqi Intelligence Service in January 2005 estimated that there were at least 40,000 hardcore fighters participating in the insurgency.

INSURGENCY AND SECTARIANISM

Iraq has seen an alarming increase in sectarian violence and rhetoric, mainly between Arab Sunni and Shi'ite Muslims, since its first elected government took office in April 2005.

Groups at the centre of the controversy include the Supreme Council for the Islamic Revolution in Iraq (SCIRI) and the Badr Organisation, which is thought to be its militant branch. Insurgent groups such as al-Qaida's Iraq branch are thought to be involved in sectarian violence in an effort to accelerate the onset of civil war and incite violence.

A bloody turning point in the developing sectarian conflict occurred on 29 August 2003 when a car bomb exploded outside the Imam Ali mosque in Najaf, killing over 85 Shi'ite worshippers, including SCIRI's leader Ayatollah Muhammad Baqr al-Hakim. Since then, sectarian attacks have occurred with increased frequency in and around Baghdad, as well as in the Shi'ite holy cities of Najaf and Karbala. Frequent targets have been worshippers at holy sites or mosques, mourners in funeral processions, market-goers and job queues outside of police stations. The resulting spread of fear and terror reached a crisis level on 31 August 2005 when a false rumour that a suicide bomber was about to strike in the crowd of a Shi'ite religious festival caused a stampede and the deaths of hundreds of worshippers. The bombing of the Al-Askariya mosque in Samarra on 22 February 2006 led to dozens of reprisal attacks on Sunni mosques as well as increased sectarian violence. Shi'ite mosques continued to be targeted in April 2006 as 85 people were killed in a suicide attack at Buratha mosque in Baghdad and 25 were killed by a car bomb at a Shi'ite mosque near Baquba.

The sectarian attacks have been bolstered by blatantly sectarian political discourse and sermons, as well as partisan media broadcasts. Prior to the US-led invasion in April 2003 sectarianism was widespread in society but relatively undisruptive. Saddam Hussein was purportedly more interested in complete loyalty than religious affiliation; however, his most trusted aides and the core of his 'security apparatus' comprised Sunni Arabs and particularly Tikritis. Furthermore, sectarianism reared its latent head in times of crisis and Shi'ites were often the first to be targeted (as in the Iran–Iraq War and the aftermath of the First Gulf War). Ill treatment and oppression by Saddam's regime, associated with tyrannical Sunni rule, led many Shi'ites to shun the idea of power-sharing with Sunni groups during political transition. Furthermore, Iraqis lack a national identity and instead largely identify themselves by tribe, clan or religious belief. This division of society, coupled with the lack of viable political options, inevitably meant that the people would vote along sectarian lines.

As such, the rise of sectarianism has been accompanied by the utilization of mosques as a centre of political mobilisation. Groups like the SCIRI and the Da'wa party have used the mosque to assemble and communicate political messages to its worshippers. Following the bombing of the Al-Askariya mosque in Samarra, there were reports of mosques around Baghdad being used to store weapons and train insurgents. Furthermore, some mosques which previously had mixed congregations have become single-sect mosques, with haphazardly formed 'neighbourhood vigilantes' on guard to protect them.[17] Defensive Sunni Arab militias have sprung up around Baghdad in response to the presence of roving Shi'ite militias, reportedly supported at some point by US forces and the Iraqi government.[18]

On 31 May 2006, Iraqi Prime Minister Nouri al-Maliki imposed a state of emergency on the southern port of Basra in response to increasing sectarian and militia violence. Approximately 140 people were reported dead in Basra in May, most of whom were Sunni Arabs. Reportedly, Shi'ite militias in the Shi'ite-dominated city were responsible for the deaths of Sunnis in the latest wave of violence.[19] There has also been speculation that the Shi'ite militias in Basra are being supplied with money and weapons from Iran.[20]

On 5 June 2006, an audio recording was released, allegedly of the former al-Qaida leader in Iraq, Abu Musab al-Zarqawi who was killed by US forces in a raid on 8 June 2006, calling for violence against Shi'ite Muslims, which was denounced by Iraqi Prime Minister Nouri al-Maliki as 'a futile brutality, depraved mentally and morally'.[21] The speaker, who sounded like Zarqawi from previous recordings, warned Sunnis: 'don't listen to those advocating an end to sectarianism and calling for national unity. This is a weapon to get you to surrender.'[22] Zarqawi's statements are thought to have been aimed at hampering the Iraqi government's attempts to unify Iraq by disrupting the current process of creating a unity government which is to include Sunni and Shi'ite Arabs as well as Kurds.

THE INSURGENCY AND IRAQI KURDISTAN

Kurdistan has by and large escaped much of the insurgent activity that has blighted the rest of Iraq. Although the Islamist insurgent group al-Ansar was active in Kurdistan after the US-led invasion, the Kurdish authorities took a hardline approach toward them, effectively eradicating al-Ansar from the Kurdish region. Kurdish tourist resorts are experiencing a boom with a flood of Arab visitors seeking sanctuary from the violence in the south of Iraq.[23] However, insurgents have been operative in Kurdistan and there has been a recent escalation of violence in the region of Kirkuk, which is predominantly Kurdish but fully under the control of the KRG, as a part of al-Qaida's plan to deliberately provoke sectarian war in the ethnically diverse region. There have been a number of attempted suicide bombings of the KDP's local party offices in Kirkuk. On 13 June 2006, a wave of bombings hit the city, killing 14 people. It is thought that this was a show of strength by al-Qaida in the wake of Abu Musab al-Zarqawi's death.[24]

The efforts of insurgents to infiltrate Iraqi Kurdistan have largely failed. Insurgent operatives have been found and arrested and are currently in detention, though this fact has not been widely acknowledged, and some have been handed over to the US forces.[25] The Kurdish Regional Government implemented a clear strategy to counter the insurgents, incapacitating al-Ansar, who are no longer in a position to carry out attacks in Kurdistan. The KRG's efforts have been aided greatly by the cohesion between civilians and the security forces, which rely on the cooperation of civilians to inform them of foreign presences in the region. Nechirvan Barzani puts the success of the counterinsurgency in Kurdistan down to that fact that Kurdish citizens acknowledge the effort that has been required to build a stable and functioning democracy in Kurdistan, and thus will assist the security forces in maintaining peace.[26]

ALLEGED INVOLVEMENT OF SYRIA AND IRAN

Whether Iraq can maintain its territorial integrity will depend in part on the behaviour of neighbouring states. The intervention of Shi'ite Iran and Sunni-dominated Syria would have the potential to foment sectarian violence to the point of civil war.

Syria has been accused of harbouring Islamic militants who were providing funding, weapons and information to Iraqi insurgents. Many of the foreign fighters involved in the Iraqi insurgency are also thought to have smuggled arms across the Syrian border into Iraq, though Syrian officials have consistently denied this. In response to continued American pressure, Syrian intelligence agents arrested Sabawi Ibrahim Hassan, Saddam's half-brother and a financial supporter of the insurgency, and handed him over to US officials in April 2005. That event marked an increase in Syrian cooperation in the counterinsurgency; however, Syria maintains, unconvincingly, that it is not possible to secure the entire Syrian-Iraqi border.

Iran has close ties with Shi'ite politicians in the Iraqi government, although its precise involvement is difficult to gauge. There are allegations that Iran has trained and armed Shi'ite militias in Iraq; Moqtada al-Sadr and his militia, the Mahdi army, have been linked to Iran. Furthermore, both US and UK officials have expressed concern regarding Iran's alleged involvement in supporting the insurgency. On 27 May 2006, Iran and Iraq made an agreement to seal their border to insurgents. Although this move seems promising for Iran–Iraq relations, there has been wide speculation that this latest move by Iran was a public relations move to stall US intervention in its nuclear programme.[27] In addition, the agreement does not deal with the alleged training of Shi'ite militias, which would be more useful to Iran if relations between the US and Iran were to break down. Apart from supporting Shi'ite militias, Iran has reportedly established bases in Iraq from which its intelligence agents are able to 'monitor the movement of coalition forces, tend weapons caches, facilitate cross-border travel of clerics, smuggle munitions into Iraq and recruit individuals as intelligence sources'.[28] Iran and Turkey have frequently disregarded international law by conducting cross-border military operations in neighbouring countries. In particular, they have aimed at targets in Iraqi Kurdistan, where they suspect Kurdish militants from their own countries are carrying out operations. Although Iran has the option and incentive to encourage sectarian strife in Iraq, ensuring that the Shi'ite government in Iraq stabilises and takes control of the country is a strong competing interest.

CAUSES OF THE INSURGENCY

The insurgency appears to have developed gradually after the overthrow of the Ba'athist regime. It seems that these early insurgents, who were organised into small cells of fighters, fought out of resentment for the occupation and anger at dire prospects rather than for Ba'athist ideology. From the start, the insurgents developed rhetoric centred on patriotism and religious themes. Although the impact of foreign fighters increased over the course of the insurgency, they were negligible at the beginning.

The US-led coalition made mistakes that contributed to the development of the insurgency, underestimating the work needed to secure, stabilise and reconstruct Iraq after the removal of Saddam's regime. Inadequate forces were deployed along the borders of Iraq, facilitating the entry of foreign jihadists into the country. The Coalition Provisional Authority's decision not to call back the dismantled Iraqi army and security services led to the creation of a 'security vacuum', which the coalition was perhaps not in a position to fill. Furthermore, it left hundreds of thousands of trained Iraqi forces without jobs and prospects, idle and susceptible to insurgent rhetoric.

As for the Iraqi people, the coalition seems to have made the mistake of strategising from a western perspective; the Iraqi people, having lived under Saddam Hussein's totalitarian regime, should not have been expected to perceive and respond to coalition forces the way that the citizens of a democratic society would. Fear and passivity are endemic in such societies, and 'truth' is controlled by the state authority. The conversion of this type of civil society is likely to be a long and complicated process. It was therefore misguided to think that Iraqi society would welcome its 'liberators' with open arms and that order could be restored quickly.

The coalition's inability to restore basic services during the first few months after the collapse of the regime fuelled resentment and anger. However, even in areas where services had been restored to pre-war levels, there were violent outbreaks directed at coalition forces. As the insurgency developed, it increasingly appealed to religious ideology. This type of Islamic radicalism 'provided the motivation, legitimacy, and global network of support for the insurgents in Iraq'.[29]

COUNTERINSURGENCY

For a successful counterinsurgency to be mounted in Iraq, high-quality intelligence and analysis are needed as well as effective channels of communication through which to share information. Furthermore, a clear, cooperative strategy, which promotes transparency and accountability, is essential for the success of the counterinsurgency.

It is crucial that arbitrary or excessive use of force is avoided if the counterinsurgency is to maintain its legitimacy. Civilians should be well informed about what the government and coalition forces are doing; and this information should be disseminated in a way that is sensitive to the local culture and practices.

The counterinsurgency has, so far, been focused on eliminating large numbers of insurgents, targeting the insurgent leaders and their power structures, and the destruction of their bases and disruption of their channels of communication. The insurgency has maintained a relatively stable level of violence, however, due to its flexible structure and deep-seated family, tribal and local allegiances. The solution lies, therefore, in the counterinsurgency targeting the popular support and sympathy the insurgency enjoys.

Although the use of force is inevitable, for an effective counterinsurgency to be waged sheer military might must give way to political solutions. The legitimacy of the insurgency must be reduced from the perspective of the Iraqi people, and that of the Iraqi government must be similarly increased. The use of illegitimate force, torture, lack of concern for civilian casualties, and dependence on sectarian militias, all of which the Iraqi government has been accused of, are harmful to the goal of quelling the insurgency. To increase the legitimacy of the Iraqi government, sectarian militias should be disbanded in favour of regular armed forces, and the human rights of all the citizens of Iraq have to be respected. The behaviour of security forces should be monitored and those that use illegal methods should be punished, to avoid the creation of an atmosphere of impunity. Illegal acts like torture, extrajudicial killings and cruel and unusual punishments, which are currently being ignored, should be addressed and dealt with in accordance with principles of fundamental justice. An effective counterinsurgency should also deal with the problem of organised crime, which is taking hold in some areas of Iraq.

Iraqi Prime Minister Nouri al-Maliki's claim that his so-called unity government represents all Iraqis without discrimination was an attempt at inclusiveness, although his choices have been criticised as sectarian by some. Maliki has emphasised that his government will halt sectarian violence and take control of security issues, focusing on reconciliation. The next item on the political agenda for Iraq is the amendment of Iraq's constitution. Any amendments which are made should involve inclusiveness and transparency at all levels.

Coalition forces are of the view that the force of the insurgency will gradually fade as the reconstruction of Iraq develops. A US Pentagon report released in May 2006 predicted that the insurgency would hold strong in 2006 but begin to wane in 2007. The report also stated that most Sunni groups in Iraq oppose al-Qaida but either do not have the resources to fight it or believe it furthers their own political goals. Polling data has also indicated that most Iraqis are opposed to the insurgency's use of violence. The Pentagon report also cited that there have been signs of stability in Iraq, with an increase in the number of independent mass media outlets and businesses registered, and a constant level of oil production. If Iraq can continue to prosper to the benefit of ordinary Iraqis, then the popularity of the insurgents, who target any signs of reconstruction, will surely diminish.

However, this optimism must be kept in check, as all the immediate signs are that the command of the insurgency is far from declining. There have been recent reports that several Sunni Arab rejectionist insurgent groups are collaborating with al-Qaida. Moreover, as of 30 May 2006, the rate of US troop fatalities was almost double that of previous figures, and the rate of insurgent attacks was at its highest level in two years. The death of Abu Musab al-Zarqawi was hailed as a major victory for coalition forces in the fight against the insurgents. However, the insurgent forces are too decentralised for his death to have a great impact on them. Indeed, twelve days after al-Zarqawi's death, the Mujahidin Shura Council announced the new leader of al-Qaida in Iraq, Abu Hamza al-Muhajir, had personally killed two US soldiers to avenge his predecessor's death.[30] While the Bush administration has stressed the importance of eradicating al-Qaida operatives, it has been accused of exaggerating the strength of al-Qaida in an effort to legitimise the war on terror, so any effective counterinsurgency should not be designed around the elimination of al-Qaida; rather, legitimate force should only be used in conjunction with social and economic improvements in Iraq.

Aiming to weaken the Iraqi government and coalition forces through terrorism, the tactics of the insurgency have become increasingly sophisticated. Despite mainly focusing on coalition and government targets, insurgents have increasingly attacked non-military and civilian targets. The consolidation of the smaller insurgent groups on the basis of organisation and ideology has led to a short-term increase in strength and tactical advantage. The development of the insurgency has been paralleled by increasing sectarian conflict, with powerful sectarian militias, initially strengthened by the tacit approval of an overburdened government, operating outside the control of the law. The involvement of neighbouring countries in the developing sectarian conflict and insurgency may prove critical in the short term in establishing stability in Iraq.

Regarding the counterinsurgency, the ministries must ensure that dismantling militias and incorporating their members into the Iraqi security forces does not allow the militias to continue sectarian operations but with the cover of official legitimacy. Responsible actions by security forces, good intelligence, inclusiveness and transparency are values that Maliki's government must prioritise if the federal Iraqi state is to have a chance of survival.

Above all, the ministries must promote reconciliation. President Talabani has recently conducted talks with the insurgent groups[31] which seem to have laid the foundation for the 28 peace packages announced by the new Iraqi administration at the end of June 2006, to be brokered with the insurgents if they lay down their arms.[32] This package promises a halt to all US operations against insurgent strongholds as well as compensation for victims of attacks and a proposal, endorsed by the UN to withdraw the coalition forces. Despite the promise of a withdrawal, in line with its ongoing policy in the Middle East, it is clear that the US will not withdraw troops from Iraq until it is certain that its interests are protected. This peace deal is seen as a last-gasp attempt by the Iraqi administration to prevent the country from descending into civil war and is designed to split the Iraqi insurgents from the foreign al-Qaida operatives. The insurgents have yet to respond and there are major stumbling blocks posed by the plan, namely if the US would allow insurgents who had killed US troops to be granted amnesty. However, the timeline for the withdrawal of coalition troops is the crucial concession that may prove the key to ending the insurgency.

16
Current Legal and Human Rights Issues

THE COALITION PROVISIONAL AUTHORITY

The CPA is charged with exercising powers of government on a temporary basis and under CPA Regulation 1 is 'vested with all executive, legislative and judicial authority necessary to achieve its objectives, to be exercised under relevant UN Security Council resolutions, including Resolution 1483 (2003), and the laws and usages of war'.[1]

There is an initial legal inconsistency identifiable in this regulation. It entered into force on the date of signature, which was 16 May 2003, whereas the UN Security Council adopted Resolution 1483 on 22 May 2003. Therefore the CPA could not 'exercise' its powers of government under Resolution 1483 in the period between 16 May and 22 May, as it did not exist.

Applicable law in Iraq as defined in Regulation 1, are the laws in force in Iraq as of 16 April 2003, insofar as those laws are not suspended or replaced by the CPA, superseded by legislation issued by the democratic institutions of Iraq, in conflict with Regulations/ Orders issued by the CPA, or they do not prevent the CPA from carrying out its duties.[2]

HUMANITARIAN INTERNATIONAL LAW OBLIGATIONS

There are many who would challenge the legality of the war and the continued occupation of coalition forces in Iraq. However, KHRP will not endeavour to debate this controversial issue as for the purposes of this publication it is sufficient to say that the Geneva Conventions apply once a given set of factual circumstances arises, regardless of the legality of the initial resort to armed force.

In the case of occupied territory, the provisions of the Fourth Geneva Convention continue to apply beyond the general close of military operations.

The general legal consensus is that the US/UK are exercising their occupying powers *through* the CPA.[3] UN Security Council Resolution 1483 noted the letter of 8 May 2003 from the US/UK representatives to the Security Council, and recognised 'the specific authorities, responsibilities, and obligations under applicable international law of these states as occupying powers under unified command (the "Authority")'.[4]

The preamble recognises that the US/UK are obliged as states by the international laws relating to occupation but they are defined as working '*under*' the command of the CPA and not *through* the CPA. While it is quite clear that the Geneva Conventions apply to the US/UK when they are acting as states, do they apply to CPA decisions as a body? This is a very important question, as organisations such as Amnesty have criticised the CPA for promulgating laws that are outside their mandate as Occupying Powers.[5] However, if the CPA as a body is not an occupying power, which is arguable given the definitions of Resolution 1483, then these criticisms have no legal basis.

To compound this argument, the preamble of Resolution 1483 recognises the US/UK as Occupying Powers but does not specifically recognise any other coalition forces as Occupying Powers, and indeed it further notes that 'other States that are not occupying powers are working now or in the future may work under the Authority'.[6] This strengthens the argument that the CPA itself is not bound by the laws of occupation. However, what alternative legal basis in international law the CPA may have is unclear. In recent times international law has developed to recognise such bodies as the United Nations Mission in Kosovo (UNMIK), which administered that region and continues to do so. Although the CPA is not a United Nations established administration, its operation under international law may be of a similar nature.

Resolution 1483's acknowledgement that other countries are working under the CPA who are not Occupying Powers begs the question of who exactly these countries are and what criteria are used to determine their occupation status. For example, do the Geneva Conventions apply to Italian forces in Iraq although Italy has not specifically been recognised as an Occupying Power and remained non-combatant during the actual war?

As noted above, the Geneva Conventions apply from the outset of any occupation or conflict. There are two types of occupation under the Geneva Conventions. The first is the case where the occupation is 'carried out under the terms of the instrument which brings hostilities to a close: an armistice, capitulation, etc.'.[7] The International Committee of the Red Cross (ICRC) Commentary explains that 'In such cases the Convention will have been in force since the outbreak of hostilities or since the time the war was declared.'[8] The application of the Convention in this situation applies for one year after the general close of military operations. However, certain provisions of the Convention continue to apply after one year has expired so far as the Occupying Power continues to exercise governmental functions. For those states that have ratified Protocol I to the Geneva Conventions, the provisions of that Protocol and the Conventions continue to apply fully for the duration of the occupation.

The second situation is when 'cases where the occupation has taken place without a declaration of war and without hostilities, and makes provision for the entry into force of the Convention in those particular circumstances'.[9] In this case the Convention continues to apply fully for the duration of the occupation.

In relation to Iraq, it remains to be determined when occupation actually started under the Conventions as, according to the CPIC, the US is still at war.[10]

In addition, the question arises as to whether the Geneva Conventions are applicable to the *peshmerga*. Iraq did not adopt the Additional Protocol to the Conventions relating to the Protection of Victims of Non-International Armed Conflicts. The Geneva Convention relative to the Protection of Civilian Persons in Time of War applies only to state parties in relation to occupation and therefore the *peshmerga* cannot be deemed an occupier. However, the *peshmerga* are bound by Common Article 3, which defines the provisions of law relating to prohibited acts of parties in a non-international conflict and continue to remain so bound, particularly if the war is not actually over, but applies regardless as they are fighting the Ansar al-Islam and ex-Saddam loyalists who are internal threats.

INTERNATIONAL HUMAN RIGHTS LAW OBLIGATIONS

There is perhaps a danger that a fixation with crimes of the Ba'athist regime distracts attention away from the coalition's obligations to adhere to human rights standards that they claim to value and uphold.

There are three human rights modalities in which international human rights law may be applicable in Iraq. Firstly, one must explore the issue of the law of state succession as Iraq has ratified some international human rights instruments. Secondly, human rights law is incorporated into the mandate of the CPA by way of Resolution 1483 and by the UN Charter itself. Finally, human rights obligations of the governments of the coalition states may apply directly to the conduct of their troops/personnel in Iraq.

Succession

Iraq is a party to all the major human rights treaties, and as such the human rights obligations prior to the 2003 war remain binding on the current administrative authorities in Iraq. This is due to the principle of state succession, which provides for automatic succession with respect to human rights obligations.

Human rights obligations pass with control of territory and the beneficiaries of the rights are entitled to maintain them. This legal principle was clarified by the Human Rights Committee when it stated that

> once people are accorded the protection of the rights under the Covenant, such protection devolves with territory and continues to belong to them, notwithstanding change in government of the State party, including dismemberment in more than one State or State succession or any subsequent action of the State party designed to divest them of the rights guaranteed by the Covenant.[11]

Furthermore, Iraq's membership of the UN would also bind the CPA to the human rights obligations contained within the Charter. By means of Articles 55 and 56 of the Charter, the CPA is obliged to promote 'universal respect for, and observance of, human rights and fundamental freedoms for all without distinction as to race, sex, language or religion'.

The CPA acting as the current 'executive' authority in Iraq is therefore bound by the human rights obligations in these instruments.

UN mandate

In Resolution 1483, the UN Security Council recognises the creation of the CPA and expressly mandates the CPA to assist the people of Iraq through 'promoting the protection of human rights'.

As the CPA is responsible for protecting and promoting human rights under Resolution 1483, the only way that this objective can be achieved is through compliance with international human rights standards.

Furthermore, acting under Chapter VII of the Charter, the Security Council calls upon the CPA,

> consistent with the Charter of the UN and other relevant international law, to promote the welfare of the Iraqi people through effective administration of the territory, including in particular the working towards the restoration of conditions of security and stability and the creation of conditions in which the Iraqi people can freely determine their own political future.

Thus, the CPA is mandated with compliance of international human rights standards.

Do human rights obligations of coalition governments apply to their troops/personnel in Iraq?

The legal situation in Iraq is unique in the world today, as rather than being administered by the international community through the UN as in Kosovo, the CPA was established by the coalition states themselves.

In Kosovo it is difficult to establish a direct link between states and the actions of their troops/personnel since orders are given through UNMIK or the Kosovo Force (KFOR). In Iraq, on the other hand, the coalition states, particularly the UK and US, directly make the decisions and give orders to their personnel/troops.

Taking the example of obligations of the UK under the European Convention on Human Rights (ECHR) system, for acts committed in Iraq by its personnel, this issue can be examined.

According to the case law of the ECHR, when a contracting state exercises effective control of an area outside its national territory, it may be responsible for acts committed by its authorities on this territory. The persons affected by those acts are considered to fall 'within the jurisdiction' of that state and the state is therefore obliged to secure their Convention rights. Accordingly, a victim of a violation of the Convention, which occurred in the territory effectively controlled by a state, can file an application in Strasbourg against that state.[12] Therefore, if it could be shown that the armies of the UK exercise an effective control over the area they are in charge of, and a violation of the ECHR occurs, there is a prima facie case under the Convention.

The case of troops/personnel from one member state of the Coalition following orders from another member state

In Iraq the situation may arise where one state's troops are put under the command or follow orders of another's. Were such a situation to lead to human rights abuses, the question arises as to which state action should be pursued against.

It appears logical that a case be brought against the state that gives the orders, even if those orders are carried out by troops from another state. However, the troops following the orders are obliged not to engage in acts which are contrary to the human rights obligations of their own state. Therefore a case could be pursued against both states in question.

Filing an application

According to Article 1 of the ECHR the 'High Contracting Parties' to the Convention shall secure to everyone 'within their jurisdiction' the rights and freedoms defined in the Convention. This same rule applies to other human rights mechanisms.

Therefore an application under a human rights mechanism could not be taken against the CPA itself. Such an application would no doubt be declared inadmissible by the courts as being incompatible rationae personae (that is, does not fall within the jurisdiction of the relevant body) within the provisions of the mechanisms.

A victim would therefore need to establish a direct chain of command to a given state or states, assess what human rights instruments they have ratified and violated in this instance, and then take the case before the relevant judicial authority.

Exhausting domestic remedies

Before filing an application to any human rights mechanism, a petitioner must in principle use all the procedural means that are available within the domestic legal system of the violating state.[13] This includes both judicial and non-judicial procedures.

In the context of Iraq this could mean that an applicant would have to submit his or her case to the domestic courts of the state concerned. The main reason for this is that the principle of exhaustion of domestic remedies under the ECHR for example is based on the subsidiary nature of the competence of the court: the state, whose authorities are accused of having violated the Convention, must be offered the possibility of redressing the situation before the Strasbourg

Court intervenes. The domestic courts in Iraq, although under the authority of the CPA, are not directly under one member state and therefore could not be used to exhaust domestic remedies. Secondly, it could be argued that since there is local immunity for the acts of CPA officials in all capacities, then the remedies that are normally available in Iraq would not be effective.

An applicant from Iraq may be exempt from bringing a case to the member state's domestic court on the basis of the reasoning in the Issa case of 2000. Here it was found that it was too expensive for victims to bring a case to Turkey and therefore they could not be expected to exhaust domestic remedies.

If the argument is that domestic remedies are not effective and therefore a victim is exempt from exhausting such remedies, the application should be filed in Strasbourg within six months following the date when the facts of which the applicant complains occurred.

Furthermore, exhaustion of domestic remedies would not have to be established where an 'administrative practice' (namely where a clear repetition of acts incompatible with the human rights mechanism and their official tolerance by the authorities) has been shown to exist and is of such a nature as to make proceedings futile or ineffective.[14]

17
The Question of Autonomy

With uncertainty hovering over the 'fundamental law' of Iraq as well as the final constitution, how best to preserve Iraqi Kurdistan's existing autonomous powers within a new political framework is still being negotiated. However, it is assumed that Iraqi Kurdistan will enjoy unprecedented autonomy recognised both by the constitution and the international community.

In December 2003, the Kurdish parties submitted a draft for a voluntary federation of Iraqi Kurdistan with the rest of Iraq to the Governing Council. The draft details that all the territories which belonged to Iraqi Kurdistan when Mosul was forcibly annexed to Iraq in the aftermath of the First World War should become officially part of Iraqi Kurdistan. Furthermore, all cities that had a Kurdish majority based on the 1957 census should be part of the voluntary federation.

Both the coalition and the Arab factions are proposing a federalist plan at governorate levels, which means that Kurdistan as an entity would disappear in exchange for a decentralised rule, without any guarantees for the Kurds.

It remains to be seen what the coalition and Arab parties will make of this proposal. However, as for the right and the future of self-determination and autonomy in Iraqi Kurdistan, this will be dealt with in Part III.

18
The Anfal Campaigns:
The War Crimes Tribunal

AN ENDURING LEGACY

The Anfal campaigns left a mark not only in the collective memory of the Kurdish people but also on the daily lives of its immediate victims. An estimated 7,000 families are the direct survivors of Anfal, dependent on the charity the government is able to provide, or on short-term labour opportunities for themselves or their children. Old men and women crowd outside the offices of the Ministry of Human Rights in Sulaimaniya, still hoping for information about their loved ones, or to be housed outside of the old resettlement complexes that rise imperceptibly out of the dusty plains of north-eastern Iraq; their inhabitants kept apart from the rest of Kurdish society, entertaining little hope of being properly integrated.

Fifteen years is perhaps a shorter time in the life of an individual than it is in the news-jaded world at large. The memories of survivors are fresh, 15 years after the event. One man, Kamal Jalal, described how on 5 May 1988, the Republican Guard and the *jash* came to his village near the town of Qoi and took his father, mother, three sisters and six brothers away before burning the village. By the time Kamal was a 14-year-old *peshmerga* in 1991,

All of the young men that had survived Anfal joined the uprising. I went to the town of Harija and I found an official who could tell me about my family. I said, 'Tell me what happened to my sisters, brothers and mother or I'll kill you.' He said, 'They're all dead. They died at [the prison camp] Nugrat Selman. If they weren't executed, they starved to death.' I have no hope that they'll ever come back.

Others still cling to the hope that with the end of Saddam Hussein, disappeared loved ones might reappear.[1]

At least in the PUK areas, where the majority of Anfal survivors now live, the regional government insists[2] that its assistance makes a positive and worthwhile difference to their lives. The ministries provide access to health facilities, a pension of approximately US$ 40 per family per month, and educational benefits, including positive discrimination for children of Anfalak families, to increase their chances of going to university. In Sulaimaniya a Ministry of Human Rights, Displaced Persons and Anfal was established by the Kurdish administration in 1999, before which, according to its director of Anfal issues, no organisation dealt methodically with the plight of an estimated 7,000 remaining families directly affected by the Anfal campaigns.[3] The ministry coordinates social services, landmine removal and facilitates returns to destroyed villages.

But despite government help and worldwide concern, depression, self-harm, and suicide attempts are commonplace amongst 'Anfalak'. With the end of Saddam's regime, many experienced a renewed flush of hope that disappeared loved ones will reappear – only to grieve again. The director of a local women's NGO in Erbil described how 'Anfal widows are unable to move on, they still wear black and they can't be persuaded to move on.'[4] Social isolation and lack of counselling contribute to the difficulties faced by victims.

The discovery of mass graves in Iraq at the end of hostilities in 2003 has begun to shed light on the fate of the 'disappeared'. As many as 300,000 victims are believed to have been buried in 263 mass graves across Iraq.[5] The largest grave is estimated to contain the bodies of up to 2,000 people.[6]

THE IRAQI SPECIAL TRIBUNAL

Plans for a tribunal have been discussed for several years among human rights campaigners and opponents of Saddam's regime, to bring those responsible for crimes against humanity to justice. For obvious reasons the end of the Ba'athist regime has opened up the possibilities for justice to be sought on behalf of victims of the Iraqi government, whether Kurds, Sunni or Shi'ite.

On 10 December 2003, the Statute of the Iraqi Special Tribunal, to try members of Saddam's regime for genocide, war crimes and crimes against humanity, became law.[7] The Tribunal has jurisdiction over any Iraqi national or resident, accused of committing these crimes between the period 17 July 1968 up to and including 1 May 2003.[8]

The Tribunal will deal with crimes against the people of Iraq, including the Kurds, Arabs, Turcomans, Assyrians, Shi'ites and Sunnis, whether or not they were committed during armed conflict.[9]

Furthermore, it includes crimes committed outside Iraq, for example during the wars with the Islamic Republic of Iran and the State of Kuwait.[10] Defendants may also be tried in absentia as according to Ahmad Chalabi, a member of the Governing Council, Saddam would have been 'accused and charged for committing major crimes against humanity and against the Iraqi people, and he will certainly fall under the jurisdiction of this court' in absentia.[11] Since his capture on 13 December 2003, this circumstance is no longer applicable for Saddam. However, the statement is significant for other members of his regime as they may be tried in absentia.

There was no clear date set for the Tribunal to commence work but it has been indicated that trials will not start for months.[12] Prosecutors will use the collection of documents seized from the former regime by US forces as evidence. Evidence will also come from the excavation of some of the 270 mass graves in Iraq that are believed to hold at least 300,000 sets of remains. The new court is expected to cost £70 million[13] and the funding will come from the regular budget of the Government of Iraq.

The trials will be open to the public, human rights groups and news media, which suggests that they could be televised. Defendants will have the right to a lawyer and to appeal, and the Iraqi penal code, except for some additions introduced by Saddam's regime, will be applicable.

THE DEFENDANTS

Some of the chief perpetrators of the crimes outlined in the Statute of the Tribunal, including Saddam Hussein and 'Chemical Ali', are already in the custody of coalition forces. The first suspects brought to trial could include the top officials on the US 55 'most wanted' list. Furthermore, there are currently over 5,500 detainees in US custody, but it is not clear how many of these are war crimes suspects.

It is unclear whether the Governing Council wishes to bring more than the 55 people on the US list to the Tribunal. There is a danger that if they do, the court will become overloaded with cases and will not be able to work effectively, in a similar fashion to the European Court of Human Rights. In the Nuremberg trials following the Second World War only 23 cases were tried, and the War Crimes Tribunal for the former Yugoslavia has indicted less than 100 people in eight years.

THE DEATH PENALTY

The Governing Council is insisting that the Tribunal will be given the authority to impose the death penalty. The death penalty, which was suspended by the CPA, remains in Iraq's statute books, and is popular with Iraqis as well as the US. It is understood that the transitional government, scheduled to take over sovereignty in July 2004, will make the decision on the death penalty.[14] However, from an Iraqi perspective it appears a foregone conclusion that the Tribunal will have the power to impose the death penalty.

The outcome of the decision on the death penalty poses not only issues relating to human rights in general, but also practical issues relating to European coalition partners such as Britain, Italy, Poland and Spain, as they would be forbidden by the European Convention on Human Rights from handing over prisoners to a court with the power to sentence them to death.

INTERNATIONAL JUDGES

A further contentious issue with the Statute is the role of international judges on the court's panel or international prosecutors. An initial discrepancy can be noted in the Statute as Article 4 states that the tribunal may 'appoint non-Iraqi judges who have experience in the crimes encompassed in this statute'. However, Article 28 provides that 'the judges ... shall be Iraqi nationals'. Iraqi lawyers will argue the cases and will be assisted by international advisors who will also monitor the proceedings. The Statute does not require that judges and prosecutors have experience working on complex criminal cases and cases involving serious human rights crimes. Nor does the law permit the appointment of non-Iraqi prosecutors or investigative judges, even if they have relevant experience investigating and prosecuting serious human rights crimes. In the Yugoslav and Rwandan tribunals international experts argued the cases and international judges decided the cases. The Iraqi structure poses difficulties for a number of reasons.

Iraqi judges have not had any experience in these types of cases, and given their complexity there is a fear that the trials will not be carried out expediently and judiciously. A committee has been set up to remove all judicial officials that had links to Saddam's Ba'ath party. During Saddam's regime, all the senior judges were Ba'ath party members, while most legal officials were at least nominal members of the party. This committee is reviewing every judge and prosecutor in Iraq for membership of the Ba'ath party and complicity for human rights violations or corruption. If any judge or prosecutor is found to be in violation of these standards, the committee will dismiss him or her from office. Paul Bremer stated that the goal of these actions was to rebuild an independent and transparent judicial system, but stressed that it is an ongoing process which would inevitably take some time. Therefore it will be extremely difficult to find Iraqi lawyers with experience and who have no proven links to the Ba'ath party.

Furthermore, by using members of the Iraqi judiciary alone there is another concern as to whether 'the Iraqi population would consider individuals who were part of the legal system under Saddam Hussein's presidency to possess the required neutrality, since in countless instances they would be adjudicating cases involving the Saddam Hussein government'.[15]

On a practical level this clearance process may stall the work of the Tribunal, in that the Tribunal may need to wait for an investigation of lawyers/judges to be completed before being able to commence a case, even if all the evidence is collated and the case is ready to begin.

On the other hand, the defendant is entitled to have non-Iraqi legal counsel but only if the principal lawyer is Iraqi. The accused will face serious charges and therefore should have the right to choose the best person to represent him or her regardless of that person's nationality. Furthermore, it impacts the weight of a conviction as it could be argued that the only reason the defendant was convicted was because he or she did not have access to the best principal lawyer for the job but was confined by nationality.

These issues combined with the wisdom of letting victims of the regime try their own tormentors diminish the credibility of the Tribunal both nationally and internationally. International support is vital to offset any criticisms that the Tribunal is a coalition tool to perform 'victors' justice'.

THE CRIMES

For the purposes of the Statute, 'genocide' is defined in accordance with the Convention on the Prevention and Punishment of the Crime of Genocide as ratified by Iraq. As described in previous chapters, the Anfal campaigns at the very least pointed to a prima facie case of genocide, confirmed under Article 1 of the Convention on the Prevention and Punishment of the Crime of Genocide.[16] For such a crime to be proven it would have to be established that there existed the requisite intent to destroy a group in whole, or in part.

The Special Rapporteur on Iraq stated that the Iraqi government's operations may well have amounted to genocide within the meaning of the Convention and that 'the Anfal Operations constituted genocide type activities which did in fact result in the extermination of a part of this population and which continue to have an impact on the lives of the people as a whole'.[17] Article 4 of the Convention envisages such acts being tried by a competent tribunal where the act was committed, or by an international penal tribunal having jurisdiction.

One possibility may have been for other state parties to the Genocide Convention to submit disputes relating to 'the interpretation, application or fulfilment' of the Convention, including state responsibility for genocide, to the International Court of Justice (ICJ). But the outcome of such a submission would have been limited. Reparations for the Kurds could be sought, including compensation for destroyed or confiscated property, since the purpose of an international claim for reparation is that 'reparation must, as far as possible, wipe out all the consequences of the illegal act and re-establish the situation which would, in all probability have existed if that act had not been committed'.[18] Court orders for the cessation of illegal acts, for compensation for the victims or for other forms of redress might be possible – even for an undertaking to change legislation or practices to prevent further violations. But though it is open to the ICJ to determine a state's responsibility for acts prohibited by the Convention and issue orders for reparations, it has as such no criminal jurisdiction. Moreover, enforcement would have been impossible.

The establishment of the Tribunal in Iraq should satisfy the requirements of Article 4 and lead to some form of justice for the Kurdish victims of genocide if a case can be proven. However, there is a danger that a defendant could argue successfully that the Tribunal is not 'competent' within the meaning of Article 4. Moreover, if the court is clouded with scepticism as to its capabilities and impartiality, it will have a detrimental effect on the overall justice and recognition for the crime of genocide in relation to the Kurds.

'Crimes against humanity' are defined in Article 12 of the Statute and a number of acts are listed 'when committed as part of a widespread or systematic attack directed against any civilian population, with knowledge of the attack'. Interestingly, although international law instruments are referred to expressly for the purposes of defining genocide and war crimes, no mention is made of a specific international instrument when defining crimes against humanity. However, Article 12 does refer to the 'fundamental norms' of international law.

In defining 'war crimes' the Statute refers to the Geneva Conventions and customary international law, as well as attacks against 'personnel, installations, material, units, or vehicles involved in a peacekeeping mission in accordance with the Charter of the United Nations'. The Tribunal also has the power to prosecute persons who have committed crimes under Iraqi law. Furthermore, there is no statute of limitations on these crimes.

In interpreting the Articles dealing with the various crimes, the Trial Chambers and the Appellate Chamber may resort to relevant decisions of international courts or tribunals as persuasive authority for their decisions. This highlights another concern relating to the Tribunal that such huge crimes are being prosecuted in a court with no established legal history.

There are many other criticisms of the Statute. One example is that it does not require the standard of proof to be beyond a reasonable doubt, and another is that there is a lack of protection of witnesses and victims or security for the tribunal and its staff. This has proved to be a major issue in the Yugoslav War Crimes Tribunal[19] and yet it is not adequately addressed in the Statute.

It is essential that justice when done is impartial, rigorous and obeys the highest standards of probity – to resort to quick-fix 'victors' justice' or political showcase trials the conclusion of which is foregone, would be to do an injustice not only to defendants but to the victims and their families. According to the head of Iraq's Governing Council, Saddam and other defendants will appear before the Iraqi Tribunal and get a fair trial before this Iraqi court. However, with all the concerns expressed over the Statute it is hard to see how this will be achieved.

19
The Continuing Problem of Internal Displacement

The displacement of so much of the Kurdish population of Iraq remains an enduring legacy of the treatment of the Kurds by the Ba'athist regime. Prior to the invasion of Iraq in March 2003, 800,000 people, mainly of Kurdish origin but also Assyrians and Turcomans, were displaced in northern and central Iraq. In the south, between 100,000 and 200,000 Marsh Arabs and at least 25,000 Arab Shi'ites were displaced.

The 2003 conflict which resulted in the fall of the former government of Iraq and the subsequent periodic fighting and insurgency has led to further population movements throughout the country. Displacement has continued even after the proclaimed liberation by the US-led multinational forces, thanks mainly to the instability of the region and the insurgent fighting.[1] Kirkuk and Mosul were among the cities targeted by military operations and fighting. Insecurity in these areas led to further internal displacement as families fled the region because of the growing violence and ethno-religious tensions.[2]

In September 2003, the London based NGO KHRP sent a fact-finding mission to a number of camps in the area around Sulaimaniya and witnessed the appalling conditions in which many IDPs subsist. The origins of the camps vary. Many victims of the Anfal campaigns, displaced almost 16 years ago, still inhabit the resettlement complexes 'provided' by the Ba'athists at the time their villages were destroyed. However, it appears that the most recent arrivals endure some of the worst conditions.

The Takiyeh camp is perhaps indicative of a number of others spread out upon the arid plains around Sulaimaniya. Most of the camp's inhabitants have been expelled from the Kirkuk region, or have returned from Iran where they had been granted refugee status. In total the camp houses some 400 families. Shelter is minimal and is largely in the form of UN standard-issue tents designed for emergency relief, the majority of which have almost certainly been used several times before. The canvas, in many cases, is splitting and patched. Some of the structures have been built with extremely limited resources, by the inhabitants themselves and at their own expense. Water for domestic consumption arrives by tanker and is stored in aluminium drums without shade or other cooling apparatus. It must therefore be drunk at room temperature or cooled with the aid of ice-blocks, which the inhabitants of Takiyeh must purchase. Cooking is undertaken in communal mud-built ovens. In the absence of any other form of fuel, residents forage for scraps of wood in an almost completely barren environment. Transport to Sulaimaniya and back, the nearest centre of any kind of employment opportunity, costs 10 dinar a day; yet the earnings that temporary labourers from Takiyeh can expect are little more than 20 dinar per day (approximately US$ 2).[3]

Resentment of UN agencies, NGOs and the local administration is high amongst the inhabitants, who have been promised imminent improvements to their living conditions that have yet to be realised. One resident told the KHRP mission, to the audible agreement of other camp inhabitants, that they had effectively been ignored by every institution that had the capability to positively affect their lives. The ultimate dream, he said, of his family and others, was to return to Kirkuk from where almost all of them had been expelled. His frustration lay in the fact that they had not been given any assistance in returning to Kirkuk, nor, as a temporary measure, in improving conditions in the camp;

It's possible to go back but we have no proof of ownership of property. I can do nothing. Our only hope is to get help from the international organisations. There are thousands of them, but they never do anything. Imagine what it's like here for the children. They have no future, no education, nothing. And imagine what it's like in the winter. The snow here can be a metre deep. Children die every day. There are no jobs because we're too far from the centre of Sulaimaniya. Sometimes the international organisations come here. They write reports and take photographs, and we never see them again. The Red Cross came here, and never came back. Once, some Americans came. One of them opened up a bag full of hundreds dollars and said, 'You see this money? It's all for helping you and your family.' And then they got into their Land cruisers and drove away. That was about a year ago. Next time an NGO comes here with empty promises, we'll just kick them out. We've been neglected and ignored.[4]

Given the conditions in which IDPs live in camps such as Takiyeh, these complaints are understandable; though perhaps given the scale of the IDP problem in the region, it is sadly inevitable that some will continue to inhabit inadequate settlements for the short to medium future.

The village of Suresh, near Chamchamal is a resettlement camp originating from the Anfal campaigns of 1988. After the destruction of their villages, those who had not been taken away to prison camps or who had not fled towards Iran were directed towards camps such as these, often bare patches of scrub without buildings or shelter, and there rehoused, tens or hundreds of kilometres away from the places where their villages had been. The Suresh camp lies off the Kirkuk–Sulaimaniya road. Most of its inhabitants lived originally in the villages around Qader Karam, roughly 80 kilometres to the south.

The camp as it now exists consists of a few hundred single-storey buildings, largely constructed by breeze-blocks built from the inhabitants, who have dubbed the settlement 'New Qader Karam'. Most are victims of the third Anfal campaign conducted in the Germian area between 7 and 20 April 1988. As in Takiyeh, tankers bring water. As victims of the Anfal campaigns, each family is paid a monthly pension of 400 dinar per family by the local administration (approximately US$ 40). Because of their distance from any major settlement, it is difficult for the inhabitants to find work; no employment opportunities exist within the Anfal camps themselves.

The UN-HABITAT constructed settlement of 450 houses at Bazian is a positive indication of what can be achieved by a concerted allocation of resources. Although some distance from Sulaimaniya, the settlement is close to the main road and, for those with private transport, access to the city is good. The houses are well-constructed bungalows with front yards and parking space. The majority appear to be equipped with satellite television. The village is widely regarded as a model for future development (although at current rates of construction it will be some decades before all the displaced persons in Iraqi Kurdistan are accommodated in anything approaching comparable conditions).

Amongst the inhabitants, the main concern is the lack of adequate facilities and services, with one individual reporting that

There's a small hospital quite nearby, but it isn't really big enough. We only have eight hours of electricity a day, which isn't long enough, and we have to buy water, which is brought every day by tanker. The children have to go to school in Sulaimaniya.[5]

Despite some privations, including a lack of running water, shortage of electricity, and distance from medical and educational facilities, the UN-HABITAT settlement is built to a high standard and provides a model for further construction. But it only addresses the needs of a fraction of the IDPs in the region.

Currently, nearly 60 per cent of IDPs in Iraqi Kurdistan live in collective towns. Many families own their houses, and have, according to UN-HABITAT, established the necessary socio-economic framework to continue living in these towns. UN-HABITAT also believes that it should be a priority to give attention to the upgrading of these towns in order to meet the fundamental objective of the Settlement Rehabilitation Programme which is to ensure adequate living conditions within sustainable human settlements.

The original homes of many of the IDPs in the northern governorates are, or were prior to their destruction, located in sites within the Kurdish autonomous region (KAR). The reasons behind the IDP's reluctance or inability to return home were numerous. In many cases whole villages and towns have been destroyed, and with them complete social and physical infrastructures. The presence of minefields is another disincentive. UNOPS, alongside dedicated mine-action groups such as MAG, have operated mine-clearing schemes since 1996. UNOPS noted that while the number of mines laid is unknown, it had nevertheless identified by September 2001, '3,400 mined areas covering 900 square kilometres of land required for reconstruction, resettlement, agricultural purposes and the rehabilitation of basic services such as electricity and water, affecting approximately 1100 communities'.[6] In 1998, the Secretary-General of the UN reported that minefield clearance would take between 35 and 75 years.[7]

While progress has been made to rehouse displaced persons (and where possible return them to their former homes) within the Kurdish-administered region, the end of the recent conflict in Iraq vastly increases the extent of the scope of the resettlement. Along with this new opportunity, however, came the potential for new conflicts to be unleashed, as Kurds crossed the border of the autonomous region into what was Saddam's Iraq.

The international community's apparent inability or lack of willingness to establish even the most basic mediation or conflict resolution mechanisms by which property disputes could be resolved exacerbated the impression of an unregulated free-for-all which resulted from the end of major combat operations. Both of the main Kurdish political parties, the KDP and the PUK, expressed their commitment to a suitable legal mechanism by which property claims could be adjudicated.[8]

Nonetheless, even among some liberals within the Kurdish diasporas, otherwise committed to the rule of law and a multiethnicity in the 'new Iraq', there exists a perception that justice, however rough, was being done.[9] Those brought into the Kurdish region by the Saddam Hussein regime are largely believed to have been Tikriti Arabs, 'fascists', pro-Saddam, fervent supporters of the regime, and compensated for their move with money, property and other considerations. In addition, Kurds point out that after the uprisings of 1991, many Arabs seized the opportunity to vacate the region and return to their traditional homelands. In the present circumstances, the argument is that they will once more leave of their own accord.

Elections in Kirkuk for a new, 30-member municipal council, held under the auspices of the US military, seemed to ease some of the simmering tensions between the many groups in the city, but the resettlement, property restitution and ethnic tensions between Kurds, Arabs and Turcomans remain ongoing issues which the international community will have to monitor closely.

THE CURRENT SITUATION

The collapse of Saddam Hussein's regime in April 2003 provided the impetus for thousands of displaced Kurds and Turcomans to return to Kirkuk and other regions in Kurdistan which had been 'Arabised' under Ba'athist policies. The spontaneous return of these IDPs to their areas of origin has in many cases produced further displacement of other groups already residing in the region. The Kurds who were displaced were mainly living in the northern governorates of Dohuk, Erbil and Sulaimaniya. They returned to their places of origin below the 'green line', in the province of Tameem, Diayala, Salah al-Din and Ninawa. In August–September 2004, a second population movement occurred, following a national census. There were allegations – instigated it is thought by political representatives – that the census would have an effect on political representation in the area.[10] As a result of the influx of Kurds, thousands of Arabs who had migrated to the area under Saddaam's 'Arabisation' programme began to flee the region. Some were evicted by the returning Kurdish IDPs, while others fled out of fear of revenge attacks. According to the Arab Displacement Union (ADU), a local NGO, more than 4,000 Arab families have become homeless since the conflict in 2003.[11]

The return of the former Kurdish residences has also bolstered the political support of the Kurdish authorities in areas such as Kirkuk. During the January 2005 elections, the Kurdish political parties threatened to boycott the elections because Kurdish residents of Kirkuk, expelled by the former regime in the 1980s and 1990s, were not allowed to vote in the province. Under increasing pressure, the Iraqi Electoral Commission announced on 14 January 2005 its decision to allow 100,000 displaced Kurds to vote locally. Arab and Turcomen leaders roundly condemned this decision, an indicator of the ethnic tensions that have arisen due to the return of the IDPs.

Achieving some semblance of normality has been difficult for many of the returning Kurdish IDPs. The slow resolution of land and property rights and the shortage of housing, especially in the Kirkuk area, have left many of the returning Kurdish families still displaced. Local authorities have said that nearly 16,830 Kurdish families have moved to Kirkuk since March 2004 and are living in old government buildings or are camping on the outskirts of the city because they do not have property or have been unable to reclaim their homes.[12] The difficulties for their resettlement lie in the fact that, unlike the rural farmers who were expelled en masse from villages all through the north, the urban expulsions of Kirkuk were conducted on an individual basis and the majority of the expelled urban Kurds do not have property claims of the same legal strength as their rural counterparts.[13]

20
Current Economic/Humanitarian Issues in Iraqi Kurdistan

SANCTIONS AND EMBARGOES

The UN has lifted the full economic sanctions that were imposed against Iraq in 1990 and obviously with the fall of Saddam, the Baghdad embargoes no longer apply. The only measures remaining are an arms embargo, a ban on the trade of stolen Iraqi cultural property, and a requirement to transfer to the Development Fund for Iraq all assets belonging to Saddam Hussein, senior members of his regime or entities controlled by them.

THE OIL-FOR-FOOD PROGRAMME

On 21 November 2003 the OFFP run by the UN ended in Iraq. Security Council Resolution 1483 authorised the termination of the programme on 21 November and the handover of all activities to the CPA. In Resolution 1511, the Iraqi Governing Council was recognised as a legitimate Iraqi entity and to that end the CPA has transferred the responsibility for the programme to them. The programme will continue to run until the end of June 2004, at which stage the Transitional National Assembly should be functioning.

In Iraqi Kurdistan, the Governing Council turned over responsibility for the uncompleted projects of the three northern governorates of Duhok, Erbil and Sulaimaniya to the KRG's Office of Project Coordination located in Erbil. The CPA agreed to provide support to the Office of Project Coordination via providing specialists in procurement and international contracting to advise on relevant issues.

Of the US$ 8 billion raised through the OFFP in Iraq, at least half remains unspent. Under Resolution 1483, the monies as yet unused are to be placed in a central fund for the development of Iraq. US$ 3 billion has already been transferred and the remainder will be transferred when the programme closes.

Over the summer of 2003 the Iraqi ministries and the CPA re-evaluated the contracts agreed under the OFFP and purport to have made considerable savings where corrupt interventions by the previous regime have been stopped. However, 80 per cent of the contracts eligible for review by the CPA will continue and the remaining contracts will be held until an internationally recognised Government of Iraq decides on their future.

Although the authority to manage the programme has transferred, regarding the actual distribution of the food it was agreed that control of this task would remain with the World Food Programme until June 2003. In anticipation of transferring this task to national officials, the WFP continues to train Iraqis to manage transportation, warehousing and databases, as well as monitor and renegotiate contracts to keep the food aid flowing. Since April 2003, the WFP has supplied the Iraqi population with more than 2.1 million tons of food.

CURRENCY

On 15 October 2003 the public in the whole of Iraq were able to start exchanging the Old Iraqi Dinar (OID) banknotes for a new set of banknotes with a wider range of denominations and much improved security features. The exchange, which is a simple 1:1 conversion of the Old Iraqi Dinar and a 1:150 exchange for the 'Swiss' dinar notes that circulated in the Kurdish north of Iraq, is bringing a standard currency to the whole country for the first time in many years. The banknote exchange is coinciding with the start of foreign exchange auctions run by the central bank, which are bringing stability to the value of the dinar.

Initially, after the war the value of the dinar rose sharply in Iraqi Kurdistan. In the months leading up to the US-led invasion of Iraq, it was widely speculated in the money markets of Kurdish towns and cities that the US invasion would precipitate a return to pre-1991 currency values and that the OID would revert to a value of US$ 3 to 1 OID. In this expectation, those with dollar savings bought up OID; with the presence of US troops and injections of dollar capital into the local economy, those in possession of dollars continued to buy up OID where they could, with the value of the dollar plunging as a result.

As the US government largely took on responsibility for the payment of dollar wages of government employees in Iraqi Kurdistan, an estimated 300,000 heads of household, spending power for many families has been substantially curtailed.

In its attempt to simplify salary claims, the US administration devised a ten-point status-based pay scale. So far, payment of salaries has not met expectations, nor has it met anything like pre-war levels. As of mid-June 2003, the monthly salaries of teachers, once in the dollar-equivalent range of US$ 250–400, had declined to US$ 80. Some categories of employee, including the *peshmerga* forces whose assistance was so valuable to US military aims, have received no payment at all.

NON-GOVERNMENTAL ORGANISATIONS
AND INTERNATIONAL ORGANISATIONS

UN work in Iraq has virtually come to a halt since the bombing of the UN headquarters, as the Secretary-General has moved all UN staff to neighbouring countries.

Aid workers in Iraqi Kurdistan have also been affected by the recent security assaults on NGOs and the UN, as well as the truck bombings in Erbil, in August. However, MAG did not withdraw from the area as they reasoned that the threats to the population of Iraqi Kurdistan from mines is greater than to their employees from bomb blasts.

The UN did withdraw many of their international staff from the once safe haven of the north. The World Food Programme also closed their offices, but handed the food distribution to the US. The ICRC continues to maintain a reduced presence in the north despite the closure of its offices in the south.

On 27 November 2003, it was reported that Japan will provide US$ 1.9 million in grants to help the reconstruction of communities in Iraqi Kurdistan. The money will help finance the reconstruction of schools and renovation of sewer systems in Mosul. It will also provide ambulances to the health and welfare bureau and upgrade waterworks in Ninev.

The US military have spent US$ 100 million on 13,000 humanitarian projects in Iraq and infrastructure improvements. This money has come from assets of Saddam's regime that were seized by US troops. How much of this money is being spent in Iraqi Kurdistan is unclear and the information is not readily available.

Although some international aid workers have left Iraq since the attacks on the UN and Red Cross, NGOs have been expanding as funders have increased the amount of aid to Iraq. In particular, groups that are funded by USAID and DfID (Department for International Development) have been expanding rapidly due to the financing of reconstruction projects. A spokeswoman for USAID stated that 'our NGOs are doing fine. We just don't want them named ... They're continuing to expand.'[1] Again it is unclear how many are based in Iraqi Kurdistan and receiving funds from USAID.

Many of the new members of NGOs are Iraqi nationals who are aware of the topography, culture and languages of Iraq, which makes it safer for them than for international personnel.

On 27 November 2003, the CPA promulgated Order Number 45 on Non-Governmental Organisations, which requires NGOs to register in Iraq, and unless they register they may not carry out programmes in Iraq. International organisations are obliged to be accredited by the Ministry of Foreign Affairs but not to register. There are a number of duties imposed on NGOs seeking to operate in Iraq: providing complete lists of any previous visits or activities in Iraq; complete statements of revenue and expenses and assets and liabilities for the current year and the previous three years; and projected budgets for the next two years. For local NGOs, particularly in Iraqi Kurdistan as they remain poorly funded, it may be extremely difficult to provide this information and it is at the discretion of the NGO Assistance Office to authorise registration in this type of circumstance.

It remains to be seen what impact Order 45 and the current security situation will have on NGO operations in Iraq in the future.

OIL

Since the war, experts have identified expected problems relating to water seeping into oil deposits in both the southern and northern oilfields of Iraq. They have stated that years of poor management damaged the fields and some warn that the US drive to return to pre-war production may lead to a reduction in their productivity in the long term.

CPA officials have acknowledged the problems, but are counting on oil revenues to help to pay for Iraq's reconstruction. To achieve this they have adopted a policy of aggressively managing the oilfields to keep the oil flowing. External repairs are being made to the pipelines, but the CPA have not considered delving below the surface to assess the extent of the problem, as they are worried that the Arab world would see this as further evidence of the US intending to control Iraq's oil.

In a recent interview, however, Rob McKee, the senior oil advisor for the CPA, stated that while some might overstate the underground problems, he believed that the reservoirs did demand attention.

US$ 1.7 billion has already been set aside for maintaining Iraq's oil supply, and the money has been split between paying for imported fuel and fixing the Iraqi pipes, pumps and transfer stations, according to officials. Approximately US$ 2 billion has been approved for oil infrastructure repairs in 2004, including about US$ 40 million to begin the study of the reservoirs. This work is particularly important, because while Iraq sits on one of the world's largest deposits of oil, most of it is drawn from two older fields, Rumaila in the south and Kirkuk in the north.

Recent estimates of Kirkuk's condition are also bleak, with an American oil executive saying that Iraqi engineers had recently informed him that they were now expecting recovery rates of only 9 per cent in Kirkuk, without more advanced technology. At the time of writing, the pipeline bypasses the IT-2 pipeline, 90 miles south of the Turkish border. The IT-1 and IT-1a pumping stations (and the Zakho metering station straddling the Iraqi–Turkish border) are functional, though require substantial overhauling.

There is not yet a firm price tag for modernising Iraq's oil industry, but it will clearly be enormous.

The oilfields suffer from another problem in the post-Saddam era; explosions. At the end of November in Kirkuk there were three separate explosions within minutes of each other. Oilfields have been struck almost weekly since 1 May in Iraq, at pumping stations and along the miles of pipelines that are difficult to protect. The attacks have all but shut down the flow of barrels of exported crude through Kirkuk's pipelines.

This insurgency has also cost the coalition in terms of revenues for reconstructing Iraq and adding to the cost of repairs. Although the coalition forces are patrolling the pipelines, the attacks are virtually impossible to thwart and the Iraqi national fund continues to lose money.

These two issues have cast doubt on the predictions that Iraqi oil production will return to pre-war capacity of 3 million barrels per day by the end of 2004.

Quite how the nascent government of the Kurdish region intends to manage contracts signed with foreign investors during the regime of Saddam Hussein is unknown. In March 2003, Barham Saleh, Prime Minister in the PUK region of Iraqi Kurdistan, insisted that they 'would not be honoured'.[2] While numerous agreements ran into difficulty well before the beginning of hostilities in 2003, the Russians in particular have extensive interests in the northern oilfields: Tatneft and Zarubhezneft have signed (UN-approved) contracts at Bai Hassan, Saddam and Kirkuk oilfields – Tatneft to drill 33 new wells, Zarubhezneft to drill a number of wells at Kirkuk. In total, Deutsche Bank estimated in late 2002 that Iraq had signed contracts worth up to US$ 38 billion with oil companies from Russia, France (TotalFina Elf), Spain (Repsol-YPF), Italy (ENI), India (ONGC) and China (CNPC), a number of which related to concessions in and around Kirkuk.

Part III
The Future

21
Self-Determination and Autonomy[1]

WHAT IS SELF-DETERMINATION?

Self-determination – the right of peoples freely to determine their political status and to pursue their economic, social and cultural development – is a compelling legal concept for many groups seeking greater autonomy, protection and freedom from a repressive authoritarian regime. The precise scope of the principle of self-determination – both as to its substantive content, the legal rights it confers and the entities to which it applies – is still vaguely defined. This tends to make it particularly attractive as an elastic principle, which can be moulded to fit a variety of very different situations and aspirations.

Yet its very lack of precise definition and application have made self-determination a highly controversial, politicised and confused concept. This, coupled with the tendency to associate claims by non-state entities to self-determination as capable of being met only by the achievement of full independence as a sovereign state, has limited its value as an objective legal basis for the protection and defence of human rights and as the impetus for political change within a state. This is regrettable since the objective and fair application of the elements of the principle of self-determination could provide the basis in many situations for measures to protect human rights, to guarantee the fair treatment of minority groups, to foster democratic institutions and to serve as an engine for political, social and economic development without necessarily bringing about the dismemberment of a state.

The right of self-determination is now generally accepted as a recognised international legal principle, even if its precise scope is unclear. The UN Charter includes as one of its basic purposes in Article 1(2) 'to develop friendly relations among nations based on respect for the principle of equal rights and self-determination of peoples ... '. The same phrase occurs in Article 55 which calls for the promotion of economic and social cooperation, including observance of human rights, in order to create the conditions necessary for 'peaceful and friendly relations among nations based on respect for the principle of equal rights and self-determination of peoples'.

The right to self-determination and the duty on all states to promote it is also incorporated as Article 1 in both the International Covenant on Civil and Political Rights and the International Covenant on Economic, Social and Cultural Rights.

The principle of self-determination has been most commonly invoked in respect of colonial territories, in particular the two types of territory placed under a special regime by the UN Charter – trust and non-self-governing territories. The Declaration on the Granting of Independence to Colonial Countries and Peoples, contained in General Assembly Resolution 1514(XV) of 1960, reaffirmed the right of peoples to self-determination in the context of calling for a speedy and unconditional end to colonialism in all its forms.[2] It recalled the important role of the UN in assisting the movement for independence in trust and non-self-governing territories. The International Court of Justice has also held that the principle of self-determination applies to all colonies.[3]

Trust territories and non-self-governing territories are terms of art developed by the UN; there is no comprehensive legal definition of such territories. The Trusteeship System, established in Chapter XII of the UN Charter, essentially replaced the League of Nations' system of mandate territories. The Charter states that the trusteeship system applies to existing mandate territories, to territories 'detached from enemy states as a result of the Second World War' and to territories voluntarily placed under the system by the states responsible for their administration. The purpose of the trusteeship system was four-fold and underscored the linkage between the different elements, the furtherance of international peace and security, the progressive development of the territories towards self-government or independence in accordance with the freely expressed wishes of the people, encouraging respect for human rights and recognition of global interdependence, and equality of treatment for all UN member states and their nationals.

It was initially left up to states to determine which territories they considered to be 'non-self-governing' and thereby subject to the provisions of Chapter XI of the Charter. In 1959 the General Assembly established a Special Committee to study the criteria and in 1960 adopted Resolution 1514(XV) setting out some rather restrictive guidelines as to which territories should be included in the definition.

The principal characteristic was a territory that was 'geographically separate' and 'ethnically distinct' from the country administering it. If that was met, other historical, political, economic and other factors which arbitrarily placed the territory in a subordinate position became relevant. The General Assembly has, on several occasions, determined that a particular territory qualified as non-self-governing with or without the approval of the administering state but it has generally followed the basic criterion of geographical separateness which would exclude from the concept many groups struggling for some form of autonomy within the territorial borders of a state. States responsible for such territories were expected to protect the people against abuses, ensure their political and social advancement and to develop their self-government and free political institutions taking account of their political aspirations.

The 1960 Colonial Declaration, which reaffirmed the right of 'all peoples' to self-determination, suggested, however, that self-determination is not limited to colonial territories but might have a wider application. Ten years later the Declaration on the Principles of International Law concerning Friendly Relations and Co-operation among States in accordance with the Charter of the UN, annexed to Resolution 2625(XXV) of 1970, stated that every state has an obligation to promote the realisation of the right of self-determination and a duty to respect this right of peoples in order to promote friendly relations among states and to bring a speedy end to colonialism.[4] Other references to self-determination in international instruments and subsequent, but inconsistent, state practice indicates that the right is not limited to colonial situations, although it is still not possible to delineate with any legal certainty a category of territories or peoples to which the right clearly applies.[5]

There is no general agreement on the definition of 'peoples' for the purposes of self-determination. Although common characteristics such as ethnicity, language and religion, a territorial connection, a common historical tradition and self-identification as a distinct group, would all be relevant, it is certainly not accepted that every minority or indigenous group automatically has a legitimate claim to self-determination. The territorial approach has resulted in the principle being applied to territorial units which contain a mix of different groups. It is also invoked to defend the rights of entire states to determine their own political, economic and social systems, free of external interference.

The issue is further complicated by the fact that UN references to self-determination are almost always accompanied by statements defending the territorial integrity of states. The Colonial Declaration stated that 'any attempt aimed at the partial or total disruption of the national unity and the territorial integrity of a country is incompatible with the purposes and principles of the Charter of the UN'. A similar reference appears in the 1970 Declaration on Friendly Relations but here it is limited to states 'conducting themselves in compliance with the principle of equal rights and self-determination of peoples ... and thus possessed of a government representing the whole people belonging to the territory without distinction as to race, creed or colour'.

In as much as a claim to self-determination is sought to be exercised by secession, international law is effectively neutral. There is no generally accepted right of secession but it is not necessarily prohibited and once secession has occurred in practice it may have legal consequences. A secessionist group that is militarily successful in its attempts to break away from an existing state and that fulfils the basic criteria of statehood[6] may be able to function as an independent state and may subsequently be recognised as such by all or some of the international community, depending on the political context in which secession has occurred.

It has been suggested that, in addition to colonial territories and existing states, there may be another category of 'self-determination units': 'entities part of a metropolitan State but which have been governed in such a way as to make them in effect non-self-governing territories'.[7] The Committee of Rapporteurs, appointed by the League of Nations to investigate aspects of the dispute over the Aaland Islands, stated that the 'separation of a minority from the State of which it forms a part and its incorporation in another State can only be considered as an altogether exceptional situation, a last resort when the State lacks either the will or the power to enact and apply just and effective guarantees'. There is, however, no conclusive body of legal principles or state practice to clarify application of the right of self-determination in respect of this possible third category, which remains 'acutely controversial'.

THE KURDISH CLAIM TO SELF-DETERMINATION

Kurds in Iraq are concerned that their political ambitions are being swallowed up by political, ethnic and security problems in the rest of the country.[8] A claim to self-determination by the Kurds if actual or perceived to be a claim for independence from Iraq would meet with little, if any, political support today. The US would be hesitant to allow the Kurds to take this step for a number of reasons: Turkey, Iran and Syria are opposed to a Kurdish free state on the borders with their countries due to their large Kurdish population and therefore Turkey would more than likely act on its continuous threats to invade Iraqi Kurdistan; Kurdish self-rule would lead to a situation in the rest of the country whereby the Muslim Shi'ite population would be a majority, turning Iraq into another Islamic Republic mirroring Iran; and the control of the Kirkuk and Mosul oilfields by the Kurds would leave the Sunni triangle without any source of financial earnings. The international community has consistently defended Iraq's territorial integrity and have been at pains to stress that they do not challenge the territorial integrity of Iraq nor would they support an independent political entity in Iraqi Kurdistan.

Furthermore, even if the case can be made that the Kurds are a 'people' for the purposes of self-determination, the legal and practical difficulties are enormous in claiming self-determination in respect of a people divided between a number of states. It would have to be determined whether self-determination was claimed on behalf of the Kurdish people as a whole, which implies a high degree of commonality of political goals shared by the Kurdish populations in all the states they currently inhabit, or simply by the Kurds in one of these countries, a claim which might not enjoy the same degree of international legitimacy.

The principle of self-determination is not, however, relevant only to claims for full independence. The term has two distinct meanings: 'the sovereign equality of existing States, and in particular the right of a State to choose its own form of government without intervention' and 'the right of a specific territory (people) to choose its own form of government irrespective of the wishes of the rest of the State of which that territory is a part'. Resolution 1514(XV) envisaged the exercise of self-determination through the options of free association or integration with an independent state, with safeguards to ensure that these options were exercised by a people freely and voluntarily through informed and democratic processes. Integration depended on an advanced state of self-government with free political institutions and had to be opted for in full knowledge and through impartial democratic processes. The 1970 Declaration on Friendly Relations added another option – 'the emergence into any other political status freely determined by a people'.

This confirms that the principle of self-determination not only has an external aspect (such as emergence as an independent state) but also has internal aspects by which peoples have the right to determine their political and form of government and to pursue their development within a given territory. Free and participatory choice on the basis of equality are the conditions for the exercise of the internal aspects of self-determination. The Covenant on Civil and Political Rights is intended to make the right of self-determination of political status through democratic means applicable to all nations' citizens. When the Covenant came into force, self-determination ceased to be applicable only to specific areas and became a universal right. It also became a principle of inclusion – the right to participate – rather than exclusion (secession). The right now allows the peoples of all states to participate freely, fairly and openly in the democratic process of governance freely chosen by each state.

There are close links between self-determination, the existence of a representative government and the protection of human rights. The Human Rights Committee in its General Comment on Article 1 of the International Covenant on Civil and Political Rights stated that the realisation of self-determination is an 'essential condition for the effective guarantee and observance of individual human rights … '. A government such as that in Iraq which was not freely elected and continues not to be freely elected, denies its people the most fundamental human rights in not fulfilling its obligations to guarantee self-determination for its people.

The right to self-determination extends beyond protection from violence and repression and implies the free determination of political status, the existence of open and participatory institutions that reflect and safeguard that status, and the opportunity to pursue economic, social and cultural development.

The development of the concept, scope and legal principles of internal self-determination is still in its infancy, particularly the extent to which the concept relates to specific self-determination rights of oppressed groups within a state as opposed to the right of the state population as a whole. It has been suggested that human rights norms and standards may provide a framework of legal rules to balance the competing rights and interests inherent in claims to self-determination. The advantages of reliance on self-determination are that it is a collective right of a people, rather than the sum of the rights of individuals, and one in respect of which all states share an obligation to promote its realisation. The drawbacks are that it does not yet provide a firm basis of clearly defined rights applicable in identifiable political contexts and that reliance on it inevitably raises the fear of secession and the fragmentation of states. This is not to say that the principle of self-determination is irrelevant in the Kurdish context, but only that it probably does not provide a sufficiently firm basis at the present time on which to ground international responsibility.

AUTONOMY

'Unless they believe that their position within a future Iraq will ... consolidate their hard-won autonomy, it is uncertain that a majority would opt to remain within the current boundaries, despite what their more pragmatic leaders may tell them.'[9] Some of the younger generation of Kurds do not speak Arabic and wonder what benefit it would be to be part of the rest of the state when they have had a de facto independent state for twelve years.[10]

There is no generally accepted definition of the concept of 'autonomy' in international law. Autonomous regions are regions of a state that are usually in possession of cultural and/or ethnic distinctiveness, and that have been granted separate powers of internal administration without any detachment from the state of which the region is a part. Such regions, however, are not recognised as states, and may never be deemed thus until they have reached an advanced stage of self-government.

There is presently no generally internationally recognised right to any form of autonomous status. However, the development of minority rights protection beyond the traditional areas of language, culture and religion to encompass measures to protect and promote the identity of minorities and to secure their participation in decision-making and public life envisage far more extensive political and economic rights for minorities. The full exercise of these rights in some situations may well require a form of autonomous status. According to a 1990 UN report, autonomy 'represents the highest possible level of minority rights'.

Autonomy is, however, increasingly recognised as a useful concept and means by which to address competing claims for political and minority rights. State practice offers a wealth of different autonomy and internal self-governing arrangements to respond to a wide variety of political contexts, claims to minority protection and the realisation of other international rights and obligations. However, while regional autonomous entities are accorded only limited status under international law, the increasing frequency of claims to autonomy, and the effect upon the international legal order that such claims will have, make the concept of autonomy ripe for review.

Autonomy for a group or part of a territory within a state is generally the result of an internal political and legislative arrangement, which may well enjoy entrenched constitutional or other special protection. It will not usually grant the area any internationally recognised status or devolve powers normally associated with statehood, such as in the areas of defence or foreign affairs. In some cases, however, an autonomous area may have a limited capacity to enter into international agreements on issues within the scope of its reserved powers, such as cultural or economic matters. It will usually encompass a local or regional executive, legislature and judiciary and may grant authority in a wide range of matters such as education, health, housing, social welfare, culture, religion, land, resources and local security as well as providing for some means of financing itself through taxation or otherwise.

Autonomy has long been accepted as a political option in Iraq and must be at least the starting point for discussions on the status of Iraqi Kurdistan. Iraq committed itself over 25 years ago to the principle of Kurdish autonomy and did establish the basic parameters and institutional structures for such autonomy (whatever the shortcomings of these arrangements and however imperfectly they have been implemented since). Since then it has held out the autonomy arrangements for the Kurds as evidence of its accommodation of and commitment to the promotion and protection of the rights of the Kurdish minority. However, an acceptable autonomy arrangement must be one which is acceptable to the Kurds, which allows them to preserve and develop their identity as a group and which fosters open and participatory institutions of self-government. It must genuinely secure the promotion and protection of all the rights guaranteed to them under legally binding treaties as well as the principles and standards set out in the 1992 UN Declaration on the rights of minorities. Most importantly, it must reflect the will of the Kurdish people and be developed in a process which allows them full and equal participation.

Previous experience has shown that there can be no confidence in the international community's commitment to any form of genuine autonomy for the Kurds. It is imperative that future negotiations be conducted under international supervision, not just with the coalition, and that recognised international guarantees are secured.

A UN MANDATE?

There have been many who have called for the UN to take over administration of Iraq from the US-led coalition. A number of the UN's recent peace-keeping operations have also imposed a high degree of international protection and supervision in various countries. In Cambodia, for example, the UN established a Transitional Authority with considerable powers to oversee the process leading to elections. The 1989 Paris Conference brought together 18 countries, the Cambodian parties and the UN Secretary-General to negotiate a political settlement under UN supervision. It included the five permanent members of the Security Council and key regional powers. The Agreements on a Comprehensive Political Settlement in Cambodia were signed in October 1991 and endorsed by the Security Council which also approved and supervised the implementation plan. The UN Transitional Authority in Cambodia (UNTAC) comprised military and civilian components, including an extensive human rights monitoring operation. Cambodian administrative bodies in the areas of foreign affairs, defence, public security and information were placed under the direct control of UNTAC which also had control and supervisory powers over any administrative bodies which could influence the elections and the authority to reassign or remove any government personnel. The interim national authority, the Supreme National Council, delegated to the UN all powers necessary to implement the political settlement. UNTAC remained in place until free elections had been held and a new government was installed.

In Kosovo, following the 1999 conflict, the UN established UNMIK, an interim administration which was unprecedented in both scope and structure.[11] UNMIK is made up of other multilateral organisations such as the EU and the OSCE working under a UN leadership. There are some similarities between Kosovo and Iraqi Kurdistan in that both are provinces of another country rather than states in their own right. However, in Kosovo UNMIK has transferred responsibilities to local institutions as part of its commitment to 'gradually introduce self-government to Kosovo'.[12] Furthermore, on 12 December 2003, the UN Security Council issued a presidential statement expressing support for the 'standards for Kosovo'.[13] These written standards include functioning of democratic institutions, rule of law, freedom of movement, returns and reintegration, economy and property rights, and Kosovo's status will ultimately be determined by its institutions' abilities to meet these standards.[14]

It is not, of course, suggested that any of these prior international arrangements can or should provide a blueprint for the future international protection of Iraqi Kurdistan. Each was tailored to a particular historical and political context. The special circumstances, characteristics and needs of each situation must dictate the form and nature of supervision and protection. Moreover, although it is not too late for the UN to adopt overall control over the transition to independence in Iraq, it is highly doubtful that it would do so given the establishment of the CPA and the gulf between the go-it-alone attitude of the US and the multilateral approach of the UN since the beginning of the road to war. These examples do, however, indicate considerable international creativity in devising special arrangements to meet the particular needs of a territory where there is the political will to act. If the international community is willing to face up to its responsibilities in Iraqi Kurdistan, it is quite possible to devise an arrangement that meets the political and security needs of this particular situation.

There are a number of reasons why some sort of a UN mandate is necessary for Iraq. As regards security, the notion of coalition forces remaining in Iraq following the transfer of power will continue to cause a backlash of violence within Iraq and lead to further security problems. A UN mandate would also impact the security situation for NGOs as they would not be working under the auspices of the 'hated' US but rather the UN. Furthermore, if the Transitional Assembly continues to host those that were once 'invaders' and Occupying Powers they won't be seen as impartial and it will detract from their ability to govern the country. It is important to bear in mind that a government can retain UN-authorised peace-keepers for a period of several years without forfeiting its sovereignty, as for example the UN peace-keeping mission to Cyprus.[15]

There are several specific areas that the UN should assume responsibility as a matter of urgency: the UN should participate in the creation of an effective war crimes tribunal and a land commission, and it should assist with elections and the transfer of power to Iraqis. Moreover, the UN should expediently adopt a resolution specifically recognising the new plan for Iraqi transition by 1 July 2004. Such a resolution should also recognise the US/UK forces remaining in Iraq as peace-keepers, if UN peace-keepers themselves do not take over from them. As regards Iraqi Kurdistan it is imperative that the UN recognises that the Kurdish region is the only part of Iraq that has the elements in place for immediate self-government.

ECONOMIC ISSUES

Despite its considerable shortfalls, the Oil-for-Food Programme constitutes the mainstay of the economy of Iraqi Kurdistan, and one of its only assured sources of income. Landlocked, mountainous, and traditionally reliant on an agrarian economy, now damaged by decades of conflict and insecurity, the reconstruction of Iraqi Kurdistan poses numerous challenges and is beset by uncertainty. The safe haven was a de facto state established by the no-fly zone above the 36th Parallel; revenues raised from the charging of border tariffs – one of the few significant supplements to oil-for-food revenue – is, likewise, a de facto form of taxation. As at time of writing, the status of Kirkuk – and hence its oil production facilities – is uncertain. What is probable is that regardless of the eventual form of the Iraqi constitution, a revenue-sharing formula will be developed between the Iraqi central government and the KRG, or reconstituted regional government of Iraqi Kurdistan.

Oil and international assistance should not be seen as the be-all-and-end-all of the economy of Iraqi Kurdistan. Key to the region's long-term survival is the regeneration of agriculture and the development of relevant industries. Research is and must continue to be undertaken regarding the flight of rural communities to overburdened towns and cities: agriculture is a mainstay of the Kurdish economy. But to restore the agricultural economy to full capacity will require the continued reconstruction of rural towns, drainage, water provisions, health and education services, if displaced families are to be encouraged to return. In Kurdish areas outside of the safe haven, the legacy of the Arabisation policy needs to be tackled, leading eventually both to the restitution of property and the creation of a system of property registration that will encourage capital flow through micro-lending. Research also needs to be adopted into the impact of the Arabisation process into farming patterns and land tenure.

For the foreseeable future, the public sector will remain the largest employer in the region. At the time of writing, the majority of government employees have received little or no pay for several months; they are, however, saved from the mass redundancies seen elsewhere in Iraq under coalition administration. However, the knock-on effect of a crisis in the rest of Iraq could be considerable. Degradation of the economy of northern Iraq has precipitated feuds between the two main Kurdish parties before. Both parties are now working toward regeneration of the economy and declare old enmities to be a thing of the past; nonetheless, outside observers suggest that fault lines could well be reopened if regional economic security is not met.

Since the creation of the safe haven, Iraqi Kurdistan has made considerable strides towards a stable economy but outside assistance from multilateral and other sources will continue to be needed in substantial volume if the region is to thrive.

22
Kirkuk

The city of Kirkuk has been the source of most of the tension between Iraqi Kurdistan and Baghdad. Control of Kirkuk is essential if the Kurds are to gain full independence and autonomy from the rest of Iraq. The region's large oil reserves as well as its location, astride northern and central Iraq, mean that Kirkuk is of immense strategic and economic importance to the Kurds, and also to the ethnically diverse inhabitants of the region.

The Kurds' proximity to Turkish, Persian and Arab empires throughout history shaped the development of the cultural identity of the Kurdish people, preventing the organisation and union of the whole Kurdish nation. Kurds, Turcomans and Arabs have all laid claim to the city, and this antagonism between its ethnically diverse inhabitants remains an impediment to peace in the region.

HISTORY OF KIRKUK

Historically, the Kirkuk region has been highly coveted due to its numerous trade routes and proximity to mountain passes, leading rulers of Kurdish regions to attempt to take control of the region by destroying existing Kurdish emirates. In the early sixteenth century, most Kurds in the region were under the rule of the Ottoman Empire; however, many Kurds lived under the rule of the bordering Saffawi Empire. The Ottomans, who controlled the province, or *vilayet*, of Mosul, which encompasses the Kurdish region of modern-day Iraq, initially granted a measure of sovereignty to the Kurds in areas including Kirkuk. This was undertaken in an attempt to win their favour and lead them to fight against the neighbouring Saffawis.[1] Although the boundary lines between the Saffawi and Ottoman Empires shifted several times, they remained more or less intact until the end of the First World War.

After the breakdown of the Ottoman Empire during the First World War, the British Empire took control of the provinces that make up most of modern-day Iraq. The Treaty of Sèvres, signed in 1920, was to pave the way for the creation of a Kurdish state including the *vilayet* of

Mosul. However, this proposal met with opposition from Kurdistan's neighbours. King Faisal of Iraq pushed for the annexation of Mosul to Iraq, and the formation of the Turkish state brought about Turkey's interest in controlling the province. The council of the League of Nations conducted an inquiry in Mosul after the Treaty of Lausanne was signed in July 1923, which found that the Kurdish language and identity was undeniably distinct from that of the Turks and the Arabs. Despite that, it was finally decided to attach the province of Mosul to the kingdom of Iraq in 1925, promising a measure of autonomy as well as recognition of the rights of the Kurds. However, this recognition failed to materialise as the 1930 Anglo-Iraqi Treaty setting out Iraqi independence from British rule did not mention the Kurds. This led to political unrest, demonstrations and arrests of Kurdish nationalists.

THE SETTLEMENT OF TURCOMANS IN THE KIRKUK REGION

The importance of Kirkuk to trade and transport was obvious to the Ottoman rulers of Kurdistan. Both the Ottoman and Saffawi Empires had an interest in controlling the trade routes of Kirkuk, which connected modern-day Turkey, Iraq and Iran. This was not only because of the trade and transport advantages, but also because of the logistical advantages it would confer in wartime. Therefore, both sides increased the presence of their subjects in and around the Kirkuk region.

The history of the arrival of Turcomans in Kirkuk is unclear. While some believe that Turcomans originally came to the region as mercenaries in the seventeenth century, Turcomans themselves claim that they were originally sought out by rulers during the Amawi and Abbasid eras in the twelfth to thirteenth centuries because of their 'prowess in battle'.[2] They further claim to have settled in the thirteenth centuries under the Seljouki reign, and expanded under the Ottoman Empire. The composition of Kirkuk in the late twentieth century corroborates the claim that Turcomans settled in Kirkuk only by forced migration. That is, less than half of them belong to the Shi'ite sect of the Saffawids known as Kizilbashi, the rest subscribe to the Hanafit school of Sunni Islam, which was the official sect of the Ottoman rulers. Regardless, during the periods of coexistence, Kurds and Turcomans interacted and engaged in commerce, which led to an exchange of values and traditions.

Statistics from the time show that Turcomans living in Iraq in the 1920s and 1930s made up around 2.1–2.4 per cent of the Iraqi population. In 1957, Iraqi officials confirmed that the Turcomans made up 21.4 per cent of the population of Kirkuk. The Arabisation policies of the Ba'athist regimes in the 1960s and onwards led to a decrease in the Turcoman population to 16.75 per cent in the 1977 census.

Although many Turcoman civil servants were transferred from Kirkuk to other parts of Iraq, Sunni Turcomans continued to dominate trade and commerce as well as hold senior positions in the Iraqi Petroleum Company. This situation led many Kurds to change their ethnic identity in an effect to secure civil service jobs. Intermarriage of Kurds and Turcomans further contributed to the change in the ethnic make-up of Kirkuk between the periods of Ottoman and Ba'athist rule. Furthermore, Arabs were encouraged to settle in Kirkuk throughout the period of the monarchy in the Kingdom of Iraq. Arabisation had begun, but the period of Ba'athist rule represents the era of most intense ethnic cleansing.

THE ARABISATION OF KIRKUK

Due to the strategic and economic importance of the Kirkuk region, successive Iraqi governments have adopted intricate Arabisation policies towards the Kurdish regions. During the monarchical period, Arabs were appointed in favour of Kurds and Turcomans to key positions in the administration and military of the Kirkuk region.

The discovery of oil brought more Arabs to the region. The petroleum industry was established in 1925, leading to significant changes in the social and ethnic make-up of Kirkuk. Kirkuk's regional oil company, the Turkish Petroleum Company (later renamed the Iraqi Petroleum Company, IPC), exploited much of the land in north-eastern Iraq, bringing large numbers of Arab, Assyrian and Armenian workers from outside Kirkuk, marginalising local Kurds and Turcomans. This rapid influx of IPC employees resulted in the creation of predominantly Assyrian and Arabic neighbourhoods in the vicinity of the oil company, altering the ethnic composition of Kirkuk.

There is evidence that the settlement of Arabs in Kirkuk was a policy of the monarchical government. It built the Haweeja irrigation project for the settlement of the Arabs, especially in the south-west of Kirkuk, where there was a lack of water and agricultural problems. The irrigation plan involved the construction of a large canal to provide the area with water. The government brought in nomadic Arab tribes who knew nothing about agriculture, built modern villages and distributed the land among them. Most of the Arab families received grants from the government, in addition to the other privileges. It is likely that this was the first Arab settlement in Kirkuk.

The monarchy was overthrown in a 1958 military coup d'état. This led to further discrimination against Kurds and Turcomans in Kirkuk. In the late 1950s, many Kurds and Turcomans were arrested by Abdul Karim Kassem's military regime, ostensibly for being supporters of the deposed monarchy and opponents of the new regime. Twenty-seven Kurds and one Turcoman were sentenced to death in the Kassem era and eventually executed under the Aref regime in Kirkuk in 1963.

Following the 1958 coup, security forces waged an indiscriminate campaign of harassment on Kurds, provoking many Kurds to leave the city, including civil servants who asked to be transferred to other areas for security reasons. This situation continued until the military coup of February 1963 led by Colonel Abd al-Salam Aref, the military, and members of the Ba'ath party. This new regime continued the campaign of terror against the Kurds, and Kurdish villages, particularly those near the oilfields, were destroyed. Furthermore, Kurds were expelled from certain villages and replaced by Arabs, and Kurdish employees of the IPC were dismissed or transferred outside of Kirkuk. Colonel Aref's regime provided Arab settlers with housing and employment in government institutions such as the police department and the military.

The Arabisation of Kurdistan, and in particular Kirkuk, became a demonstrable policy of the Iraqi governments from 1963 onwards. It was carried out by forcibly removing Kurds from the city of Kirkuk and settling Arab families in their place who were brought from central and southern Iraq. Large numbers of Kurds were expelled from their villages and towns between 1962 and 1990, along with thousands of others who were forced to flee the city because of bombings carried out by the Republican Guard units when it recaptured the city following the collapse of the uprising in April 1991. The administrative structure was also ethnically altered as Kurdish civil servants were transferred to other governorates, while others were coerced to leave.

The Arabisation of Kirkuk continued systematically after the 1968 coup, which saw the Ba'ath Socialist Party return to power. At that point, existing property in Kirkuk could only be conveyed to Arabs. Moreover, Kurds were prevented from buying homes and property and were even denied permission to renovate their homes, regardless of the state of dilapidation. Kurdish youths were arrested arbitrarily, and Kurdish villages, schools and streets were given Arabic names. Similar policies were implemented throughout the region, in particular by the Turkish and Iranian governments, toward their own Kurdish populations.

POST-GULF WAR DEVELOPMENTS

Thousands of Kurdish families, facing heavy shelling and aerial bombardment, fled Kirkuk during the 1991 conflict between the Kurdish *peshmerga* and Iraqi forces. After Iraqi forces took over the city, the escapees were not permitted to return to Kirkuk. Furthermore, their homes and businesses were looted, and many were forced to live in camps in the liberated area of Kurdistan.

The Ba'athist regime continued to systematically relocate Arab tribes from southern and central Iraq to be settled in the Kirkuk governorate. Kurds were not only discriminated against and marginalised, but also hundreds of Kurdish villages were destroyed and hundreds of thousands of Kurds were evacuated from their ancestral homes in Kirkuk to parts unknown. The Kurds that remained in the region were given the option of moving to southern Iraq and keeping their possessions, or leaving all their possessions behind and moving into the autonomous region of Kurdistan. In 1996, under the direction of then governor of Kirkuk, Ali Hassan al-Majid (known to Kurds as 'Chemical Ali' for his role in the Halabja massacre), Kurdish and Turcoman residents were made to register as Arabs or face eviction to southern Iraq.

KURDISH ASPIRATIONS FOR KIRKUK

Kirkuk, encompassing some of Iraq's biggest oilfields, has been the subject of much debate and conflict, ultimately over the control of the oil revenue. While it is unclear whose claim to the land will win out, it is evident that the outcome of the Kirkuk issue, which has been an area of major focus in the post-war conflict, will have a significant effect on both the long- and short-term stability of Iraq. Interethnic tensions have been spurred by the interest of the Iraqi Kurds, the Turks and the Arabs in controlling Kirkuk. Furthermore, the new Iraqi government has a stake in controlling the city because of its oil resources and strategic importance.

The Kurds as a whole have long considered Kirkuk to be an integral part of a Kurdish federal region. Turkey has repeatedly expressed its concern over Kurdish aspirations for Kirkuk, stating that Kurdish control of Kirkuk could fuel Kurdish nationalism in the region and undermine the rights of Turcoman residents in Kirkuk. Some Turks also lay historical claim to Kirkuk, which has led to interference on the part of Turkey, with decisions regarding control of the city. Although Kurds have given up a claim for independence for the time being, handing control of Kirkuk to Kurdish authorities would fortify any future bid for independence by affording a source of economic power to the Kurdish region.

To the Kurds, the Kirkuk question has been paramount for a long time. Over the last three decades, Kurdish authorities have attempted to attain control of Kirkuk through negotiation with Baghdad or, failing that, by force. The KDP, led by Barzani, reached an Autonomy Agreement with the Ba'athist regime in 1970 to establish an autonomous Kurdish region in Kurdish-dominated areas of northern Iraq. Article 14 of the agreement called for a census to determine the status of disputed areas, including Kirkuk. However, the Iraqi government maintained and reinforced its policy of Arab settlement after the agreement was reached, weakening Kurdish claims to the region and rendering the agreement worthless. Further negotiations could not resolve the biggest point of contention between the Kurds and Iraq, the Kirkuk question, leading to the outbreak of war in 1974. Negotiations started up again in 1984, this time between the PUK and the Iraqi government. When the Iraqi government refused to grant control of Kirkuk, the PUK and a small group of Iranian Republican Guards attacked the oilfields of Kirkuk. Inflicting some minor damage, they quickly retreated. After the liberation of Kuwait in late February of 1991, a Kurdish uprising led to the Kurdish occupation of Kirkuk. The Kurds occupied Kirkuk for about a week in March 1991 before they were driven out by Iraqi forces. Further negotiations in 1992 broke down again over the issue of Kirkuk.

After the fall of Saddam's regime in Baghdad in March 2003, the Kurds perceived a genuine opportunity to gain control of Kirkuk at last. Kurdish forces took over the city of Kirkuk in April 2003, entering despite an agreement with US forces to stay outside the city.[3] The Kurdish *peshmerga* were able to protect the city's hospitals and other important locations; however, they were not permitted by the coalition forces to take full control of the city. US forces took control of the city after approximately a week of Kurdish control, after which Kurdish authorities were able to provide 'civilian defense units, traffic police, and medical staff for the hospitals in order to fill the vacuum left behind when Iraq government forces and officials fled Kirkuk'.[4] During this time, anti-Arab sentiments developed and there were allegations of Kurdish militias pressuring Arab residents to leave Kirkuk. It is unclear whether these Kurdish groups were official *peshmerga* forces or rogue factions operating without the knowledge or consent of Kurdish authorities.[5]

There have been a number of violent incidents in Kirkuk relating to control of the city. May 2003 saw gunfights between Arabs and Kurds; in August 2003 there were violent protests in Kirkuk, which led to many people being killed; in December of the same year, a demonstration was staged by Arabs and Turkmans outside of the PUK office in Kirkuk, shouting 'No to federalism, Kirkuk is Iraqi.'[6] Despite these developments, Kirkuk has remained largely under Kurdish control since 2003.[7] More recently, on 13 June 2006, four suicide bombers killed at least 16 people in the city.

According to Nechirvan Barzani, the Prime Minster of the newly united Kurdish Regional Government, Kurds seek nothing less than a fair referendum on the status of Kirkuk after the boundary lines have been adjusted to their pre-Ba'ath era positions and the Kurds that were evicted during the Ba'athist Arabisation campaign have been resettled in Kirkuk. However, Barzani claims that regional control of Kirkuk would not mean a right to the area's oil revenues, which, he maintains, would benefit all Iraqis.[8] A provision in the Iraqi constitution allows for the displaced Kurdish victims of Arabisation to receive compensation or resettle in Kirkuk, and grants compensation for relocation to the newly displaced Arabs. This resettling process is meant to take place before the Kirkuk census and referendum that are set to take place in 2007. According to the speaker of Kurdistan's parliament, Adnan Mufti, the position of Kurdish authorities is that resettlement costs can be negotiated with Kirkuk's Arab residents; however, they must leave Kirkuk and return to the lands they came from.[9] According to the Iraq Property Claims Commission, since it was established in 2003 to deal with property confiscated by Saddam's Ba'athist regime, over 130,000 claims had been filed and one-third of those came from Kirkuk. [10] Several thousand of these claims have been settled; however, an effective legal mechanism does not exist to execute eviction orders on Arab occupants.[11] According to US and Iraqi official estimates, approximately 350,000 Kurds that were forced out of Kirkuk during the Ba'athist Arabisation campaign have returned.[12]

RECENT DEVELOPMENTS IN THE REGION

Turkey has not been reluctant in the past to express its interest in controlling Kirkuk. The 'Kirkuk issue' was one of the main topics discussed when the then Prime Minister of Iraq, Ibrahim al-Jaafari, visited Ankara in February 2006. The Turkish government stressed to al-Jaafari their interest in a swift and equitable solution to the Kirkuk issue, due to the large numbers of Turcoman residents. It also urged the Prime Minister to strengthen the central government and disband the *peshmerga*, which would take considerable power away from the Kurds. Turkey's main concern is that positive developments for the Kurds in South Kurdistan will establish a precedent that will lead its own restive Kurdish population to demand similar reforms.

As recently as May 2006, Arab and Turcoman leaders have alleged intimidation and illegal arrests on the part of Kurdish authorities. US officials have reported retaliatory attacks on the Kurdish population. Despite the presence of the ethnically motivated attacks and killings, US officials are unable to determine how extensive they are or who is carrying them out.[13]

The US embassy's Kirkuk office has indicated that Moqtada al-Sadr has sent hundreds of fighters to the region under the auspices of protecting their people and holy structures from Kurdish forces. Kurdish officials have stated that the presence of the militias has led to an increase in the number of kidnappings and killings in Kirkuk. The Kurds have increased the presence of *peshmergas* as well as private security workers in Kirkuk in response to the influx of Shi'ite militias.[14]

The deputy governor of Kirkuk, Rebwar Talabani, believes, however, that the reports of an influx of Arab militiamen to Kirkuk may have been exaggerated. Furthermore, Talabani claimed that US reports of a massive migration of Kurdish returnees to Kirkuk was also exaggerated. There are 'Iraqi laws designed to preserve the fragile ethnic balance of the city' which require returnees to obtain the permission of the governorate to move into the city, and 'that permission has not been granted'.[15]

According to reports, Turkish commandos crossed the border in early May 2006 to pursue PKK fighters that had set up camps in Iraq. In the same week, Iran bombed Kurdish villages in northern

Iraq, targeting PKK rebels seeking autonomy in Iran. Both countries have a stake in the outcome of the Kirkuk question. Any steps toward autonomy that Kurds in Iraq may take threaten to stir up the nationalistic desires of their own sizeable Kurdish populations.

The united Kurdish Regional Government (KRG) officially took office in May 2006. Despite years of in-fighting (armed conflict ceased in 1997), the PUK and the KDP have been able to come together in response to the US-led invasion and effectively bargain with Iraqi authorities for the interests of Kurdistan as a whole. This official unification will likely increase Kurdish negotiating power, allowing them to push for decentralisation and federalism, improve the infrastructure and growth of Kurdistan, as well as promote Kurdistan on an international level. Furthermore, the KRG will negotiate for control of natural resources and revenues within Kurdish territory. The KRG also insisted on controlling security (through its defence ministry – the *peshmerga*), and prohibiting the Iraqi military from entering Kurdistan. The Kurds withstood pressure from the central government and coalition forces to disband the *peshmerga*, insisting that their experience in and commitment to the region were necessary to the preservation of peace and security in Iraqi Kurdistan. Although the unification appears to be a step towards reconciliation of the long-standing differences between the Kurdish factions, upon closer inspection, the KRG has given control of whole ministries to either party, rather than sharing the responsibilities. Furthermore, control of fragile portfolios such as the ministries of defence and finance were divided by region, effectively creating two separate ministries, akin to the old divided system.[16] These issues must be resolved by the Kurdish Regional Government in order to most effectively administrate the Kurdish region.

The KRG is now looking to secure the economic future of the region. The KRG has become frustrated with the rate of reconstruction taking place in southern Iraq and has independently approved at least two oil exploration deals in Kurdistan.[17] The KRG has signed contracts with DNO (a Norwegian oil firm), as well as the Canadian company, Western Oil Sands. Oil exploration is permitted by the Iraqi constitution, but repairing existing oilfields has to be negotiated with the Oil Ministry in Baghdad and the oilfields in Kirkuk, which contain 15 per cent of Iraq's oil wealth, have not yet been restored.[18] According to Iraqi Oil Ministry officials, the Kirkuk region is not secure enough to justify rebuilding at this time which will hinder the exportation of oil from the north of Iraq.[19]

The outcome of the Kirkuk question will have repercussions on the Kurds, the future of Iraq and the stability of the region. The presence of oil in the region and its strategic location in Iraq mean that Kirkuk will continue to attract the attention of any Iraqi administration. Moreover, relations between the opposing groups in the region are delicately balanced. The alleged influx into Kirkuk of Shi'ite Arab militias, the interest of Turkey and Iran in the region and the unification of the KRG have further increased the tension that existed between the ethnic groups in the region. An escalation in factional violence in the Kirkuk region could lead the whole country into civil war.

Kurdish aspirations for autonomy rely on the control of Kirkuk, not only for its economic wealth, but also because of the emotional link many Kurds have to the region which was amplified by their forced expulsion. The sentiment among Kurds is that the Kurdish region will not be complete without the inclusion of Kirkuk, indicating that as long as the Kirkuk issue remains unresolved, the larger Kurdish question will continue to hang over Iraq. It now appears that a political solution is being sought as the fate of the city will be determined by a referendum, scheduled for June 2007. This vote should see Kirkuk officially recognised within Iraqi Kurdistan. However, this will not be without profound repercussions for the rest of Iraq, with many fearing that this could lead the Shi'ites in the south to demand a semi-autonomous region of their own and the effective fragmentation of the country into three independent states.

23
The Tribunal and the Victims

INTRODUCTION

Clearly, there is a need for impartiality in the operation of any tribunal. It must be fair, respecting the basic norms of procedural and substantive due process required under international law,[1] and include the rights of the accused as enshrined in the defining documents of international human rights law.[2] In addition, any tribunal must be (and, critically, must be seen to be) independent; difficult if controlled by a new Iraqi government or the US-led occupation forces.

KHRP is troubled that the current structure for the tribunal is not concerned with justice due to its structure and the strong possibility of the authority imposing the death penalty.[3]

A UN TRIBUNAL

It is clear that an international tribunal would enjoy greater legitimacy in the eyes of the world, and benefit from the considerable experience of previous tribunals. An international contingent of judges representing the combined jurisprudential and experience of a cross-section of legal systems would create the requisite impression of impartiality.

The US administration, however, is thought to have been opposed to using the Rwanda and Yugoslavia models as templates, largely on account of their costliness and duration. Each has cost somewhere in the region of US$ 80–100 million per annum, and is of indefinite duration. Neither do they make provision for the death penalty, which the US and Iraq are particularly keen to maintain.[4]

The first two of these reservations seem surmountable. Given the huge scale of atrocities committed by the Ba'athists and the breadth of their victims – Shi'ite Arabs, Marsh Arabs, dissidents, Turcomans and Assyrians in addition to Kurds – it can only be expected that if justice is to be done to the proceedings they will be time-consuming. Nonetheless, there is little or no reason why a cap could not have been placed on the length of any UN-created tribunal, and indeed in the current Iraqi Statute there is no cap mentioned. The ultimate cost of rebuilding Iraq (and the cost of failing to do so successfully) and the financial scale of the international tribunals, while substantial, are almost certainly worth paying if they promote justice, accountability, the resumption of the rule of law, and Iraq's reintegration into the community of nations. The Rwandan and Yugoslavian trials were almost universally perceived as impartial, fair and independent (although charges of 'victors' justice' have sometimes been levelled at the International Criminal Tribunal for the former Yugoslavia (ICTY)).

Putting aside the morality of the death penalty, as the London Director of Human Rights Watch observed, 'the example of the Romanian dictator Nicolae Ceausescu – shot after a summary trial in 1989 – reminds us how things should not be done. That execution hindered long-term justice in Romania.'[5]

Furthermore, a UN tribunal would have a mandate under Chapter VII of the UN Charter, which would require all member states of the UN to comply with the tribunal's orders, including its indictments and arrest orders for high-profile figures. Both the ICTY and the ICTR (International Criminal Tribunal for Rwanda) have Chapter VII mandates.

Thus, an ad hoc tribunal operated under the auspices of the UN would offer international legitimacy and practical legal experience to the Iraqi people.[6] In addition 'by allowing the United Nations to perform a job at which it excels and for which it has a proven track record, the United States will finally get what we tried so desperately hard, and failed, to obtain before invading Iraq: broad-based international support'.[7]

A HYBRID COURT

A UN tribunal could embrace Iraqi participation by including Iraqi judges and prosecutors. In 2000, following a UN resolution, it was decided to establish the only hybrid court in existence – the Special Court for Sierra Leone. Unlike the Rwandan or former Yugoslav tribunals, the court sits in the country where the crimes were committed. One of the primary differences between this type of court and the ICTY or ICTR, is the mandate under which they were created. The latter were established by the Security Council under the auspices of Chapter VII of the UN Charter. Therefore, these tribunals operate under UN jurisdiction and not the domestic governments concerned. The Special Court for Sierra Leone, however, was created by a treaty between the UN and the Sierra Leone government which put it under joint UN–Sierra Leonean jurisdiction. Both local and international judges and prosecutors staff the Sierra Leone court. The Chief Prosecutor was appointed by the UN and the Deputy by the Sierra Leonean government, with the Chief Prosecutor taking responsibility for final decisions.

This model is favoured for Iraq for a number of reasons: the ICTY proceedings in The Hague, and ICTR proceedings in Arusha, made it practically impossible for ordinary citizens to follow the tribunal's cases; and locating a court in the country involved assists local judicial officials in gleaning knowledge from internationals to rebuild the country's judicial system. The drawback of not being able to assert primacy over other states as in Sierra Leone could be defused in Iraq by placing a hybrid tribunal under Chapter VII of the Charter. There is no legal reason why this could not be done. As regards costs, the hybrid model is believed to be cheaper than the ICTY and ICTR and more efficient, which addresses any budget concerns of the US.

With the prior establishment of this type of court in Sierra Leone, Iraq and the US could learn from their mistakes and set up a hybrid court to deal with Iraqi war crimes which has the benefit of the wisdom of precedence.

THE INTERNATIONAL CRIMINAL COURT (ICC)

As regards the International Criminal Court (ICC), Iraq is not a signatory and neither is the US. The US has spent considerable time opposing the ICC and could not be expected to cooperate with it on Iraq. Regardless of these issues the new court is not retrospective and can only preside over crimes committed after its establishment in July 2002. Furthermore, the ICC will try a case only in the event of domestic courts being unwilling or unable to act.

Although Saddam and his officials have committed crimes since July 2002, even if Iraq were to ratify the Statute of the Court, KHRP would not advocate this route, as the bulk of his crimes would be excluded. This would not provide justice for all of Saddam's victims and recognition of his heinous crimes towards the Kurds, particularly during the Anfal campaigns.

A TRUTH AND RECONCILIATION COMMISSION

Several organisations have called for an Iraqi truth commission that would paint a full picture of human rights abuse in Iraq over the past 25 years. A legitimate Iraqi government should consider such a commission to give victims a voice, consider means to assist victims and prevent further violations. The commission should not grant amnesty for international crimes as it would undermine the rule of law and provoke anger and cynicism among victims.

The commission could explore ways of promoting reconciliation and harmony between the ethnic groups in Iraq. It could also examine the role other countries have played in supporting and sustaining Saddam's rule. It would serve as a potent reminder to the international community of the consequences of supporting repressive rule in the world.

Edie Vandy, a Sierra Leone national and political analyst, stated of the Truth and Reconciliation Commission's hearings stage in Sierra Leone that 'For the victims, it provided a forum to speak out and to be heard ... and by speaking out, there was an innate healing power behind it all, regardless of any material or physical compensation that might be provided at the end of the day.'[8] He further added, 'One critical element that ushered in the war, and which was re-echoed throughout the deliberations, was the denial of justice, or the lack of it.'[9]

THE WAY FORWARD

KHRP advocates that a hybrid tribunal is established under the auspices of the UN and in consultation with other organisations in this field.

The Governing Council drafted the Statute without consulting any outside parties or allowing for public comment. KHRP agrees with Human Rights Watch that a group of experts should have been created to suggest appropriate ways for the tribunal to function, particularly in relation to accountability mechanisms, evidence and selection of judges/prosecutors.[10] Should Iraq insist on continuing down the path of a domestic tribunal it is still possible to convene such a group and alter the Statute appropriately.

KHRP has specialised in working with Kurdish victims of human rights abuses for over ten years and has represented hundreds of victims at the European Court of Human Rights. KHRP has also engaged in fact-finding missions to northern Iraq. In relation to legal structures KHRP, in conjunction with other non-governmental organisations, drafted a Joint Response to Proposals for Reform of the European Convention of Human Rights. For these reasons KHRP is adept, in partnership with other organisations, to advise on how best to meet the needs of the victims and establish a Tribunal, which has the highest legal regard.

Justice Murphy wrote in the Yamashita case: 'If we are ever to develop an orderly international community based upon a recognition of human dignity, it is of the utmost importance that the necessary punishment of those guilty of atrocities be as free as possible from the ugly stigma of revenge and vindictiveness.'[11] KHRP fears that in the case of Iraq this will not be the outcome if the present course is maintained.

24
The Land Question

I thought the Kurds would want revenge on Iraq Arabs for the things Saddam did to them. In fact most of them blame the Ba'athists, not the Arabs themselves, and here every Kurd has welcomed us.[1]

While the 'Arabisation' process has deeply scarred Iraq, and admittedly in the first few days following the liberation of Kirkuk and Mosul posed a security threat, things have quietened down since then. However, the land ownership issue needs to be addressed as expediently as possible not only for human rights reasons but also to ensure that security problems do not arise from internal sources. Jay Garner, the retired general overseeing Iraq's post-war reconstruction, promised a Bosnia-style commission to resolve disputes between Arabs, Kurds and Turcomans displaced in Iraqi Kurdistan during Saddam Hussein's regime in April.[2] This has not happened.

THE IRAQI PROPERTY RECONCILIATION FACILITY

CPA Regulation 4 established an Iraqi Property Reconciliation Facility (IPRF) to resolve claims resulting from the Arabisation process in Iraq.[3] It is tasked with collecting property claims and resolving such claims 'on a voluntary basis in a fair and judicious manner'. Under this regulation a fund may also be established to be used in connection with the work of the IPRF.

There are a number of uncertainties in Regulation 4. Firstly, it is unclear whether the IPRF would apply Iraqi law in relation to property rights and what its relationship would be with the courts. Furthermore, it does not deal with procedures in relation to cases being referred from the courts. Moreover, it does not indicate whether victims will actually receive compensation or whether the fund will be used merely for operational purposes. There are no procedures outlined for an enforcement mechanism, nor is there any indication of what status the facility will have in relation to the Iraqi legal system.

The International Organisation for Migration (IOM) was contracted to implement critical aspects of the IPRF. It was tasked with conducting a fact-finding and information campaign; developing a standardised claim form; establishing a series of claim registration offices; and offering facilities where property disputes could be settled through voluntary mediation.[4] Furthermore, IOM agreed to develop a long-term strategy for dealing with such disputes.

However, due to security concerns, IOM was unable to implement its programme and withdrew its staff.[5] IOM has also asserted that it failed to implement the project as a result of 'lack of expertise and insufficient staffing'.[6] Moreover, 'concerns arose about IOM's unwillingness to engage with experienced humanitarian and human rights actors to ensure that the process reflected sensitivity to the human rights dimension of the property claims issue'.[7] In response, IOM admitted that it did not attend regular meetings with humanitarian and human rights groups and rarely sought consultation with such groups.[8]

> Concerns about the lack of consultation with such groups, IOM's position as a contractee of the occupation administration and not an independent humanitarian organization, and IOM's lack of expertise and capacity caused intergovernmental and nongovernmental organizations to distance themselves from the IPRF process. The process remains in limbo.[9]

THE WAY FORWARD

The establishment of an effective property dispute mechanism is imperative as the deprivation of a person's right to his or her property is a fundamental human rights violation. However, a balanced mechanism should be put in place with consultation with such organisations as KHRP, which has a background in legal procedure, knowledge of procedures in other countries such as Kosovo, and more importantly local knowledge of victims' needs and the events which caused the land disputes in the first instance.

KHRP, although advocating a property commission, understands that victims of forced displacement have the right to reclaim their former property but this right must be balanced against the rights and humanitarian needs of the current occupants as many have lived there for more than a decade. Lessons can be learnt from other property mechanisms such as Bosnia and Kosovo, although all processes are designed for the particular situation in an individual country.

In the first instance it is necessary to establish a retrospective cut-off date for claims to be handled as it is not dealt with in Regulation 4. The coalition should draw on the resources of organisations and groups who have been involved in Iraq for a number of years to propose an acceptable date. Provisions for implementing the facilities' decisions should also be included in the regulation. The amount of funding needs to be decided as well as sources of funding for the future in order that the IPRF is not rendered inefficient at a later date due to lack of funding. Those who are displaced because of IPRF decisions need to be provided for in advance. There is adequate government-owned land in Iraq for this purpose, but social and human rights concerns must be taken into consideration. Objective criteria need to be decided upon to sort out which claims will be dealt with first. Either earliest claims first, or last claims first, or the like. Information on the process needs to be publicised worldwide to inform Iraqis outside of Iraq of the ability to take case under the procedure.

In addition, the regulation does not provide for enough offices. Mobile teams should be established to target the people who live in rural areas. The regulation does state that international staff will work in the offices; however, it should be made clear what role they take. They should be hired as Chairs of committees to ensure that no prejudices influence decisions. There should also be a definition of the qualifications necessary to work for the IPRF, which include some legally trained personnel, and the international staff members should have experience of such cases.

A property commission is not specifically provided for under the Fourth Geneva Convention, but the IPRF could secure legality by establishing it for the purposes of public security, which is the case in Iraq. A thorough assessment needs to be made (if not previously undertaken by the CPA) of whether certain provisions of Iraqi law need to be suspended for the IPRF to be working within domestic law, as although CPA regulations currently supersede Iraqi law, in the future the IPRF cannot operate if conflicting with domestic provisions. Furthermore, the UN should adopt a resolution authorising the IPRF. There should be no opportunity in the future for doubts as to the IPRF's legality.

The urgency of establishing an operational mechanism is not only for the purposes of justice, but it is also essential that a property restitution process is in place before reintegration of returnees, so as to ensure that an outbreak of violence does not occur upon their return. Moreover, given the extreme poverty of the displaced it is important to have a system established to support them so that they do not have to resort to criminal or other activities to survive.

International assistance should be obtained from the Permanent Court of Arbitration in The Hague, the OSCE, the IOM, the UN and non-governmental organisations.

Addendum

Since the writing of this publication, CPA Order 5 'Establishment of the Iraqi De-Baathification Council' has been rescinded. KHRP contacted the CPIC by telephone on 23 December 2003 to enquire why this regulation was rescinded but has not received a response to date. CPA Order 1 'De-Baathfication of Iraqi Society' has not been rescinded to date.

What bearing the rescinding of Order 5 will have in the operation of the Iraqi Special Tribunal in relation to the vetting process for judges and lawyers remains to be seen.

Appendix I
Articles of the 1920 Treaty of
Sèvres Relating to Kurdistan

SECTION III
KURDISTAN

Article 62

A Commission sitting at Constantinople and composed of three members appointed by the British, French and Italian Governments respectively shall draft within six months from the coming into force of the present Treaty a scheme of local autonomy for the predominantly Kurdish areas lying east of the Euphrates, south of the southern boundary of Armenia as it may be hereafter determined, and north of the frontier of Turkey with Syria and Mesopotamia, as defined in Article 27, II (2) and (3). If unanimity cannot be secured on any question, it will be referred by the members of the Commission to their respective Governments. The scheme shall contain full safeguards for the protection of the Assyro-Chaldeans and other racial or religious minorities within these areas, and with this object a Commission composed of British, French, Italian, Persian and Kurdish representatives shall visit the spot to examine and decide what rectifications, if any, should be made in the Turkish frontier where, under the provisions of the present Treaty, that frontier coincides with that of Persia.

Article 63

The Turkish Government hereby agrees to accept and execute the decisions of both the Commissions mentioned in Article 62 within three months from their communication to the said Government.

Article 64

If within one year from the coming into force of the present Treaty the Kurdish peoples within the areas defined in Article 62 shall address themselves to the Council of the League of Nations in such a manner as to show that a majority of the population of these areas desires independence from Turkey, and if the Council then considers that these peoples are capable of such independence and recommends that it should be granted to them, Turkey hereby agrees to execute such a recommendation, and to renounce all rights and title over these areas.

The detailed provisions for such renunciation will form the subject of a separate agreement between the Principal Allied Powers and Turkey.

If and when such renunciation takes place, no objection will be raised by the Principal Allied Powers to the voluntary adhesion to such an independent Kurdish State of the Kurds inhabiting that part of Kurdistan which has hitherto been included in the Mosul vilayet.

Appendix II
The Kurdistan Regional Government Provisional Constitution for the Federal Republic of Iraq

PART I – ESTABLISHING THE FEDERAL STATE

Article 1

Iraq is a federal state with a democratic, parliamentarian, pluralistic, republican system that will be called the Federal Republic of Iraq.

Article 2

The Federal Republic of Iraq consists of two regions:

i) The Arabic Region that includes the middle and southern regions of Iraq along with the Province of Ninevah in the north excepting the districts and sub-districts that have a Kurdish majority as mentioned in the item below.

ii) The Kurdish Region that includes the Provinces of Kirkuk, Sulaimaniya and Erbil within their administrative boundaries before 1970 and the Province of Duhok and the districts of Aqra, Sheihkan, Sinjar and the sub-district of Zimar in the Province of Ninevah and the districts of Khaniqin and Mandali in the Province of Diyala and the district of Badra in the Province of Al-Wasit.

Article 3

Power is inherent in the people as they are the source of its legitimacy.

Article 4

The people of Iraq consist of the two principal Arabic and Kurdish nationalities and this Constitution affirms the national rights of the Kurdish people and their enjoyment of them within the Kurdistan Region based on federalism as it also affirms the legitimate rights of the minorities within the framework of the Federal Republic of Iraq.

Article 5

Baghdad shall be the capitol of the Federal Republic of Iraq.

Article 6

The Federal Republic of Iraq shall have a flag, an emblem, and a national anthem that shall reflect the union between the Kurds and the Arabs and that shall be regulated by law.

Article 7

The state religion is Islam.

Article 8

Arabic is the official language of the federal state and the Arab region. Kurdish shall be the official language of the Kurdistan Region.

PART II – BASIC RIGHTS AND RESPONSIBILITIES

Article 9

i) Citizens are equal under the law without discrimination due to sex, race, colour, language, religion, or ethnic origin.
ii) All are guaranteed equal opportunity under the law.

Article 10

The family unit is the foundation of the community, the protection and support of which is guaranteed by the state. Mothers and children are also afforded protection under the law. The law upholds the basic moral and ethical values of the community among its citizens.

Article 11

i) An accused person is presumed innocent until proven guilty in a court of law.
ii) The right to legal defence is guaranteed at all stages of an investigation and trial in accordance with the law.
iii) Trial proceedings must be open unless otherwise declared closed by the court.
iv) Punishment is personal. Nothing can be treated as a crime, nor can any punishment be ordered and carried out unless defined in the law. No act is punishable unless it is considered to be a crime at the time of commission. No punishment can be administered that is greater than what is written in the law.

Article 12

i) The integrity of the individual shall be protected and all types of torture, physical or psychological, are prohibited.

ii) No one can be captured, detained, jailed, or searched except in circumstances defined in law.

iii) The sanctity of the home shall be protected and cannot be entered or searched except in accordance with procedures laid out in the law.

Article 13

The privacy of postal, cable and telephone communications is guaranteed and cannot be disclosed except when deemed necessary to serve the needs of justice and security in accordance with the parameters and procedures laid out in the law.

Article 14

A citizen cannot be prevented from travelling abroad or outside the country nor prevented from returning home to the country. Movements within the country shall not be restricted unless specified in the law.

Article 15

Freedom of religion, belief, and the practice of religious duties is guaranteed provided they do not conflict with provisions of this Constitution and the Regional Constitutions or with federal laws and provided they do not go against general moral and ethical standards.

Article 16

Primary education is compulsory. The federal and regional governments shall combat illiteracy, guarantee for their citizens the right to a free education in all its stages of primary, secondary, and university, and guarantee the development of technical and vocational studies.

Article 17

The right of academic research shall be guaranteed. Outstanding achievement, innovation and creativity shall be encouraged and rewarded.

Article 18

Freedom of expression, publication, printing, press, assembly, demonstration, and forming of political parties, unions and associations shall be guaranteed by law.

Article 19

The right to political asylum for all those persecuted because of their political beliefs shall be guaranteed. Political refugees shall not be extradited.

Article 20

i) Work is a right and duty of every citizen and the federal and regional governments shall make efforts to create work opportunities for every capable citizen.

ii) The state shall guarantee good working conditions, work towards raising the standard of living as well as the skills and knowledge of all working individuals. The state shall provide social security benefits in cases of illness, disability, unemployment, or old age.

iii) No individual shall be forced to carry out a job unless the purpose is to carry out a public service according to the law or in the case of emergency or natural disaster.

Article 21

The state and regional governments shall guarantee the right of ownership and this shall be regulated by law.

Article 22

The state guarantees to protect public health through consistent efforts to provide medical services in the fields of prevention, treatment and medication.

Article 23

Paying taxes is a duty of every citizen and such taxes shall not be levied, collected or amended except by law.

Article 24

Citizens have the guaranteed right to raise complaints and write petitions to the proper authorities and the authorities shall consider these within a reasonable period of time.

Article 25

The judiciary is the source of the protection of rights mentioned in this part. The Courts will decide what punishment and/or fine is warranted from any of the parties concerned.

PART III – FEDERAL GOVERNMENT AUTHORITIES
CHAPTER 1 – FEDERAL LEGISLATIVE AUTHORITY

Article 26

The federal legislative authority, the 'federal parliament', is made up of two chambers – the National Assembly (Chamber of Deputies) and the Assembly of the Regions.

Section 1 – National Assembly

Article 27

i) The National Assembly is made up of representatives of the people within the two regions elected through direct, secret, general ballot as regulated by law.
ii) Each citizen, 18 years of age or older, of sound mind and in good standing in the community has the right to vote.
iii) Each citizen, 25 years of age or older, of sound mind and in good standing in the community has the right to stand for election to the National Assembly.

Article 28

The Federal Parliament has a five-year term commencing with the holding of its first session.

Article 29

The electoral process and its procedures shall be regulated by law.

Article 30

i) No individual can hold a position in the National Assembly, the Assembly of the Regions, the Regional Parliament, or the local municipal and administrative councils, at the same time.
ii) A member of the National Assembly cannot hold another public position or office at the same time.

iii) A member of the National Assembly shall be considered to have resigned from any public position or office from the date that he/she swears the oath of office.

Article 31

The National Assembly shall hold its first session presided over by the oldest member. A president, vice president and secretary shall be elected from among its members through secret ballot.

Article 32

The National Assembly can meet with the presence of a simple majority of members present. Votes are also by simple majority.

Section 2 – The Assembly of the Regions

Article 33

The Assembly of the Regions is made up from representatives from each of the Arab and Kurdistan regions provided that the principle of equal representation is upheld.

Article 34

Each region evaluates the performance and can dismiss its representatives in accordance with the methods specified in the Regional Constitution and/or law.

Article 35

The Assembly of the Regions participates on an equal footing with the National Assembly in the practice of the federal legislative authority.

CHAPTER 2 – FEDERAL PARLIAMENT AUTHORITIES

Article 36

The Federal Parliament shall have the following authorities:

i) Declare war and conclude peace where a 2/3 majority will be required
ii) Amend the Federal Constitution
iii) Ratify international treaties and agreements where a 2/3 majority will be required

iv) Enact federal legislation

v) Vote of confidence in the federal cabinet and its members as well as withdrawal of such confidence

vi) Approve the federal budget

vii) Levy, regulate, and abolish taxes and duties

viii) Supervise the work of the federal executive authority

ix) Draft internal rules and procedures for personnel and staffing, determine positions, appoint staff, determine salaries, and approve the budget of the Federal Parliament

x) Look into and verify the membership in the National Assembly and the formation of the committees.

CHAPTER 3 – FEDERAL EXECUTIVE AUTHORITY

Section 1 – President of the Federal Republic of Iraq

Article 37

The President of the Federal Republic of Iraq is the head of state and the Commander-in-Chief of the Armed Forces.

Article 38

The President shall be elected through direct, general, secret ballot for a period of five years and may stand for re-election once.

Article 39

All candidates for President shall be:

i) an Iraqi citizen whose parents must both have been born in Iraq

ii) at least 40 years of age

iii) a citizen in good standing in both his/her civil and political rights

Article 40

The President of the Federal Republic of Iraq shall take the following oath of office in the presence of a joint session of the Federal Parliament:

'I swear, by God Almighty, to respect the Constitution of the Federal Republic of Iraq, to defend the independence and sovereignty of the country, and to work diligently for the realization of the interests of the people, freedom and honor.'

Article 41

In the case of the resignation, demise, or inability to perform the duties of the President of the Republic of Iraq, his/her deputy shall take over the duties of the presidency for the remainder of the term of office.

Article 42

The President of the Federal Republic of Iraq represents the federal state abroad and concludes treaties in its names and acknowledges and receives foreign diplomats and missions.

Article 43

The President of the Federal Republic of Iraq shall assume the following duties and responsibilities:

i) Protecting the independence and territorial integrity, and the internal and external security of the Federal Republic of Iraq
ii) Appointing the Vice President of the Federal Republic of Iraq after having been nominated by the Assembly of the Regions
iii) Announcing the federal cabinet after it has won a vote of confidence from the National Assembly
iv) Calling general elections for the National Assembly
v) Proclaiming federal legislation
vi) Appointing Iraqi diplomats and representatives to Arab and other foreign countries and to international organizations and conferences
vii) Instructing the Armed Forces and Internal Security in accordance with national interests
viii) Declaring states of emergency, which shall be regulated by law
ix) Conferring military ranks on members of the Armed Forces and the Internal Security as well as dismissing or retiring members from those services
x) Conferring medals or awards
xi) Appointing individuals of special ranks such as those in the judiciary, the chief prosecutor, general prosecutor and the deputies in the federal state

Article 44

The President of the Republic of Iraq shall be indicted by a 2/3 majority of the Federal Parliament and shall be put on trial in a joint session of the High Court and the Assembly of the Regions presided over by the President of the High Court and any sentence passed must be by a 2/3 majority.

Article 45

The President of the Republic of Iraq shall remain in office carrying out his/her duties during the period of his/her indictment and trial.

Section 2 – Council of Ministers (Cabinet)

Article 46

The Council of Ministers constitutes the highest executive authority in the Federal Republic of Iraq and practises its responsibilities under the supervision and guidance of the President of the Republic of Iraq.

Article 47

The Council of Ministers shall be made up the prime minister, his/her deputies and a number of ministers who shall represent both regions in proportion to the regions populations.

Article 48

Upon the election of the President of the Republic of Iraq from one region, the Prime Minister shall be appointed from the other.

Article 49

i) The Prime Minister designate shall submit the names of his/her cabinet to the President of the Republic of Iraq for his/her approval.
ii) Following approval by the President, the Prime Minister designate shall introduce his/her cabinet to both the National Assembly and the Assembly of the Regions for a vote of confidence following which the President shall issue the necessary decree for the formation of the cabinet.

Article 50

The Council of Ministers shall assume the following responsibilities:

i) Carrying out federal legislation
ii) Protecting the safety and security of the land

iii) Preparing federal draft legislation and submitting it to the Federal Parliament

iv) Preparing the federal budget

v) Supervising the federal ministries, institutions and public agencies

vi) Issuing federal orders and regulations

vii) Concluding loans, grants and supervising financial affairs

viii) Appointing, promoting, and retiring federal civil servants

Article 51

The President of the Republic of Iraq may chair meetings of the Council of Ministers and request special performance reports from the Council and the Ministries.

Article 52

i) The Federal Parliament may withdraw confidence from

a. The cabinet and it shall be considered no longer in office from the date of the withdrawal of confidence;

b. A minister and he/she shall be considered no longer in office from the date of the withdrawal of confidence.

ii) The cabinet shall continue in office until a new cabinet is formed.

CHAPTER 4 – HIGH COURT (CONSTITUTIONAL COURT)

Article 53

The High Court shall consist of a number of members, persons of high integrity, qualifications, and experience, chosen from among the judiciary and law professors teaching at universities who have had at least 20 years of practice or teaching and each region shall designate half of the members of the Court.

Article 54

The President of the High Court shall be on a rotational basis. Each member shall assume the presidency for a period of one year at a time.

Article 55

Members of the High Court cannot be dismissed except in the case of indictment due to lack of integrity. Their indictment, trial and sentencing shall be carried out by the Assembly of the Regions.

Article 56

Members of the High Court shall not be retired due to age unless there is a personal request to that effect.

Article 57

The High Court shall look into and adjudicate the following:

i) Interpretation of the Constitution with regard to conflicts that arise in relation to the rights and duties of the federal institutions or conflicts within the various authorities;
ii) Conflicts arising out of the implementation of the Constitution between the federal and regional levels;
iii) Conflicts that arise out of the implementation of the Constitution or those that may occur among the regions.

Article 58

The High Court shall issue its decisions on a simple majority basis and, in the case of an even split, the President of the High Court shall decide.

CHAPTER 5 – RESPONSIBILITIES OF THE FEDERAL GOVERNMENT

Article 59

The federal government shall assume the following responsibilities:

i) Declaring war and concluding peace
ii) Setting out foreign policy and diplomatic and consular representations
iii) Concluding international treaties and agreements
iv) Defending the country by utilizing all branches of the Armed Forces
v) Issuing currency and planning monetary and banking policy
vi) Defining standards for weights and measures and designating salary policy
vii) Drafting general economic planning aimed at development in the regions in the areas of industry, commerce and agriculture
viii) Ordering federal general audits
ix) Overseeing federal security affairs
x) Citizenship, residency and foreigners' affairs
xi) Oil resources
xii) Nuclear power

PART IV – REGIONAL CONSTITUTIONAL STRUCTURE

Article 60

Each region shall draw up its own constitution taking into consideration the following:

i) Shall adopt the republican system
ii) shall not contradict the terms of this Constitution

Article 61

Citizens of the region shall, through direct, general and secret ballot, elect their representatives to the Regional Assembly, the 'Regional Parliament,' and the electoral process and ratio of representation shall be regulated by a law.

Article 62

The responsibilities of the Regional Assembly and its relation with other authorities shall be set out in the Regional Constitution.

Article 63

The regional executive authority shall be made up of:

i) Regional President
ii) Regional Council of Ministers

Article 64

Citizens of the region shall elect a President, to be called the Regional President, and he/she shall be the head of the executive authority and he/she will also represent the President of the Federal Republic of Iraq within the region on official state occasions.

Article 65

Rules and procedures for the election of the Regional President, his/her term of office, responsibilities, relationship to the Regional Council of Ministers, and to other public authorities in the region shall be designated in the Regional Constitution.

Article 66

The Regional Council of Ministers consists of the prime minister, his/her deputies and a number of ministers and the Council shall carry out its regional executive responsibilities under the supervision and guidance of the Regional President.

Article 67

The rules and procedures to form the cabinet and its responsibilities and its relation to the Regional President shall be designated in the Regional Constitution.

Article 68

The independent judicial powers in the region that will consist of all levels of courts including the Regional Cassation Court which shall look into civil and criminal and other cases and this shall be regulated by a regional law.

Article 69

The region shall assume various responsibilities except those delegated to the federal government in accordance with this Constitution and in particular in Chapter 4 of Part III.

Article 70

Conflicts that may arise between the federal and regional authorities among the regional authorities in relation to the responsibilities designated in this Constitution shall be referred to the High Court, 'Constitutional Court' for adjudication.

PART V – FISCAL RESPONSIBILITIES

Article 71

Taxes shall not be levied, collected or altered unless by a federal or regional law.

Article 72

The federal authorities alone may levy and collect export and import, 'custom,' duties.

Article 73

The Regional authorities shall levy the following taxes:

i) income
ii) inheritance
iii) agricultural land and property taxes
iv) property registration fees
v) court fees

vi) licence fees

vii) water and electricity charges

Article 74

Each region shall have a share of the revenues from the oil wealth, grants, and foreign aid and loans in proportion to their population in relation to that of the total population of the country.

PART VI – MISCELLANEOUS

Article 75

No changes to the borders of the two regions can be made except with the approval of the Assembly of the region concerned.

Article 76

i) Citizens of the Kurdistan Region shall be appointed to the various positions in the federal ministries and other bodies both inside and outside the country and in particular in the deputy minister, director general, or other high level positions according to the ratio of the regional population to the total population of the Federal Republic of Iraq.

ii) The above-mentioned principle shall apply to the following:

a. Appointment of ambassadors, members of diplomatic and consular corps and federal representatives in international and regional organizations and bodies

b. Appointment to the Armed Forces and Federal Security

c. Participation in official Iraqi delegations and negotiations for the purpose of concluding international treaties

d. Acceptance of students for fellowships and scholarships as well as study abroad

e. Admission of students to academies, military and police colleges, and training programmes both inside and outside the country

Article 77

The *peshmerga* forces and their various divisions shall constitute a part of the Armed Forces of the Federal Republic of Iraq.

Article 78

Redress the effects of Arabization and deportations that took place in some parts of the Kurdistan Region. The deported Kurdish citizens from areas of the Province of Kirkuk and from Makhmoor, Sinjar, Zimar, Sheikhan, Khaniqin, Mandali, and others should return to their previous homes in those areas. As well, the Arab citizens who were brought by the authorities into those areas at any time since 1957 should return to their original homes.

Article 79

This Constitution shall be the highest law of the land and all other laws issued in contradiction to it shall be considered null and void.

Article 80

The terms of this Constitution cannot be amended unless through a 2/3 majority vote by members of both the Federal and Regional Assemblies.

Article 81

The Federal Republic of Iraq shall be accountable to the United Nations organization for guaranteeing the rights, the boundaries, and powers of the two regions designated in this Constitution and the Regional Constitutions.

Article 82

The structure of the Federal Republic of Iraq and its political system as laid out in this Constitution cannot be changed unless through a decision by the legislative authorities in the Federal and Regional levels. Action contrary to this shall afford the people of the Kurdistan Region the right of self-determination.

Appendix III
United Nations Guiding Principles on Internal Displacement

INTRODUCTION: SCOPE AND PURPOSE

1. These Guiding Principles address the specific needs of internally displaced persons worldwide. They identify rights and guarantees relevant to the protection of persons from forced displacement and to their protection and assistance during displacement as well as during return or resettlement and reintegration.

2. For the purposes of these Principles, internally displaced persons are persons or groups of persons who have been forced or obliged to flee or to leave their homes or places of habitual residence, in particular as a result of or in order to avoid the effects of armed conflict, situations of generalized violence, violations of human rights or natural or human-made disasters, and who have not crossed an internationally recognized State border.

3. These Principles reflect and are consistent with international human rights law and international humanitarian law. They provide guidance to:

(a) The Representative of the Secretary-General on internally displaced persons in carrying out his mandate;
(b) States when faced with the phenomenon of internal displacement;
(c) All other authorities, groups and persons in their relations with internally displaced persons; and
(d) Intergovernmental and non-governmental organizations when addressing internal displacement.

4. These Guiding Principles should be disseminated and applied as widely as possible.

SECTION I – GENERAL PRINCIPLES

Principle 1

1. Internally displaced persons shall enjoy, in full equality, the same rights and freedoms under international and domestic law as do other persons in their country. They shall not be discriminated against in the enjoyment of any rights and freedoms on the ground that they are internally displaced.

2. These Principles are without prejudice to individual criminal responsibility under international law, in particular relating to genocide, crimes against humanity and war crimes.

Principle 2

1. These Principles shall be observed by all authorities, groups and persons irrespective of their legal status and applied without any adverse distinction. The observance of these Principles shall not affect the legal status of any authorities, groups or persons involved.

2. These Principles shall not be interpreted as restricting, modifying or impairing the provisions of any international human rights or international humanitarian law instrument or rights granted to persons under domestic law. In particular, these Principles are without prejudice to the right to seek and enjoy asylum in other countries.

Principle 3

1. National authorities have the primary duty and responsibility to provide protection and humanitarian assistance to internally displaced persons within their jurisdiction.

2. Internally displaced persons have the right to request and to receive protection and humanitarian assistance from these authorities. They shall not be persecuted or punished for making such a request.

Principle 4

1. These Principles shall be applied without discrimination of any kind, such as race, colour, sex, language, religion or belief, political or other opinion, national, ethnic or social origin, legal or social status, age, disability, property, birth, or on any other similar criteria.

2. Certain internally displaced persons, such as children, especially unaccompanied minors, expectant mothers, mothers with young children, female heads of household, persons with disabilities and elderly persons, shall be entitled to protection and assistance required by their condition and to treatment which takes into account their special needs.

SECTION II – PRINCIPLES RELATING
TO PROTECTION FROM DISPLACEMENT

Principle 5

All authorities and international actors shall respect and ensure respect for their obligations under international law, including human rights and humanitarian law, in all circumstances, so as to prevent and avoid conditions that might lead to displacement of persons.

Principle 6

1. Every human being shall have the right to be protected against being arbitrarily displaced from his or her home or place of habitual residence.
2. The prohibition of arbitrary displacement includes displacement:

(a) When it is based on policies of apartheid, 'ethnic cleansing' or similar practices aimed at/or resulting in altering the ethnic, religious or racial composition of the affected population;
(b) In situations of armed conflict, unless the security of the civilians involved or imperative military reasons so demand;
(c) In cases of large-scale development projects, which are not justified by compelling and overriding public interests;
(d) In cases of disasters, unless the safety and health of those affected requires their evacuation; and
(e) When it is used as a collective punishment.

3. Displacement shall last no longer than required by the circumstances.

Principle 7

1. Prior to any decision requiring the displacement of persons, the authorities concerned shall ensure that all feasible alternatives are explored in order to avoid displacement altogether. Where no alternatives exist, all measures shall be taken to minimize displacement and its adverse effects.
2. The authorities undertaking such displacement shall ensure, to the greatest practicable extent, that proper accommodation is provided to the displaced persons, that such displacements are effected in satisfactory conditions of safety, nutrition, health and hygiene, and that members of the same family are not separated.

3. If displacement occurs in situations other than during the emergency stages of armed conflicts and disasters, the following guarantees shall be complied with:

(a) A specific decision shall be taken by a State authority empowered by law to order such measures;
(b) Adequate measures shall be taken to guarantee to those to be displaced full information on the reasons and procedures for their displacement and, where applicable, on compensation and relocation;
(c) The free and informed consent of those to be displaced shall be sought;
(d) The authorities concerned shall endeavour to involve those affected, particularly women, in the planning and management of their relocation;
(e) Law enforcement measures, where required, shall be carried out by competent legal authorities; and
(f) The right to an effective remedy, including the review of such decisions by appropriate judicial authorities, shall be respected.

Principle 8

Displacement shall not be carried out in a manner that violates the rights to life, dignity, liberty and security of those affected.

Principle 9

States are under a particular obligation to protect against the displacement of indigenous peoples, minorities, peasants, pastoralists and other groups with a special dependency on and attachment to their lands.

SECTION III – PRINCIPLES RELATING
TO PROTECTION DURING DISPLACEMENT

Principle 10

1. Every human being has the inherent right to life which shall be protected by law. No one shall be arbitrarily deprived of his or her life. Internally displaced persons shall be protected in particular against:

(a) Genocide;
(b) Murder;

(c)   Summary or arbitrary executions; and
(d)   Enforced disappearances, including abduction or unacknowledged detention, threatening or resulting in death.

Threats and incitement to commit any of the foregoing acts shall be prohibited.

2. Attacks or other acts of violence against internally displaced persons who do not or no longer participate in hostilities are prohibited in all circumstances. Internally displaced persons shall be protected, in particular, against:

(a)   Direct or indiscriminate attacks or other acts of violence, including the creation of areas wherein attacks on civilians are permitted;
(b)   Starvation as a method of combat;
(c)   Their use to shield military objectives from attack or to shield, favour or impede military operations;
(d)   Attacks against their camps or settlements; and
(e)   The use of anti-personnel landmines.

Principle 11

1. Every human being has the right to dignity and physical, mental and moral integrity.

2. Internally displaced persons, whether or not their liberty has been restricted, shall be protected in particular against:

(a)   Rape, mutilation, torture, cruel, inhuman or degrading treatment or punishment, and other outrages upon personal dignity, such as acts of gender-specific violence, forced prostitution and any form of indecent assault;
(b)   Slavery or any contemporary form of slavery, such as sale into marriage, sexual exploitation, or forced labour of children; and
(c)   Acts of violence intended to spread terror among internally displaced persons.

Threats and incitement to commit any of the foregoing acts shall be prohibited.

Principle 12

1. Every human being has the right to liberty and security of person. No one shall be subjected to arbitrary arrest or detention.

2. To give effect to this right for internally displaced persons, they shall not be interned in or confined to a camp. If in exceptional circumstances such internment or confinement is absolutely necessary, it shall not last longer than required by the circumstances.

3. Internally displaced persons shall be protected from discriminatory arrest and detention as a result of their displacement.

4. In no case shall internally displaced persons be taken hostage.

Principle 13

1. In no circumstances shall displaced children be recruited nor be required or permitted to take part in hostilities.

2. Internally displaced persons shall be protected against discriminatory practices of recruitment into any armed forces or groups as a result of their displacement. In particular any cruel, inhuman or degrading practices that compel compliance or punish non-compliance with recruitment are prohibited in all circumstances.

Principle 14

1. Every internally displaced person has the right to liberty of movement and freedom to choose his or her residence.

2. In particular, internally displaced persons have the right to move freely in and out of camps or other settlements.

Principle 15

Internally displaced persons have:

(a)   The right to seek safety in another part of the country;
(b)   The right to leave their country;
(c)   The right to seek asylum in another country; and
(d)   The right to be protected against forcible return to or resettlement in any place where their life, safety, liberty and/or health would be at risk.

Principle 16

1. All internally displaced persons have the right to know the fate and whereabouts of missing relatives.

2. The authorities concerned shall endeavour to establish the fate and whereabouts of internally displaced persons reported missing, and cooperate with relevant international organizations engaged in this task. They shall inform the next of kin on the progress of the investigation and notify them of any result.

3. The authorities concerned shall endeavour to collect and identify the mortal remains of those deceased, prevent their despoliation or mutilation, and facilitate the return of those remains to the next of kin or dispose of them respectfully.

4. Grave sites of internally displaced persons should be protected and respected in all circumstances. Internally displaced persons should have the right of access to the grave sites of their deceased relatives.

Principle 17

1. Every human being has the right to respect of his or her family life.

2. To give effect to this right for internally displaced persons, family members who wish to remain together shall be allowed to do so.

3. Families which are separated by displacement should be reunited as quickly as possible. All appropriate steps shall be taken to expedite the reunion of such families, particularly when children are involved. The responsible authorities shall facilitate inquiries made by family members and encourage and cooperate with the work of humanitarian organizations engaged in the task of family reunification.

4. Members of internally displaced families whose personal liberty has been restricted by internment or confinement in camps shall have the right to remain together.

Principle 18

1. All internally displaced persons have the right to an adequate standard of living.

2. At the minimum, regardless of the circumstances, and without discrimination, competent authorities shall provide internally displaced persons with and ensure safe access to:

(a)   Essential food and potable water;
(b)   Basic shelter and housing;
(c)   Appropriate clothing; and
(d)   Essential medical services and sanitation.

3. Special efforts should be made to ensure the full participation of women in the planning and distribution of these basic supplies.

Principle 19

1. All wounded and sick internally displaced persons as well as those with disabilities shall receive to the fullest extent practicable and

with the least possible delay, the medical care and attention they require, without distinction on any grounds other than medical ones. When necessary, internally displaced persons shall have access to psychological and social services.

2. Special attention should be paid to the health needs of women, including access to female health care providers and services, such as reproductive health care, as well as appropriate counselling for victims of sexual and other abuses.

3. Special attention should also be given to the prevention of contagious and infectious diseases, including AIDS, among internally displaced persons.

Principle 20

1. Every human being has the right to recognition everywhere as a person before the law.

2. To give effect to this right for internally displaced persons, the authorities concerned shall issue to them all documents necessary for the enjoyment and exercise of their legal rights, such as passports, personal identification documents, birth certificates and marriage certificates. In particular, the authorities shall facilitate the issuance of new documents or the replacement of documents lost in the course of displacement, without imposing unreasonable conditions, such as requiring the return to one's area of habitual residence in order to obtain these or other required documents.

3. Women and men shall have equal rights to obtain such necessary documents and shall have the right to have such documentation issued in their own names.

Principle 21

1. No one shall be arbitrarily deprived of property and possessions.

2. The property and possessions of internally displaced persons shall in all circumstances be protected, in particular, against the following acts:

(a) Pillage;
(b) Direct or indiscriminate attacks or other acts of violence;
(c) Being used to shield military operations or objectives;
(d) Being made the object of reprisal; and
(e) Being destroyed or appropriated as a form of collective punishment.

3. Property and possessions left behind by internally displaced persons should be protected against destruction and arbitrary and illegal appropriation, occupation or use.

Principle 22

1. Internally displaced persons, whether or not they are living in camps, shall not be discriminated against as a result of their displacement in the enjoyment of the following rights:

(a) The rights to freedom of thought, conscience, religion or belief, opinion and expression;
(b) The right to seek freely opportunities for employment and to participate in economic activities;
(c) The right to associate freely and participate equally in community affairs;
(d) The right to vote and to participate in governmental and public affairs, including the right to have access to the means necessary to exercise this right; and
(e) The right to communicate in a language they understand.

Principle 23

1. Every human being has the right to education.
2. To give effect to this right for internally displaced persons, the authorities concerned shall ensure that such persons, in particular displaced children, receive education which shall be free and compulsory at the primary level. Education should respect their cultural identity, language and religion.
3. Special efforts should be made to ensure the full and equal participation of women and girls in educational programmes.
4. Education and training facilities shall be made available to internally displaced persons, in particular adolescents and women, whether or not living in camps, as soon as conditions permit.

SECTION IV – PRINCIPLES RELATING TO HUMANITARIAN ASSISTANCE

Principle 24

1. All humanitarian assistance shall be carried out in accordance with the principles of humanity and impartiality and without discrimination.

2. Humanitarian assistance to internally displaced persons shall not be diverted, in particular for political or military reasons.

Principle 25

1. The primary duty and responsibility for providing humanitarian assistance to internally displaced persons lies with national authorities.
2. International humanitarian organizations and other appropriate actors have the right to offer their services in support of the internally displaced. Such an offer shall not be regarded as an unfriendly act or an interference in a State's internal affairs and shall be considered in good faith. Consent thereto shall not be arbitrarily withheld, particularly when authorities concerned are unable or unwilling to provide the required humanitarian assistance.
3. All authorities concerned shall grant and facilitate the free passage of humanitarian assistance and grant persons engaged in the provision of such assistance rapid and unimpeded access to the internally displaced.

Principle 26

Persons engaged in humanitarian assistance, their transport and supplies shall be respected and protected. They shall not be the object of attack or other acts of violence.

Principle 27

1. International humanitarian organizations and other appropriate actors when providing assistance should give due regard to the protection needs and human rights of internally displaced persons and take appropriate measures in this regard. In so doing, these organizations and actors should respect relevant international standards and codes of conduct.
2. The preceding paragraph is without prejudice to the protection responsibilities of international organizations mandated for this purpose, whose services may be offered or requested by States.

SECTION V – PRINCIPLES RELATING TO RETURN, RESETTLEMENT AND REINTEGRATION

Principle 28

1. Competent authorities have the primary duty and responsibility to establish conditions, as well as provide the means, which allow

internally displaced persons to return voluntarily, in safety and with dignity, to their homes or places of habitual residence, or to resettle voluntarily in another part of the country. Such authorities shall endeavour to facilitate the reintegration of returned or resettled internally displaced persons.

2. Special efforts should be made to ensure the full participation of internally displaced persons in the planning and management of their return or resettlement and reintegration.

Principle 29

1. Internally displaced persons who have returned to their homes or places of habitual residence or who have resettled in another part of the country shall not be discriminated against as a result of their having been displaced. They shall have the right to participate fully and equally in public affairs at all levels and have equal access to public services.

2. Competent authorities have the duty and responsibility to assist returned and/or resettled internally displaced persons to recover, to the extent possible, their property and possessions which they left behind or were dispossessed of upon their displacement. When recovery of such property and possessions is not possible, competent authorities shall provide or assist these persons in obtaining appropriate compensation or another form of just reparation.

Principle 30

All authorities concerned shall grant and facilitate for international humanitarian organizations and other appropriate actors, in the exercise of their respective mandates, rapid and unimpeded access to internally displaced persons to assist in their return or resettlement and reintegration.

Notes

Web addresses are given where it is believed they will remain stable for some time. Articles from newspapers are mostly from the online version of the newspaper and can be found online for free (at the time of writing) using their URL.

INTRODUCTION

1. Benedict Anderson, *Imagined Communities: Reflections on the Origin and Spread of Nationalism* (London: Verso, 1991).
2. KHRP, *After the War: The Report of the KHRP Fact-Finding Mission to Iraqi Kurdistan* (London: KHRP, 2003).
3. KHRP, FFM (fact-finding mission) interviews, Taxi driver: Kawa, Erbil, 30 August 2003.
4. KHRP, FFM interviews, Anfal survivors, near Sulaimaniya, 31 August 2003.

1 THE KURDS

1. Mehrdad A. Izady, 'History: Origins', *The Encyclopaedia of Kurdistan* <www.kurdistanica.com/english/history/histroy-frame.html>.
2. Ibid.
3. KHRP, *The Safe Haven in Northern Iraq* (London: KHRP, 1995), p.6.
4. Dr Vera Saeedpour, *Meet the Kurds* (London: Cobblestone Publishing, 1999) <www.cobblestonepub.com/pages/Kurds.htm>.
5. David McDowall, 'The Land of the Kurds', *The Encyclopaedia of Kurdistan* <www.kurdistanica.com/english/geography/geography-frame.html>.
6. Ibid.
7. Joyce Blau, 'The Kurdish Language and Literature', *InstituteKurde.org* <www.institutkurde.org/ikpweba/kurdora/llitt.htm>.
8. Culturalorientation.net, *Language Issues, Iraqi Kurds: Their History and Culture, Refugee Fact Sheet* No. 13, <www.culturalorientation.net/kurds/klang.html>.
9. Ibid.
10. KHRP, *Safe Haven*, p.6.

2 THE TREATY OF SÈVRES AND THE CREATION OF IRAQ

1. Updated excerpts from KHRP, *The Safe Haven in Northern Iraq* (London: KHRP, 1995).
2. Woodrow Wilson's Fourteen Points, delivered 8 January 1918, available at <www.historyguide.org/europe/14points.html>.

3. David McDowall, *A Modern History of the Kurds* (London: I.B. Tauris, 2001) p.132.
4. Mosul was a former vilayet or province of the Ottoman Empire, subsequently occupied by the British, along with the vilayets of Basra and Baghdad.
5. Kom, 'The Men Who Put the Kurds Into Iraq: Percy Cox and Arnold T. Wilson', *Kurdish Affairs*, Vol. 1, No. 2 (September 1994).
6. Barham Salih, 'A Kurdish Model for Iraq', *The Iraq Foundation* (10 December 2002) <www.iraqfoundation.org/studies/2002/dec/10_model.html>.
7. Kom, 'The Men Who Put the Kurds Into Iraq'.
8. In any event, the question of voluntary adhesion by the inhabitants of Mosul to an independent Kurdish state was rendered moot by the collapse of the Treaty of Sèvres.
9. Historical sources include: McDowall, *Modern History of the Kurds*; KHRP, *Safe Haven*; and Marion Farouk-Sluglett and Peter Sluglett, *Iraq Since 1958: From Revolution to Dictatorship* (London: I.B. Tauris, 2001).
10. In 1918 Sheikh Mahmud had presented a document signed by 40 tribal chiefs to Sir Arnold Wilson demanding the granting of certain rights to the Kurdish people. He then revolted against British rule in Sulaimaniya in 1919 and was captured.
11. Gerard Chaliand, *The Kurdish Tragedy* (London: Palgrave Macmillan, 1994), pp.53–4.

3 THE KURDS UNDER BARZANI

1. Kurdish term meaning 'one who faces death'.
2. A process designed to change the ethnic balance from Kurdish to Arab.
3. Marion Farouk-Sluglett and Peter Sluglett, *Iraq Since 1958: From Revolution to Dictatorship* (London: I.B. Tauris, 2001).
4. Ibid., p.129.
5. *Kurdish Language Policy of Monarchy and Republican Iraq* available at <www.cogsci.ed.ac.uk/~siamakr/Kurdish/KURDICA/1999/FEB/Iraq-policy3.html>.
6. Human Rights Watch, *Iraq: Forcible Expulsion of Ethnic Minorities*, Vol. 15, No. 3(E), March 2003, available at <www.hrw.org/reports/2003/iraq0303/Kirkuk0303.pdf>.
7. Ibid.
8. For history and analysis of the 1974 autonomy law see Farouk-Sluglett and Sluglett, *Iraq Since 1958*, Chapter 6; and David McDowall, *A Modern History of the Kurds* (London: I.B. Tauris, 2001), Chapter 16.
9. Jonathan C. Randal, *After Such Knowledge, What Forgiveness? My Encounters with Kurdistan* (London: Westview Press, 1999).
10. Ibid., p.156.
11. McDowall, *Modern History of the Kurds*, p.337.
12. Middle East Watch Report, *Genocide in Iraq: The Anfal Campaign Against the Kurds* (Human Rights Watch, 1993) available at <www.hrw.org/reports/1993/iraqanfal/>.

4 THE ANFAL CAMPAIGNS

1. See <www.road-to-heaven.com/quran/english/8.htm>.
2. For more information on relations between the KDP and PUK see Chapter 6, this volume.
3. A Middle East Watch Report, *Genocide in Iraq: The Anfal campaign against the Kurds* (Human Rights Watch, 1993) Appendix B, 'The Perpetrators of Anfal: A Road-Map to the Principal Agencies and Individuals', available at <www.hrw.org/reports/1993/iraqanfal/APPENDIXB.htm>.
4. Ibid.
5. Ibid.
6. Kurdish villagers loyal to and paid by the Ba'ath party, and led by a headman or *mustashar*. *Jash* in its literal translation means 'donkey' and they were used throughout the campaigns as armed auxiliaries to the Iraqi military, flushing out villages, and delivering up prisoners to regular forces.
7. KHRP, FFM interviews, Northern Iraq, August 2003.
8. Middle East Watch Report, *Genocide in Iraq*, 'Introduction', available at <www.hrw.org/reports/1993/iraqanfal/ANFALINT.htm>.
9. Middle East Watch Report, *Genocide in Iraq*, 'First Anfal: The Siege of Sergalou and Bergalou, February 23–March 19 1988', available at <www.hrw.org/reports/1993/iraqanfal/ANFAL3.htm>.
10. Ibid.
11. Ibid.
12. Middle East Watch Report, *Genocide in Iraq*, 'Second Anfal: Qara Dagh, March 22–April 1 1988', available at <www.hrw.org/reports/1993/iraqanfal/ANFAL4.htm>.
13. Middle East Watch Report, *Genocide in Iraq*, 'Third Anfal: Germian, April 7–20 1988', available at <www.hrw.org/reports/1993/iraqanfal/ANFAL5.htm>.
14. Ibid.
15. Middle East Watch Report, *Genocide in Iraq*, 'The Camps', available at <www.hrw.org/reports/1993/iraqanfal/ANFAL8.htm>.
16. Middle East Watch Report, *Genocide in Iraq*, 'The Amnesty and its Exclusions', available at <www.hrw.org/reports/1993/iraqanfal/ANFAL11.htm>.
17. Ibid.
18. 'Anfalak' was a term adopted to describe those affected by Anfal campaigns.
19. Middle East Watch Report, *Genocide in Iraq*, 'The Amnesty and its Exclusions'.
20. 'The True History of the Gulf War: An Exchange', *The New York Review of Books*, Vol. 39, No. 6, 26 March 1992, available at <www.nybooks.com/articles/2978>.
21. Report of a Medical Mission to Turkish Kurdistan by Physicians for Human Rights, *Winds of Death: Iraq's Use of Poison Gas Against its Kurdish Population*, 1989, available at <www.phrusa.org/research/iraq/winds.html>.
22. Ibid.

23. Ibid.
24. Ibid.
25. Testimony of Dr Christine M. Gosden before the Senate Judiciary Subcommittee on Technology, Terrorism and the Government, and the Senate Select Committee on Intelligence, 22 April 1998, available at <www.senate.gov/~judiciary/oldsite/gosden.htm>.
26. Ibid.
27. Raju Thomas, 'Report Suppressed: Iran Gassed Kurds, Not Iraq', *Times of India*, 16 September 2002 <www.the7thfire.com/Politics%20and%20History/GaseousLies.htm>.
28. Political statements to which parliamentarians can sign up and support.
29. Marion Farouk-Sluglett and Peter Sluglett, *Iraq Since 1958: From Revolution to Dictatorship* (London: I.B. Tauris, 1990), p.270.
30. Ibid.
31. Full text of Resolution 620 1988 available at <http://ods-dds-ny.un.org/doc/RESOLUTION/GEN/NR0/541/47/IMG/NR054147.pdf?OpenElement>.

5 THE FIRST GULF WAR: FROM UPRISING TO DEMOCRACY

1. Falaq al-Din Kakai, 'The Kurdish Parliament', *Iraq Since the Gulf War: Prospects for Democracy* (ed. Fran Hazelton) (London and New Jersey: Zed Books, 1994), p.119.
2. Ibid p.97.
3. Ibid.
4. 'War of Propaganda US v Iraq 1991: Voice of the Gulf', *Clandestine Radio.com* <www.clandestineradio.com/dossier/iraq/gulf.htm>.
5. Kakai, 'The Kurdish Parliament'.
6. Faleh 'Abd al-Jabbar, 'Why the Intifada Failed', *Iraq Since the Gulf War: Prospects for Democracy* (ed. Fran Hazelton) (London and New Jersey: Zed Books, 1994), p.106.
7. Sheri Laizer, *Martyrs, Traitors and Patriots* (London: Zed Books, 1996).
8. Ibid.
9. Ibid.
10. 'Even After the Gulf War, the US Helped Saddam Hussein Stay in Power', *Representative Press* <www.representativepress.org/evenafter.html>.
11. Al-Jabbar, 'Why the Intifada Failed', p.106.
12. Lawyers Committee for Human Rights, *Asylum Under Attack: A Report on the Protection of Iraqi Refugees and Displaced Persons One Year After the Humanitarian Emergency in Iraq*, April 1992.
13. Ibid.
14. Physicians for Human Rights, *Iraqi Kurdistan: Medical Assessment of Kurdish Refugees on the Turkey–Iraq Border*, August 1991, available at <www.phrusa.org/research/health_effects/humiraqkurd.html>.
15. *Independent*, 11 April 1991.
16. David McDowall, *A Modern History of the Kurds* (London: I.B. Tauris, 2001), p.375.

17. KHRP, *The Safe Haven in Northern Iraq* (London: KHRP, 1995), p.39.
18. Ibid.
19. Full text of Resolution 688 available at <http://ods-dds-ny.un.org/doc/RESOLUTION/GEN/NR0/596/24/IMG/NR059624.pdf?OpenElement>.
20. KHRP, *The Safe Haven in Northern Iraq*, p.36.
21. Full text of Resolution 687 1991 available at <http://ods-dds-ny.un.org/doc/RESOLUTION/GEN/NR0/596/23/IMG/NR059623.pdf?OpenElement>.
22. CRS Issue Brief for Congress, 20 September 1991.
23. Full text of the UN Charter available at <www.un.org/aboutun/charter/index.html>.
24. Lawyers Committee for Human Rights, *Asylum under Attack*, p.30.
25. McDowall, *A Modern History of the Kurds*, p.375.
26. Iran had no formal relationship with UNHCR.
27. Lawyers Committee for Human Rights, *Asylum under Attack*, p.57.
28. Albert B. Prados, *The Kurds in Iraq, Status, Protection and Prospects*, Congressional Research Service Report, 12 May 1994, p.4.
29. News Conference, 16 April 1991, cited in Lawrence Freedman and David Boren, 'Safe Havens for Kurds in Post-War Iraq', *To Loose the Bands of Wickedness* (ed. Nigel Rodley) (London and New York: Brasseys, 1992).
30. Letter to the UN Secretary-General, UN Doc S/22513.
31. KHRP, *The Safe Haven in Northern Iraq*, p.42.
32. UNHCR, *Report on Northern Iraq April 1991 – May 1992*, 1992.
33. KHRP, *The Safe Haven in Northern Iraq*, p.149.
34. Freedman and Boren, 'Safe Havens for Kurds in Post-War Iraq', p.71.
35. KHRP, *The Safe Haven in Northern Iraq*, p.46.
36. European Council Declaration on the Situation in Iraq, Luxembourg, 28–29 June 1991.
37. Saleh Barham, *Observer*, 21 April 1991, cited in McDowall, *A Modern History of the Kurds*, p.376.
38. UNHCR, *Report on Northern Iraq*, 1992, para.1.17.

6 DEMOCRACY IN IRAQI KURDISTAN

1. Falaq al-Din Kakai, 'The Kurdish Parliament', *Iraq Since the Gulf War: Prospects for Democracy* (ed. Fran Hazelton) (London and New Jersey: Zed Books, 1994), p.118.
2. Statement of Margaret Tutwiler, Spokesperson, US Department of State, 15 May 1992.
3. International Human Rights Law Group, *Ballots Without Borders*, 1992, p.21, cited in KHRP, *The Safe Haven in Northern Iraq* (London: KHRP, 1995), p.79.
4. Ibid.
5. Pax Christi, *Elections in Iraqi Kurdistan – an Experiment in Democracy*, August 1992.
6. Kakai, 'The Kurdish Parliament', p.119.
7. Ibid., p.123, and Pax Christi, *Elections in Iraqi Kurdistan*, p.32.
8. Kakai, 'The Kurdish Parliament', p.125.

9. Ibid., p.120.
10. Ibid.
11. Ibid., cited at p.130.
12. Natasha Carver, 'Is Iraq/Kurdistan a State Such That it Can be Said to Operate State Systems and Thereby Offer Protection to its Citizens?', *International Journal of Refugee Law*, Vol. 14, p.61.
13. Iraq had withdrawn the 25 dinar note from circulation, forbidding residents of the Kurdish-administered north to exchange it, at one stroke wiping out half the savings of the population.
14. Cited in *Kurdistan Review*, April 1994, p.10.
15. Michael Gunter, *The Kurdish Predicament in Iraq – A Political Analysis* (London: Macmillan, 1999), p.77.
16. For more information on the INC see Chapter 14 of this volume.
17. Gunter, *The Kurdish Predicament*, p.80.
18. Alfred B. Prados, *The Kurds: Stalemate in Iraq*, Congressional Research Service Report, 16 November 1995, p.4.
19. Gunter, *The Kurdish Predicament*, p.85.
20. Ibid., p.100.

7 HUMAN RIGHTS IN IRAQI KURDISTAN

1. Amnesty International Report, 1977.
2. David McDowall, *A Modern History of the Kurds* (London: I.B. Tauris, 2001), p.339.
3. Amnesty International Reports 1978 and 1986.
4. UNHCR, *Report on Northern Iraq April 1991 – May 1992*, 1992, Annex V-1.
5. Mine Action Group, Introduction, Programmes, Northern Iraq, <www.mag.org.uk/magtest/magwproj/projirq.htm>.
6. Human Rights Watch, *Iraq: Forcible Expulsion of Ethnic Minorities*, Vol. 15, No. 3(E), March 2003, available at <www.hrw.org/reports/2003/iraq0303/Kirkuk0303.pdf>.
7. See Chapter 8, 'Gross Violations of Human Rights in Iraq', KHRP, *The Safe Haven in Northern Iraq* (London: KHRP, 1995).
8. The following are treaties to which Iraq is a party:

   • The Convention on the Prevention and Punishment of the Crime of Genocide (date of accession: 20 January 1959)
   • The International Convention on the Suppression and Punishment of the Crime of Apartheid (date of ratification: 9 July 1975)
   • The International Covenant on Civil and Political Rights (date of ratification: 23 March 1976). Iraq has not made the declaration under Article 41 of this Convention recognising the competence of the Human Rights Committee to consider inter-state complaints. Neither has it ratified the Optional Protocol No. 1 to the Convention recognising the Committee's competence to consider complaints of violations submitted by individuals, or Optional Protocol No. 2 aimed at the abolition of the death penalty

- The International Covenant on Economic, Social and Cultural Rights (date of ratification: 3 January 1976)
- The International Convention on the Elimination of All Forms of Racial Discrimination (date of ratification: 13 February 1970). Iraq has not made the declaration under Article 14 of this Convention recognising the competence of the Committee on the Elimination of Racial Discrimination to consider complaints of violations submitted by individuals. It also made a reservation to Article 22 indicating that it did not accept the jurisdiction of the International Court of Justice over disputes between state parties as to the interpretation or application of the Convention
- The Convention on the Elimination of All Forms of Discrimination against Women (date of accession: 12 September 1986). Iraq made reservations to substantive Articles 2(f) and (g), 9 (1) and (2), and 16. It also made a reservation in respect of Article 29 (1) indicating that it did not accept the jurisdiction of the ICJ over disputes between state parties as to the interpretation or application of the Convention. It did not ratify the Optional Protocol which enables individuals to bring claims to the Committee
- The Convention on the Rights of the Child (date of ratification: 15 July 1994). Iraq made a reservation to substantive Article 14 (1) of this Convention concerning the child's freedom of religion.

9. UN Doc. E/CN.4/1992/31 at paras 103 and 153.
10. These include the Body of Principles of the Protection of All Persons Under Any Form of Detention or Imprisonment of 1988; the Declaration on the Protection of All Persons from Enforced Disappearances of 1992; the Principles on the Effective Prevention and Investigation of Extra-Legal, Arbitrary and Summary Executions of 1989; the Safeguards Guaranteeing the Protection of those Facing the Death Penalty of 1984; the Code of Conduct for Law Enforcement Officials of 1979; and the Basic Principles on the Use of Force and Firearms by Law Enforcement Officials 1990.
11. These include the Geneva Convention for the Amelioration of the Condition of the Wounded and Sick in Armed Forces in the Field; the Geneva Conventions for the Amelioration of the Condition of Wounded, Sick and Shipwrecked Members of the Armed Forces at Sea; the Geneva Convention relative to the Treatment of Prisoners of War; the Geneva Convention relative to the Protection of Civilian Persons in Time of War.
12. The following acts are absolutely prohibited: (i) violence to life and person, including murder of all kinds, mutilation, cruel treatment and torture; (ii) taking of hostages; (iii) outrages upon personal dignity, in particular humiliating and degrading treatment; (iv) the passing of sentences and the carrying out of executions without previous judgment pronounced by a regularly constituted court, affording all the judicial guarantees which are recognised as indispensable by civilised peoples.
13. Full text of Resolution 2444 (XXIII) 1968 available at <http://ods-dds-ny.un.org/doc/RESOLUTION/GEN/NR0/244/04/IMG/NR024404.pdf?OpenElement>.

14. Full text of the Declaration available at <www.unhchr.ch/html/menu3/b/24.htm>.
15. Full text of Statute available at <www.un.org/icty/legaldoc/index.htm>.
16. KHRP, *After the War: Report of the KHRP Fact-Finding Mission to Iraqi Kurdistan* (London: KHRP, 2003).
17. UNICEF, Iraq report, *Children and women in Iraq*, 1993.
18. Suha Omar, 'Women: Honour, Shame and Dictatorship', *Iraq Since the Gulf War: Prospects for Democracy* (Ed. Fran Hazelton, London & New Jersey: Zed Books, 1994).
19. Ibid.
20. Amnesty International, 'Iraq: Decades of Suffering, Now Women Deserve Better', 22 February 2005, <http://web.amnesty.org/library/pdf/MDE140012005ENGLISH/$File/MDE1400105.pdf>.
21. Taler Nadar, 'Kurds Still Seeking Lost Women', <www.peacewomen.org/news/Iraq/June04/kurds.html>.
22. 'Open Letter to Mrs Mubarak regarding Kurdish Anfal Girls', Open Letter from Françoise Brié, Director of Alliance Internationale pour la Justice to President of the National Council of Women, Cairo, Egypt, 1 August 2003, <www.kurdishmedia.com/news.asp?id=4175>.
23. Nadar, 'Kurds Still Seeking Lost Women'.
24. UN-HABITAT, *Three-Year Plan: Settlement Rehabilitation Sector in Northern Iraq 2003–2005*, December 2002.
25. Ibid.
26. KHRP, FFM interview, Director of Social Action, Cilura Hardi, Erbil, 1 September 2003.
27. Amnesty International, 'Iraq: Decades of Suffering, Now Women Deserve Better'.
28. Article 14.
29. Article 16.
30. Article 20.
31. Article 29(4).
32. Cyrille Cartier, 'Iraqi Kurdish Women Voice Hopes for Constitution', 25 April 2006, *WeNews*, <http://womensenews.org/article.cfm/dyn/aid/2717>.

8 THE DISPLACEMENT OF KURDS IN IRAQ

1. Sarah Graham-Brown, April 1998, 'The Kurds – A Regional Issue: update to April 1998', UNHCR Writenet Country Papers, available at <http://web.archive.org/web/20010408203828/www.unhcr.ch/refworld/country/writenet/wrikurd02.htm>, accessed 18 July 2002.
2. Norwegian Refugee Council/Global IDP Project, 'Profile of Internal Displacement: Iraq', July 2005, p. 9, available at <www.idpproject.org>.
3. Human Rights Watch, *Iraq: Forcible Expulsion of Ethnic Minorities*, Vol. 15, No. 3(E), March 2003, available at <www.hrw.org/reports/2003/iraq0303/Kirkuk0303.pdf>.

4. Norwegian Refugee Council/Global IDP Project, 'Profile of International Displacement: Iraq'.
5. Nouri Talabany, 'Iraq's Policy of Ethnic Cleaning: Onslaught to Change National/Demographic Characteristic of the Kirkuk Region', London, 1999, available at <www.kirkuk.kurdishpoint.com/>.
6. John Fawcett and Victor Tanner, *The Internally Displaced People of Iraq*, The Brookings Institution-SAIS Project on International Displacement, available at <www.reliefweb.int/library/documents/2002/brook-irq-31oct.pdf>.
7. Human Rights Watch, *Iraq: Forcible Expulsion of Ethnic Minorities*.
8. KHRP, FFM interview, displaced person: Ali, Takiyeh camp, near Sulaimanya, Northern Iraq, 30 August 2003.
9. Human Rights Watch, *Iraq: Forcible Expulsion Of Ethnic Minorities*.
10. Chris Dammers, 'Iraq', *Internally Displaced People: A Global Survey* (ed. Janie Hampton) (London, Earthscan 1998), p. 182.
11. UNHCR, August, Country of Origin Information – Iraq.

9 ECONOMIC/HUMANITARIAN AFFAIRS IN IRAQI KURDISTAN

1. Alexander's Oil & Gas Connections, *Iraq Report*, 2003.
2. Baker Institute, *Report on Iraq*, 2002.
3. Full text of Resolution 986 1995 available at <http://ods-dds-ny.un.org/doc/UNDOC/GEN/N95/109/88/PDF/N9510988.pdf?OpenElement>.
4. Alexander's Oil & Gas Connections, *Iraq Report*.
5. Ibid.
6. Ibid.
7. Baker Institute, *Report on Iraq*.
8. Human Rights Watch, *Iraq: Forcible Expulsion of Ethnic Minorities*, Vol. 15, No. 3(E), March 2003, available at <www.hrw.org/reports/2003/iraq0303/Kirkuk0303.pdf>.
9. David McDowall, *A Modern History of the Kurds* (London: I.B. Tauris, 2001), p.314.
10. *Arabic News*, 16 January 2001.
11. Full text of Resolution 660 1990 available at <http://ods-dds-ny.un.org/doc/RESOLUTION/GEN/NR0/575/10/IMG/NR057510.pdf?OpenElement>.
12. Full text of Resolution 661 1990 available at <http://ods-dds-ny.un.org/doc/RESOLUTION/GEN/NR0/575/11/IMG/NR057511.pdf?OpenElement>.
13. Paul Lewis, 'After The War; U.N. Survey Calls Iraq's War Damage Near-Apocalyptic', *New York Times*, 22 March 1991, available at <www.scn.org/ccpi/NYTimesAhtisaari21Mar91.html>.
14. Full text of Resolution 706 1991 available at <http://ods-dds-ny.un.org/doc/RESOLUTION/GEN/NR0/596/42/IMG/NR059642.pdf?OpenElement>.
15. Full text of Resolution 712 1991 available at <http://ods-dds-ny.un.org/doc/RESOLUTION/GEN/NR0/596/48/IMG/NR059648.pdf?OpenElement>.

16. Lewis, 'After The War'.
17. For further information (if uncritical) on the Oil-for-Food Programme and these organisations see <www.un.org/depts/oip/background/index. html>.
18. 'Since 1997 and the start of the OFFP, the situation in Northern Iraq has improved, albeit in a very uneven manner. Education, health, and water and sanitation facilities are being reconstructed and service delivery is improving, due to more imports of equipment, spares and supplies. Food rations meet the basic needs of the population. UN organisations and other international donors have carried out intensive and effective immunisation and disease control campaigns and restored clean water supplies. This has significantly improved the health status of the population.' UNICEF, *The Situation of Children in Iraq*, 2003, available at <www.unicef.org/publications/pub_children_of_iraq_en.pdf>.
19. Ibid.
20. KHRP interviews with PUK and KDP officials in London, June and July 2003.
21. UNICEF, *The Situation of Children in Iraq*.
22. Ibid.
23. Ibid.
24. KHRP, FFM interview: Minister of Human Rights, Saleh Rashid, Sulaimaniya, September 2003.
25. KHRP, FFM interview: Deputy Minister, Ministry of Humanitarian Aid Cooperation (MOHAC), Hushyar Silyari, September 2003.
26. McDowall, *A Modern History of the Kurds*, p.378.
27. Ibid.
28. KHRP, *The Safe Haven in Northern Iraq* (London: KHRP, 1995), p.65.
29. KHRP interview: Middle East Co-ordinator, Save the Children UK, Chris Saunders, London July 2003.
30. KHRP, FFM interviews, Iraq, August 2003.
31. KHRP telephone interview, David Greenhalgh, Mines Advisory Group (MAG).
32. Further information available at <www.mag.org.uk/magtest/magwproj/ projirq.htm>.
33. Further information available at <www.savethechildren.org.uk/scuk/ jsp/wherewework/country.jsp?section=middleeastnthafrica&subsectio n=iraq>.

10 THE KURDS HAVE NO FRIENDS BUT THE MOUNTAINS

1. In 2001 the PKK dissolved to be replaced by the Kurdistan Freedom and Democracy Congress (KADEK). In November 2003, KADEK also dissolved.
2. Katherine A. Wilkens, *Washington Post*, 15 September 1996.
3. David McDowall, *A Modern History of the Kurds* (London: I.B. Tauris, 2001), p.384.
4. 'Turkey's Military Offensive in Northern Iraq', *CRS Report*, 13 April 1995.

5. See for example Human Rights Watch World Report, 1999, <www.hrw. org/worldreport99/mideast/iraq.html>.
6. *Issa v. Turkey* (31821/96).
7. Reuters, 29 March 1995.
8. 'Turkey's military offensive in Northern Iraq'.
9. Leader of the PKK.
10. Vedat Turkali, 'Resistance and Repression after the Creation of the State of Turkey', *A Democratic Future for the Kurds of Turkey* (London: KHRP, 1995).
11. KHRP, *Internally Displaced Persons: The Kurds in Turkey* (London: KHRP, June 2002).
12. Martin Van Bruinessen, 'Genocide in Kurdistan? The Suppression of the Dersim Rebellion in Turkey (1937–38) and the Chemical War against the Iraqi Kurds', *Conceptual and Historical Dimensions of Genocide* (ed. George J. Andreopoulos) (Philadelphia: University of Pennsylvania Press, 1994), pp.141–70.
13. Erik J. Zurcher, *Turkey, A Modern History* (London: I.B. Tauris, 1993), p.325.
14. KHRP, *Internally Displaced Persons*.
15. Ibid.
16. 'Turkish Forces Change Tactics Against Rebel Kurds', Reuters, 30 July 1994.
17. Committee on Migration, Refugees and Demography of the Council of Europe, *Report on the Humanitarian Situation of the Kurdish Refugees and Displaced Persons in South-East Turkey and North Iraq*, Doc. 8131, June 1998, para.14.
18. KHRP, *In the Wake of the Lifting of State of Emergency Legislation: Report of the Fact-Finding Mission to Southeast Turkey*, 2002.
19. McDowall, *A Modern History of the Kurds*.
20. UN Document A/56/278.
21. McDowall, *A Modern History of the Kurds*, p.446.
22. Ibid.
23. Ibid.
24. Omar Sheikhmous Paper presented at the international conference 'Iraqi Kurdistan – Status and Prospects' organised by Awadani e.v. at *Haus der Kulturen der Welt* in Berlin, 9–10 April 1999.
25. Ibid.

11 US FOREIGN POLICY TOWARDS SADDAM: PRE-SEPTEMBER 11

1. 'Deep Roots of Bush's Hatred for Saddam', *Observer*, 16 March 2003, <http://observer.guardian.co.uk/iraq/story/0,12239,914925,00.html>.
2. Ibid.
3. Ibid.
4. Ibid.
5. Ibid.
6. 'Attack on Iraqi Anti-Aircraft Site Self-Defence, says Clinton', *Irish Examiner*, 29 December 1998, <http://archives.tcm.ie/irishexaminer/ 1998/12/29/fhead.htm>.

7. 'The Plan: Were Neo-Conservatives' 1998 Memos a Blueprint for Iraq War?', ABCnews.com, 10 March 2003, available at <www.aaiusa.org/news/must_read03_10_03abc.htm>.
8. Remarks by the President in Address to the Nation, White House, 26 June 1993, available at <www.fas.org/irp/news/1993/930626i.htm>.
9. Bradley Graham, 'US Launches More Cruise Missiles Against Iraq', WashingtonPost.com, 4 September 1996, <www.washingtonpost.com/wp-srv/inatl/longterm/iraq/timeline/090496.htm>.
10. 'Pentagon Unveils Details of Operation Desert Fox', CNN.com, 16 December 1998, <www.cnn.com/WORLD/meast/9812/16/pentagon.02/>.
11. Jason Leopold, 'When Bush First Vowed to 'Take Out' Saddam ... December 1999', Counter Punch, 17 January 2003, <www.counterpunch.org/leopold01172003.html>.
12. Johanna McGeary, 'Bush vs. Saddam the Sequel', Inside Politics, CNN.com, 19 February 2001, <http://edition.cnn.com/ALLPOLITICS/time/2001/02/26/sequal.html>.

12 THE ROAD TO WAR

1. Please note that throughout Part II, dates may vary depending on what sources were used. For example when President Bush declared war on Iraq it was 20 March 2003 in Baghdad but 19 March 2003 in the US.
2. US President George Bush, Address to a Joint Session of Congress and the American People, 20 September 2001, <www.whitehouse.gov/news/releases/2001/09/20010920-8.html>.
3. State of the Union Address, 29 January 2002, <www.whitehouse.gov/news/releases/2002/01/20020129-11.html>.
4. For more information see the Clinton Doctrine of Humanitarian Interventions at <www.globalissues.org/Geopolitics/Empire/Clinton.asp>.
5. 'China Berates Axis of Evil Remarks', CNN.com, 31 January 2002, <http://edition.cnn.com/2002/WORLD/asiapcf/east/01/31/china.bush/>.
6. Sarah Left, 'Terror Targets Condemn Bush's Speech', Guardian, 31 January 2002, <www.guardian.co.uk/bush/story/0,7369,642524,00.html>.
7. Michael White and Nicholas Watt, 'Tension Grows as Iraq Dismisses Blair Demands', Guardian, 8 April 2002, <www.guardian.co.uk/Distribution/Redirect_Artifact/0,4678,0-680622,00.html>.
8. Chris Alden, 'Defector Reveals Extent of Iraqi Weapons Programme', Guardian, 4 April 2002, <www.guardian.co.uk/Iraq/Story/0,2763,678610,00.html>.
9. Toby Helm and George Jones, 'Germany Leads Revolt Against Iraq Attack', Telegraph, 16 March 2002, <www.telegraph.co.uk/news/main.jhtml?xml=/news/2002/03/16/wsum116.xml>.
10. John Hooper and Richard Norton-Taylor, 'UN Must Sanction Iraq Strike', Guardian, 31 July 2002, <www.guardian.co.uk/international/story/0,3604,765887,00.html>.

11. Ibid.
12. 'UN Rejects Iraqi Proposal on Weapons Talks', 6 August 2002, <http://usinfo.state.gov/topical/pol/arms/02080602.htm>
13. 'Vice President Speaks at VFW 103rd National Convention', 26 August 2002, <www.whitehouse.gov/news/releases/2002/08/20020826.html>.
14. Patrick Wintour and Julian Borger, 'Bush Gives UN Last Chance', *Guardian*, 9 September 2002, <www.guardian.co.uk/Iraq/Story/0,2763,788595,00.html>.
15. Dan Plesch, Peter Beaumont and Paul Beaver, 'US Pours Arms into Gulf Region', *Observer*, 8 September 2002, <http://observer.guardian.co.uk/international/story/0,6903,788172,00.html>.
16. Statement by President Bush, United Nations General Assembly, 12 September 2002, <www.un.org/webcast/ga/57/statements/020912usaE.htm>.
17. 'Iraq Agrees to Unconditional Return of Weapons Inspectors', 16 September 2002, <www.un.org/av/photo/sc/sept1602.htm>.
18. 'Iraq's Weapons Deal May Not Satisfy UK and US', TCM Archives, 1 October 2002, <http://archives.tcm.ie/breakingnews/2002/10/01/story70712.asp>.
19. Ibid.
20. For more information see online newspapers such as the *Guardian* at <www.guardian.co.uk> or online news such as CNN at<www.cnn.com>.
21. House Joint Resolution Authorising Use of Force Against Iraq, 10 October 2002, <www.usinfo.state.gov/regional/nea/iraq/text/1010res.htm>.
22. 'Saddam wins 100% of vote', BBC news online, 16 October 2002, <http://news.bbc.co.uk/1/hi/world/middle_east/2331951.stm>.
23. Full text of Resolution 1441 2002 available at <http://ods-dds-ny.un.org/doc/UNDOC/GEN/N02/682/26/PDF/N0268226.pdf?OpenElement>.
24. 'In Quotes: Iraq MPs Condemn UN', BBC news online, 12 November 2002, <http://news.bbc.co.uk/2/hi/middle_east/2446197.stm>.
25. 'US Passes Iraq Resolution on Weapons Inspections', CNN.com/US, 8 November 2002, <http://edition.cnn.com/2002/US/11/08/iraq.resolution/>.
26. 'Iraq: Our Region Reacts', Chronology, Go Asia Pacific, <www.abc.net.au/asiapacific/specials/iraq/chronology/default9.htm>.
27. Ibid.
28. Oliver Burkeman, 'Tension Over Claim of Iraqi Violation', *Guardian*, 19 November 2002, <www.guardian.co.uk/international/story/0,3604,842960,00.html>.
29. Bill Vann, 'US, British Air Strikes Kill Iraqi Oil Workers', *World Socialist Website*, 3 December 2002, <www.wsws.org/articles/2002/dec2002/iraq-d03.shtml>.
30. Foreign & Commonwealth Office, *Saddam Hussein: Crimes and Human Rights Abuses: A Report on the Human Costs of Saddam's Policies by the Foreign & Commonwealth Office*, November 2002.
31. 'Iraq Sticks to Story', CBSnews.com, 7 December 2002, <www.cbsnews.com/stories/2002/12/08/attack/main532185.shtml>.

32. Ibid.
33. 'US Says Iraqi Declaration Constitutes Material Breach', 19 December 2002, <http://usinfo.state.gov/topical/pol/arms/02121900.htm>
34. Ibid.
35. Jack Fairweather, '50,000 Troops Sent to Gulf', *The Sun-Herald*, 22 December 2002, available at <www.smh.com.au/articles/2002/12/21/1040174438047.html>.
36. 'Iraq Shoots Down US Unmanned Drone', Fox news.com, 23 December 2002, <www.foxnews.com/story/0,2933,73735,00.html>.
37. 'Saudis to Let US Use Bases', BBC news, 29 December 2002, <http://news.bbc.co.uk/2/low/middle_east/2612455.stm>.
38. 'Britain, France get Ready for Iraq', CBSnews.com, 7 January 2003, <www.cbsnews.com/stories/2003/01/08/world/main535639.shtml>.
39. 'Full Text: Saddam's Speech', *Guardian*, 6 January 2003, <www.guardian.co.uk/Iraq/Story/0,2763,869642,00.html>.
40. Ibid.
41. Nick Paton Walsh, 'Russian Warships on Standby to Sail to Gulf', *Guardian*, 10 January 2003, <www.guardian.co.uk/international/story/0,3604,871983,00.html>.
42. 'No Smoking Guns in Iraq Arm Search', BBC News.com, 9 January 2003, <http://news.bbc.co.uk/2/hi/middle_east/2641973.stm>.
43. Vernon Loeb, IntelligenCIA, 30 January 2003, <www.washingtonpost.com/wp-dyn/nation/columns/intelligencia/>.
44. 'Nato Issues', 24 July 2003, <www.nato.int/issues/faq/index.htm#A4>.
45. David Cortright, Alistair Millar, George A. Lopez and Linda Gerber, 'UN Weapons Inspections in Iraq: a Progress Report', A Report of the Sanctions and Security Project of the Fourth Freedom Forum and the Joan B. Kroc Institute for International Peace Studies at the University of Notre Dame, 23 January 2003, <www.nd.edu/~krocinst/research/inspections_report.pdf>.
46. 'Security Council Briefed by Chief UN Weapons Experts on First 60 Days of Inspections in Iraq', Press Release, United Nations Economic and Social Commission for Western Asia, 27 January 2003, <www.escwa.org.lb/information/press/un/2003/jan/27_3.html>.
47. Ibid.
48. 'Hans Blix Delivers Report on Iraqi Inspections', ABC online home, 28 January 2003, <www.abc.net.au/am/s771061.htm>.
49. Wendy Ross, 'U.S. Says January 27 Reports Show Iraq Not Complying with UN', 27 January 2003, <http://usinfo.state.gov/topical/pol/arms/03012714.htm>.
50. Terry Cook, 'Australian Prime Minister Assists US Push for War', World Socialist Website, 30 January 2003, <www.wsws.org/articles/2003/jan2003/aust-j30.shtml>.
51. 'President Delivers State of the Union', 28 January 2003, <www.whitehouse.gov/news/releases/2003/01/20030128–19.html>.
52. Ibid.
53. 'Letter Widens Europe Rift on Iraq', CNN.com/World, 30 January 2003, <www.cnn.com/2003/WORLD/europe/01/30/sprj.irq.europe.eight.reaction/>.

54. 'Transcript of Powell's UN Presentation', CNN.com/US, 6 February 2003, <http://edition.cnn.com/2003/US/02/05/sprj.irq.powell.transcript/>.
55. 'UN Must Get Tough With Iraq: Powell', CBC news, 14 February 2003, <www.cbc.ca/stories/2003/02/14/us_reax1030214>.
56. Full text of the North Atlantic Treaty 1949 available at <www.nato.int/docu/basictxt/treaty.htm>.
57. 14 February 2003, transcript available at <www.un.org/Depts/unmovic/blix14Febasdel.htm>.
58. Andrea Koppel and Elise Labbot, 'Text: Iraq Failed to Take Final Opportunity', CNN.com/US, 24 February 2003, <http://edition.cnn.com/2003/US/02/24/sprj.irq.new.resolution/>.
59. 'Europeans Make Counter Proposal', CNN.com/World, 25 February 2003, <http://edition.cnn.com/2003/WORLD/meast/02/24/sprj.irq.iraq.germany.france/>.
60. CBS News transcript: Saddam Hussein interview available at <www.cbsnews.com/stories/2003/02/26/60II/main542151.shtml>.
61. For information on al-Samoud missiles see <www.globalsecurity.org/wmd/world/iraq/samoud.htm>.
62. Unofficial translation available at <www.cnn.com/2003/WORLD/meast/02/28/sprj.irq.letter/>.
63. 7 March 2003, transcript available at <www.un.org/Depts/unmovic/SC7asdelivered.htm>.
64. Brian Whittaker, 'UK Proposes Six Weapons Tests for Saddam', *Guardian*, 13 March 2003, <http://politics.guardian.co.uk/foreignaffairs/story/0,11538,913135,00.html>.
65. 'Foreign Secretary: UK Ready for War', FoxNews.com, 15 March 2003, <www.foxnews.com/story/0,2933,81171,00.html>.
66. 'President Bush: Monday 'Moment of Truth' for World on Iraq', 16 March 2003, <www.whitehouse.gov/news/releases/2003/03/20030316–3. html>.
67. 'Bush Counts Down to War', BBC news, 15 March 2003, <http://news.bbc.co.uk/1/hi/world/middle_east/2853295.stm>.
68. 'Belgium to Refuse Transit to US Forces if Iraq War Declared Without UN Backing', ABCnews online, 16 March 2003, <http://abc.net.au/news/newsitems/s808074.htm>.
69. 'Secretary Powell Urges Foreigners to Leave Iraq', Iraq Crisis Bulletin, 17 March 2003, <www.iraqcrisisbulletin.com/archives/031703/html/secretary__powell_urges_foreig.html>.
70. 'President Says Saddam Hussein Must Leave Iraq Within 48 Hours', 17 March 2003, <www.whitehouse.gov/news/releases/2003/03/20030317–7. html>.
71. Michael Howard, 'Militant Kurds Training al-Qaida Fighters', *Guardian*, 23 August 2002, <www.guardian.co.uk/international/story/0,3604,779223,00.html>.
72. Ibid.
73. Michael Howard, 'Kurdish Leader Shuns US Move to Oust Saddam', *Guardian*, 19 June 2003, <www.guardian.co.uk/international/story/0,3604,739786,00.html>.

74. Jonny Dymond, 'Turkey Deals a Blow to Action Against Saddam', *Guardian*, 1 August 2002, <www.guardian.co.uk/international/story/0,3604,767002,00.html>.

75. See Appendix II.

76. 'Truck, Missile Movement Reported in Iraq', Cnn.com/World, 16 August 2002, <http://edition.cnn.com/2002/WORLD/meast/08/15/iraq.us/>.

77. Ian Fisher, 'Turkey Grows More Worried Every Day About a US Attack on Iraq', *New York Times*, 28 October 2002, available at <www.geocities.com/tom_slouck/iraq/turkey_chills_to_war.html>.

78. 'Turkey Qualifies Role in UN Crisis', BBC news, 3 December 2002, <http://news.bbc.co.uk/2/hi/europe/2541025.stm>.

79. 'Turkey Ups Stakes on US Troops', BBC news, 19 February 2003, <http://news.bbc.co.uk/2/hi/europe/2773877.stm>.

80. BBC news correspondent, *The Battle for Iraq* (London: BBC Consumer Publishing, 2003), p.163.

81. 'Turkey Delays Vote on US Troops', *Guardian*, 27 February 2003, <www.guardian.co.uk/Iraq/Story/0,2763,904067,00.html>.

13 THE SECOND GULF WAR: 'OPERATION IRAQI FREEDOM'

1. Iraqi Information Minister, Mohammed Saeed al-Sahhaf, Al-Jazeera TV, 25 March 2003.

2. 'President Bush Addresses the Nation', <www.whitehouse.gov/news/releases/2003/03/20030319–17.html>.

3. 'US Launches Cruise Missiles at Saddam', CNN.com, 20 March 2003, <http://edition.cnn.com/2003/WORLD/meast/03/19/sprj.irq.main/>.

4. Amberin Zaman, 'Turkey Allows US to Use its Airspace', *Telegraph*, 22 March 2003, <www.telegraph.co.uk/news/main.jhtml;$sessionid$CIJX3IXKVNYCHQFIQMGCFF4AVCBQUIV0?xml=/news/2003/03/21/wstrat21.xml>.

5. 'Russia, China, France Blast Opening of Iraq War', PBS news, 20 March 2003, <www.pbs.org/newshour/updates/worldreaction_3–20.html>.

6. Stephanie Ho, 'US Says Number of Dropped Leaflets Reaches 28 Million', Iraq Crisis bulletin, 25 March 2003, <www.iraqcrisisbulletin.com/archives/032503/html/u_s__says_number_of_dropped_le.html>.

7. 'Saddam Fired Banned Missiles?', CBS News.com, 20 March 2003, <www.cbsnews.com/stories/2003/03/20/iraq/main544972.shtml>.

8. 'Iraq Faces Massive US Military Barrage', CBS Evening News, 24 January 2003, <www.cbsnews.com/stories/2003/01/24/eveningnews/main537928.shtml>.

9. Dietz Smith, 'The Mad Dash for Oil', *The Rant*, 31 January 2003, <www.therant.info/archive/000388.html>.

10. Abbas Diavadi, 'Turkish Troops in Northern Iraq? Yes, No, Perhaps', Eurasianet.org, 24 March 2003, <www.eurasianet.org/departments/insight/articles/pp032403_pr.shtml>.

11. Ibid.

12. BBC news correspondent, *The Battle for Iraq* (London: BBC Consumer Publishing, 2003), p.164.

13. 'Kurdish Victory as Terrorists Routed in North', Smh.com.au, 2 April 2003, <www.smh.com.au/articles/2003/04/01/1048962762243.html>.
14. Julius Strauss, 'Kurds Sweep into Kirkuk', *Telegraph*, 11 April 2003, <www.telegraph.co.uk/news/main.jhtml?xml=/news/2003/04/11/war11.xml>.
15. Daniel Williams, 'Iraqi Forces Surrender in Mosul', *Washington Post*, 11 April 2003, <www.mre.gov.br/acs/interclip2/Diario-WL/Abril-03/Materias/wpost11c.htm>.
16. Michael Howard, 'Arabs Face Evictions as Kurds Take Revenge', *Guardian*, 18 April 2003, <www.guardian.co.uk/The_Kurds/Story/0,2763,939140,00.html>.
17. Luke Harding, 'Kurdish Fighters Take Kirkuk', *Guardian*, 11 April 2003, <www.guardian.co.uk/print/0,3858,4645830–103624,00.html>.
18. Ibid.
19. Ibid.
20. Ibid.
21. Luke Harding, 'Pro-Saddam Gangs Challenge Marines' Control of Tikrit', *Guardian*, 16 April 2003, <www.guardian.co.uk/Iraq/Story/0,2763,937633,00.html>.
22. Helena Smith, 'Peshmerga Pledge May Ease Turkish Fears', *Guardian*, 11 April 2003, <www.guardian.co.uk/The_Kurds/Story/0,2763,934506,00.html>.
23. Ibid.
24. 'Turkey Sends Observers to Northern Iraq', *The Straits Times Interactive*, <straitstimes.asia1.com.sg/iraqwar/story/0,4395,182590,00.html>.
25. Nicholas Christian, 'US Risks Provoking Kurds with Turkish Peacekeeping Request', 20 April 2003, <http://209.157.64.200/focus/f-news/896692/posts>.
26. Helena Smith, 'Turkey Told US Will Remove Kurd Forces from City', *Guardian*, 11 April 2003, <www.guardian.co.uk/The_Kurds/Story/0,2763,934330,00.html>.
27. David Rohe, 'US Says Turks are Smuggling Arms into Northern Iraq City', *Kurdistan Observer*, 27 April 2003, <http://home.cogeco.ca/~kobserver/26–4–03-tky-smuggling-arms-to-kirkuk.html>.
28. 'Bush Calls End to Major Combat', CNN.com/World, 2 May 2003, <http://edition.cnn.com/2003/WORLD/meast/05/01/sprj.irq.main/>.
29. Email from CPIC Press Desk to KHRP, 8 December 2003.
30. 'Al-Qaida Fighters Arrested in Iraq', *Guardian*, 11 November 2003, <www.guardian.co.uk/international/story/0,3604,1082675,00.html>.
31. 'DHL Plane Hit by Missile in Iraq', *Airwise*, 22 November 2003, <http://news.airwise.com/stories/2003/11/1069497490.html>.
32. Rory McCarthy, 'Saddam's Arrest Fuels Insurgency', *Guardian*, 18 December 2003, <www.guardian.co.uk/international/story/0,3604,1109175,00.html>.
33. 'Great Deal of Progress made at EU Enlargement Talks', 15 December 2003, <www.number-10.gov.uk/output/Page5047.asp>.
34. ABC news, <http://abcnews.go.com/sections/wnt/World/Iraq_infiltrators_031218.html>.

35. 'Oral Answers to Questions: Defence', House of Commons, 15 December 2003, <www.parliament.the-stationery-office.co.uk/pa/cm200304/cmhansrd/cm031215/debtext/31215–01.htm>.
36. Maggy Zanger, 'Kurds Keep Iraq at Arms Length', 14 November 2003, available at <www.reliefweb.int/w/rwb.nsf/0/b86ba72a3b6e611549256de1000a7293?OpenDocument>.
37. 'Ansar Al-Islam Key Threat to US in Iraq', FoxNews.com, 23 October 2003, <www.foxnews.com/story/0,2933,101054,00.html>.
38. Michael Howard, 'Al-Qaida Linked to Bombing of Kurds', *Guardian*, 21 November 2003, <www.guardian.co.uk/international/story/0,3604,1089802,00.html>.
39. Joseph Curl, 'Bush Cites US Moves to Counter Iraq Attacks', *Washington Times*, 12 November 2003, <www.washtimes.com/national/20031111–105250–7570r.htm>.
40. Rajiv Chandrasekaran, 'US to Form Iraqi Paramilitary Force', *Washington Post*, 3 December 2003, <www.washingtonpost.com/ac2/wp-dyn?pagename=article&node=&contentId=A29753–2003Dec2&notFound=true>.
41. Ibid.

14 CURRENT EXECUTIVE STRUCTURE IN IRAQ

1. 'The Vision for Iraq', Iraqi National Congress, London, 1999, available at Iraq Watch, <www.iraqwatch.org/perspectives/INC-Vision%20for%20Iraq.htm>.
2. 'Who's Who in Iraqi Opposition', BBC News World Edition, 17 February 2003, <http://news.bbc.co.uk/2/hi/middle_east/1881381.stm>.
3. 'Defence Department to Expand Training of Iraqi Opposition', 11 December 2003, <http://usinfo.state.gov/regional/nea/iraq/text/1211rkr1.htm>.
4. Coalition Provisional Authority (CPA), *Historical Accomplishments*, available at <www.cpa-iraq.org>, accessed 13 June 2006.
5. United Nations Security Council Resolution 1483, 22 May 2003, available at <http://daccessdds.un.org/doc/UNDOC/GEN/N03/368/53/PDF/N0336853.pdf?OpenElement>, accessed 13 June 2006.
6. United Nations Security Council Resolution 1511, 16 October 2003, available at <http://daccessdds.un.org/doc/UNDOC/GEN/N03/563/91/PDF/N0356391.pdf?OpenElement>, accesssed 13 June 2006.
7. United Nations Security Council Resolution 1500, 14 August 2003, available at <http://daccessdds.un.org/doc/UNDOC/GEN/N03/467/78/PDF/N0346778.pdf?OpenElement>, accesssed 13 June 2006.
8. Bureau of Democracy, Human Rights, and Labor, *International Religious Freedom Report 2005*, available at <www.state.gov/g/drl/rls/irf/2005/51600.htm>, accesssed 13 June 2006.
9. Ed O'Keefe, 'Bremer: Insurgency "More Resilient" Than Expected', ABC News, 11 June 2006, available at <http://abcnews.go.com/ThisWeek/Politics/story?id=2063455&page=1&CMP=OTC-RSSFeeds0312>, accesssed 13 June 2006.
10. CPA, *Historical Accomplishments*.

11. CPA, ibid.

12. CPA, *Origin, Characteristics, and Institutional Authorities*. Congressional Research Service (CRS) Report for Congress, 29 April 2004, available at <www.fas.org/man/crs/RL32370.pdf>, accessed 13 June 2006.

13. Joshua Micah Marshall, Laura Rozen and Colin Soloway, *Washington Monthly's Who's Who*, December 2003, available at <www. washingtonmonthly.com/features/2003/0312.whoswho.html>, accessed 13 June 2006.

14. IGC, *Global Security*, available at <www.globalsecurity.org/military/world /iraq/igc.htm>, accessed 24 March 2006.

15. Annex to the Law for the Administration of Iraq in the Transitional Period, 1 June 2004, available at <www.cpa-iraq.org/government/TAL_Annex.html>, accessed 13 June 2006.

16. Ibid.

17. Iraq, Committee to Protect Journalists, available at <www.cpj.org/attacks04/mideast04/iraq.html>, accessed 13 June 2006.

18. Kurdish Regional Government, <www.krg.org>.

19. Patriotic Union Kurdistan: <www.puk.org/web/htm/news/knwsline/nws/alliance.html>, last accessed February 2006.

20. Kurdish regional Government, <www.krg.org/articles/article_print.asp?ArticleNr=8891>, last accessed March 2006.

21. Kurdistan Regional Government Unification Agreement, 21 January 2006, available at <www.krg.org/articles/article_detail.asp?LangNr=12&RubricNr=107&ArticleNr=8891&LNNr=28&RNNr=70>, accessed 15 June 2006.

22. Ibid.

23. Kurdistan Alliance, available at <www.puk.org/web/htm/news/nws/730.pdf>, accessed 19 June 2006.

24. Quoted from Nisar Talabany, Director of Communications of KRG-UK representation.

25. Gareth Stansfield, 'Kurdistan-Iraq: Can the Unified Regional Government Work?', Arab Reform Bulletin – Carnegie Endowment for International Peace, June 2006, available at <www.CarnegieEndowment.org>, accessed 19 June 2006.

26. The October 2005 arrest and imprisonment of Dr Kamal Said Qadar, an Austrian national of Kurdish origin, received wide condemnation from the international community. Dr Qadar was sentenced to 30 years in prison after a one-hour trial, for defamation against the Kurdish government, in response to several articles he had written on corruption and nepotism in Massoud Barzani's administration of the Kurdish region. In response to pressure from the Austrian government and complaints from the international community and human rights organisations, Dr Qadir was released in January, but not before government practices with respect to freedom of expression were scrutinised.

27. The text of the TAL can be obtained from the Coalition Provisional Authority website at <http://cpa-iraq.org/government/TAL.html>, last accessed March 2006.

28. TAL, Article 61(D).

29. Ibid., Article 61(E).

30. Ibid., Article 61(F).
31. 'The Independent Electoral Commission of Iraq', Coalition Provisional Authority Order Number 92, available at <www.cpa-iraq. org/regulations/20040531_CPAORD_92_Independent_Electoral_ commission_of_Iraq.pdf>, accessed 20 June 2006.
32. UN, *IRAQ: Electoral Fact Sheet*, available at <www.un.org/news/dh/ infocus/iraq/election-fact-sht.htm#electedwhat>, accessed 20 June 2006.
33. Ibid.
34. IECI Regulation 10/2004, 'Out of Country Registration and Voting', available at <www.uniraq.org/elections/Regulations%20English%20PD F/IECI%20Reg%2010–04%20-%20OCRV%20-%20final.pdf>, accessed 21 June 2006.
35. Kenneth Katzman, 'Iraq: Elections and New Government', CRS Report for Congress (RS21968), 24 June 2005, Congressional Research Service, at <http://fpc.state.gov/documents/organisation/50254.pdf>, accessed 21 June 2006.
36. United Nations Educational, Scientific and Cultural Organisation (UNESCO), *A Reporter's Guide to Election Coverage*, available at <http:// webworld.unesco.org/download/fed/iraq/english/election_coverage_ en.pdf>, accessed 21 June, 2006.
37. UN, *IRAQ: Electoral Fact Sheet*.
38. Katzman, 'Iraq: Elections and New Government'.
39. Frank Broadhead, 'Reframing the Iraq Election', 21 January, 2005, ZNet, <www.zmag.org/content/showarticle.cfm?itemID=7079>.
40. Mazen Ghazi, 'Forty-Seven Bodies Boycott Iraq Elections', Islam Online, <www.islamonline.com> 18 November 2004.
41. Chris Toensing, 'Another "History Day" Looms in Iraq', *Middle East Report*, 28 January 2005.
42. UN, *IRAQ: Electoral Fact Sheet*.
43. Cluster G, 'Support to the Electoral Process', available at <www. uniraq.org/operations/show_cluster.asp?Language=EN&ClusterID=G>, accessed 21 June 2006.
44. Ibid.
45. Dr Nimrod Raphaeli, 'Iraqi Elections (IV): The Results and their Implications', Middle East Media Research Institute (MEMRI), 16 February 2005, available at <www.imra.org.il/story.php3?id=24146>.
46. 'Poll Turnout Low in Iraq's Sunni provinces', 14 February 2005, available at <www.abc.net.au/news/newsitems/200502/s1301837.htm>, accessed 2 June 2006.
47. 'The First Free Election since 1953 Draws 8 Million', available at <www. bloomberg.com/apps/news?pid=10000103&sid=aYAB1J_a66a8&refer= us>, accessed 22 June 2006.
48 'Elections in Iraq – 30 January 2005: An Assessment', 2 February 2005, Panel Discussion. The Royal Society for Asian Affairs, <www.rsaa.org. uk/iraqdiscussions.pdf>.
49. Quoted in Jim Muir, BBC News, <http://newsvvote.bbc.co.uk/mpapps/ pagetools/print/news.bbc.co.uk/2/hi/middle_east/4>, last accessed March 2006.

50. Foreign News Service, Istanbul, Next Five Steps After the Iraqi Elections'. 14 February 2005, available at <www.zaman.com/ ?bl=international&alt=&hn=16542>, accessed 22 June 2006.

51. Katzman, 'Iraq: Elections and New Government'.

52. KRG, <www.krg.org>.

53. Adam Wolfe, 'The Implications of the Delayed Formulation of Iraq's Government', April 1, 2005, <http://www.globalsecurity.org/security/ issues/iraq/election/2005/0401implications.htm>.

54. Nathan J. Brown, 'Post-Election Iraq: Facing the Constitutional Challenge', Carnegie Endowment for International Peace: Policy Outlook Democracy and Rule of Law Project, February 2005, <www. carnegieendowment.org/files/PO10.brown.final.pdf>.

55. Guardian online, 'Q&A: Iraq's Constitution', available at: <www. guardian.co.uk/Iraq/Story/0,,1549574,00.html>.

56. Scheherezade Faramarzi, Kurdmeidia online, available at <www. kurdmedia.com/news.asp?id=11354>, last accessed March 2006.

57. 'Iraqi Kurds Petition UN for Independence Poll', 27 December 2004, <www.abc.net.au/news/newsitems/200412/s1272667.htm>.

58. Amnesty International, 'Iraq: Amnesty International Deplores the Removal of a Key Human Rights Provision from the Final Draft Constitution', 16 September 2005, MDE 14/035/2005 (public), <web. amnesty.org/library/Index/ENGMDE140352005?open&of=ENG-IRQ>.

59. Larry Diamond, 'Consensus and Iraq's Constitution', 15 October 2005, <www.latimes.com/news/opinion/commentary/la-oe-diamond15oct15, 0,3109329.story?coll=la-news-comment-opinions>.

60. 'Certification of the Constitutional Referendum Final Results', Independent Electoral Commission of Iraq, 25 October 2005, <www. ieciraq.org/English/Frameset_english.htm>.

61. CNN, 'Iraqi Constitution Passes, Officials Say', 26 October 2005, <http:// edition.cnn.com/2005/WORLD/meast/10/25/iraq.constitution/>.

62. Alastair Macdonald and Waleed Ibrahim, 'Analysis – After vote, Iraqi Sunnis at Crossroads', 18 October 2005, Reuters, <www.iiss.org/whats- new/iiss-in-the-press/press-coverage-2005/october-2005/after-vote- iraqi-sunnis-at-crossroads>.

63. Final Draft Iraqi Constitution, <http://portal.unesco.org/ci/en/files/ 20704/11332732681iraqi_constitution_en.pdf/iraqi_constitution_ en.pdf>.

64. Eleana Gordon, 'Open Door to Islamic Rule', 26 August 2005, <www. nationalreview.com/comment/gordon200508261002>.

65. Minority Rights Group International, 'The Constitution of Iraq: Religious and Ethnic Relations', <www.minorityrights.org/asmin/download /pdf/ Iraq.Micro2005.pdf>.

66. Amnesty International, 'Iraq: Amnesty International Deplores the Removal of a Key Human Rights Provision from the Final Draft Constitution'.

67. Iraq's Permanent Constitution: Analysis and Recommendations, <http:// portal.unesco.org/ci/en/files/20704/1133273268iraqi constitution en. pdf>.

68. 'FAQ – 15 December Electoral System', Independent Electoral Commission of Iraq.
69. Certification of the Council of Representatives Final Elections Final Results, Independent Electoral Commission of Iraq, 10 February 2006.
70. Ibid.
71. 'Final Report on the December 15, 2005, Iraqi Council of Representatives Elections', International Mission for Iraqi Elections (IMIE), 12 April, 2006.
72. Michael Howard, 'Pragmatist Who Doesn't Mince His Words, *Guardian*, <www.guardian.co.uk/Iraq/Story/0,,1759848,00.html>.
73. David Ignatius, 'In Iraqi's Choice, A Chance for Unity', 26 April 2006, <http://www.washingtonpost.com/wp-dyn/content/article/2006/04/25/AR2006042501650_pf.html>.
74. Jim Garamone, 'New Iraqi Government Approved', 20 May 2006, <www.defenselink.mil/news/May2006/20060520_5179.html>.
75. BBC News, 21 May, 2006, <http://news.bbc.co.uk/1/hi/world/middle_east/5003186.stm>.
76. Mariam Karouny and Fredrik Dahl, 'New Iraqi Government Complete with Key Security Jobs', 8 June 2006, Reuters, <www.boston.com/news/world/middleeast/articles/2006/06/08/iraq_parliament_backs_defense_interior_ministers/>.
77. Lionel Beener, 'U.S. Intervention in Iraqi Politics', 30 March 2006, Council on Foreign Relations, <www.cfr.org/publication/10314/us_intervention_in_iraqi_politics.html?breadcrumb=default>.
78. BBC News online 'Iraqi PM Unveils Unity Proposals', 25 June, 2006, <http://news.bbc.co.uk/go/pr/fr/-/1/hi/world/middle_east/5114014.stm>.
79. Henri J. Barkey, 'Turkey and Iraq: The Perlis (and Prospects) of Proximity', July 2005, United State Institute of Peace, <http://usip.org/pubs/specialreports/sr141.html>.
80. KRG, <www.krg.org>.
81. DPA Report: 'Turkey Wary of Iraqi-Kurd Plans to Export Oil', Middle East News, 26 June 2006, <www.monstersandcritics.com>.
82. Ibid.
83. Stephanie Mann, 'History of the Iraq–Syria Relationship', 17 April 2003, <www.iraqcrisisbulletin.com/archives/041703/html/history_of_the_iraq-syria_rela.html>.
84. Sami Moubayed, 'US designs on Syria's Kurds', *Asia Times* online, 9 April 2005, <www.atimes.com/atimes/Middle_East/GD09Ak01.html>.
85. Louis Meixler, 'Syrian, Turkish Leaders Meet Amid Concern Over Kurds in Iraq', 6 January 2004, available at <www.sfgate.com/sgi-bin/article.cgi?f=/news/archive/2004/01/06/international 1445EST0653.DTL>.
86. Associated Press, Syria, 'Iraq Restore Diplomatic Relations after Two Decades', 2 May 2005, <www.taipeitimes.com/News/world/archives/2005/05/02/200325285>.
87. 'Zebari Highlights Syria, Iraq Relations', 3 March 2004, <www.arabicnews.com/ansub/Daily/Day/040324/2004032408.html>.
88. Joshua Landis, 'Were the Kurdish Riots in Syria Planned in Iraq?', 28 June 2004, <http://faculty-staff.ou.edu/L/Joshua.M.Landis-1/syriablog/2004/06/were-kurdish-riots-in-syria-planned-in.htm>.

89. Anoushirovan Ehteshami, 'Iran–Iraq Relations After Saddam', *Washington Quarterly*, Autumn 2003, <www.twq.com/03autumn/docs/03autumn_ehteshami.pdf>.

90. M. Javedanfar, 'Is Talabani's Patriotic Union of Kurdistan Another Iranian Ally in the Iraqi Government?', 11 April 2005, <www.meepas.com/talebanipart1.htm>.

91. Ibid.

92. Ehteshami, 'Iran–Iraq Relations After Saddam'.

93. Amberin Zaman, 'Turkey Moves Closer to Iraqi Kurds', KRG, 5 January 2006, <http://web.krg.org/articles/article_detail.asp?showsecondimage=&RubricNr=75&ArticleNr=8525>.

94. Nisar Talabany, Director of Communications of Kurdish Regional Government – UK Representation.

95. KRG <www.krg.org/articles/article_print.asp?ArticleNr=8891>.

96. Ellen Knickmeyer, 'High Expectations of Independence', *Washington Post*, 1 August 2005, <http://wahingtonpost.com/wp-dyn/content/article/2005/07/31/AR20050731010>.

97. Turkey and Iraq.

98. Dr Asad Khailany, 'The Road to Independent Kurdistan', KurdishMedia.com, 9 December 2005, available at <www.kurdmedia.com/articles.asp?id=10593>.

99. Kurdish National Congress of North America, 'Kurdish Quest for Independence and Prospects for Statehood', KurdishMedia.com, 24 March 2006, available at <www.kurdmedia.com/articles.asp?id=11737>.

100. Knickmeyer, 'High Expectations of Independence'.

15 INSURGENCY AND SECTARIANISM

1. Steven Metz, 'Insurgency and Counterinsurgency in Iraq', *Washington Quarterly*, Winter 2003–04, <www.twq.com/04winter/docs/04winter_metz.pdf>.

2. GlobalSecurity.org, 'Iraqi Insurgency Group', <www.globalsecurity.org/military/ops/iraq_insurgency.htm>.

3. Metz, 'Insurgency and Counterinsurgency in Iraq'.

4. GlobalSecurity.org, 'Iraqi Insurgency Group'.

5. Zaineb Naji, 'Schools Hit by Insurgency' Institute for War & Peace Reporting, 31 May, 2006, <www.iwpr.net/?p=icr&s=f&o=321316&apc_state=henh>, accessed 1 June 2006.

6. The 'Fedayeen Saddam', or 'Saddam's Men of Sacrifice', was a 30,000–40,000-strong Iraqi paramilitary organization which was thought to have led attacks on coalition forces in southern Iraq 'IRAQ: What is the Fedayeen Saddam?', Council on Foreign Relations, New York, 31 March, 2003, <www.cfr.org/publication/7698/#1>, 1 June, 2006.

7. The 'Mukhabarat' or Iraqi Intelligence Service (IIS) was an intelligence branch of the state security system concerned with political and security issues Iraqi Intelligence Service, <www.globalsecurity.org/intell/world/iraq/mukhabarat.htm>, 1 June 2006.

8. 'Iraqi Insurgency Groups', <www.globalsecurity.org/military/ops/iraq_insurgency.htm>, 1 June 2006.
9. 'In Their Own Words: Reading the Iraqi Insurgency', *Middle East Report* No. 50, 15 February 2006.
10. 'Bush, Blair Admit Iraq Errors', *Seattle Times*, 26 May 2006, <http://seattletimes.nwsource.com/cgibin/PrintStory.pl?document_id=2003019878&zsection_id=2002120029&slug=iraq26&date=20060526>.
11. Robert Burns, 'Insurgency Predicted to Stay Strong All Year', 31 May 2006. <www.chicagotribune.com/news/nationworld/chi-0605310061may31, 1,4346019.story?coll=chi-newsnationworld-hed&ctrack=1&cset=true>.
12. 'In Their Own Words', *Middle East Report*.
13. Jonathan Finer, 'Iraqi Insurgents: Who's Who', 19 March 2006, <www.washingtonpost.com/wp-dyn/content/article/2006/03/17/AR2006031702087.html>.
14. The Mujahidin are a Muslim force of Muslim guerilla warriors engaged in a jihad. 'Shura' is an Arabic word for 'consultation'.
15. Finer, 'Iraqi Insurgents'.
16. 'In Their Own Words', *Middle East Report*.
17. Jonathan Steele, 'Baghdad mosques become vigilante forts as sectarianism divides suburbs' 21 April, 2006, The Guardian, <http://www.guardian.co.uk/Iraq/Story/0,,1758277,00.html>.
18. 'In Their Own Words', *Middle East Report*.
19. Kim Gamel, 'Bomb Kills 2 Construction Workers in Iraq, Associated Press, <www.washingtonpost.com/wp-dyn/content/article/2006/06/01/AR2006060100241_pf.html>, 1 June 2006.
20. Dan Murphy, 'Vying for Power, Militias Roil Basra', *Christian Science Monitor*, 2 June 2006, <www.csmonitor.com/2006/0602/p01s04-woiq.htm>.
21. Lee Keath, 'Al-Zarqawi Urges Sunni War on Shiites', Associated Press, 6 June 2006, <www.frontpagemag.com/Articles/Printable.asp?ID=22784>.
22. 'Zarqawi Urges Iraqi Sunnis to shun Shi'ites', Reuters UK, 3 June 2006, <http://today.reuters.co.uk/News/newsArticle.aspx?type=worldNews&storyID=2006–06–01T221558Z_01_L01267047_RTRUKOC_0_UK-SECURITY-IRAQ-ZARQAWI.xml>.
23. 'War-weary Arabs Flock to Kurdish Resorts', IWPR, 21 June 2006, <www.kurdmedia.com/articles.asp?id=12689>.
24. 'Bombs Kill at Least 14 in Iraq's Kirkuk', Reuters and CNN, 22 June 2006, <http://cnn.netscape.cnn.com/news/story.jsp?floc=ne-us-12-l11&idq=/ff/story/0002%2F20060613%2F0829131526.htm&sc=rontz>.
25. Lydia Khalil, 'Kurdish Officials Provide Information on al Qaeda Operatives in Custody', *Terrorism Focus*, Vol. 3, No. 22, 6 June 2006.
26. Ibid.
27. Martin Sieff, 'Interpreting the Iran–Iraq Deal' United Press International, 28 May, 2006, <www.washingtontimes.com/upi/20060528–123544–2664r.htm>.
28. Steven Simon and Ray Takeyh, 'Iran's Iraq Strategy', Washington Post, 21 May, 2006, <www.washingtonpost.com/wp-dyn/content/article/2006/05/19/AR2006051901761_pf.html>.

29. Metz, 'Insurgency and Counterinsurgency in Iraq'.
30. David Fickling, 'Al-Qaida Claims "Revenge for Zarqawi"' *Guardian Unlimited*, 20 June 2006, <www.guardian.co.uk/Iraq/Story/0,,1801920,00. html>.
31. Robert H. Reid, 'Talabani Hopeful After Meeting Insurgents', Associated Press, 1 May 2006, <www.washingtonpost.com/wp-dyn/content/ article/2006/04/30/AR2006043000127.html>.
32. 'Peace Deal Offers Iraq Insurgents an Amnesty', *The Times*, 23 June 2006, <www.timesonline.co.uk/article/0,,7374–2239088,00.html>.

16 CURRENT LEGAL AND HUMAN RIGHTS ISSUES

1. CPA/REG/16 May 2003/01, Section 1 para. 3, full text available at <www. cpa-iraq.org/regulations/REG1.pdf>.
2. CPA/REG/16 May 2003/01, Section 2.
3. 'Iraq Memorandum on Concerns Relating to Law and Order', Amnesty International, 23 July 2003, available at <http://web.amnesty.org/ library/Index/ENGMDE141572003>.
4. S/RES/1483 (2003).
5. Amnesty International have delivered extensive reports on the subject of whether the CPA has extended the limited powers of occupiers through their legislation in Iraq. The KHRP does not wish to regurgitate this work and directs you to these documents which are available on Amnesty's website at <www.amnesty.org>.
6. S/RES/1483 (2003).
7. ICRC Commentary, supra note 64, at 63.
8. Ibid., 21.
9. Ibid.
10. Email from CPIC Press Desk to KHRP, 8 December 2003, stating 'the official end of 'Major Combat Operation' Pres Bush declared was 01 MAY 03. But please do not confuse, we are still at war'.
11. General Comment No. 26, 'Issues Relating to the Continuity of Obligations to the International Covenant on Civil and Political Rights', 8 December 1997.
12. See the judgments in the case of *Loizou* v. *Turkey*, of 18 December 1996, Reports of Judgments and decisions 1996-VI, pp.2234–6, s 52 and the case of *Cyprus* v. *Turkey*, 10 May 2001, application No. 25781/94, s 75.
13. Article 35 s 1 of the European Convention on Human Rights.
14. See, *inter alia*, the judgment in the case of *Cyprus* v. *Turkey*, 10 May 2001, s 99.

18 THE ANFAL CAMPAIGNS: THE WAR CRIMES TRIBUNAL

1. The KHRP FFM met a 73-year-old man who hoped all five of his 'disappeared' sons would return. Interview, 'Abdullah', Suresh camp, Sulaimaniya, northern Iraq, 31 August 2003.
2. KHRP, FFM interview: Director-General, Anfal Affairs, Kak Mansour, Sulaimaniya, northern Iraq, 31 August 2003.

3. KHRP, FFM interview: Director-General, Department of Internally Displaced People, Mr Mansour Kariami, Sulaimaniya, northern Iraq, 31 August 2003.
4. KHRP, FFM interview, Chilura Hardi, Erbil, 1 September 2003.
5. B. Mroue and N. Price, 'Some 300,000 Saddam Opponents Believed Buried in 263 Mass Graves', Associated Press Writers, 9 November 2003.
6. BBC news, 14 May 2003.
7. Article 38, Statute of the Iraqi Special Tribunal, available at <www.cpa-iraq.org/audio/20031210_Dec10_Special_Tribunal.htm>.
8. Article 1(B), Statute of the Iraqi Special Tribunal.
9. Ibid.
10. Ibid.
11. Hamza Hendawi, 'Iraq Tribunal May Try Saddam in Absentia', Newsday. com, 10 December 2003, <www.newsday.com/news/nationworld/wire/sns-ap-iraq-war-crimes,0,4252241.story?coll=sns-ap-nationworld-headlines>.
12. James Hider and Stephen Farrell, 'Saddam and His Henchmen to Face War Crime Death Penalty', *The Times*, 11 December 2003, <www.timesonline.co.uk/article/0,,7374–927012,00.html>.
13. Ibid.
14. Ibid.
15. Human Rights Watch, 'Justice for Iraq', December 2003, available at <www.hrw.org/backgrounder/mena/iraq1217bg.htm>.
16. Genocide is defined under Article 2 as covering:

    … any of the following acts committed with intent to destroy, in whole or in part, a national, ethnical racial or religious group, as such,
    a) Killing members of the group
    b) Causing serious bodily or mental harm to members of the group
    c) Deliberately inflicting on the group conditions of life calculated to bring about its physical destruction in whole or in part;
    d) Imposing measures intended to prevent births within the group
    e) Forcibly transferring children of the group to another group.

17. UN Doc. E/CN.4/1992/31.
18. Chorzow Factory Case (1928) PCIJ Ser.A, No. 17: 47.
19. 'Serbia and Montenegro: Protection Needed for War Crimes Witness', Human Rights Watch, 11 December 2003, <www.hrw.org/press/2003/12/serbia121103.htm>.

19 THE CONTINUING PROBLEM OF INTERNAL DISPLACEMENT

1. Norwegian Refugee Council/Global IDP Project, 'Profile of Internal Displacement: Iraq', July 2005, <www.idpproject.org>.
2. United Nations Assistance Mission for Iraq (UNAMI), Situation Report 14–27 February 2005, 27 February 2005, <www.uniraq.org/library/sitreps.asp>.

3. KHRP fact-finding mission to Northern Iraq, 28 August – 4 September 2003.
4. KHRP, FFM interview, displaced person: Ali, Takiyeh camp, near Sulaimaniya, northern Iraq, 30 August 2003.
5. KHRP, FFM interview, Leyla, HABITAT settlement at Bazian, Sulaimaniya province, 1 September 2003.
6. UN Portfolio of Mine-related Projects, April 2001, p. 144.
7. Ibid.
8. KHRP interviews, PUK and KDP officials, London, June 2003.
9. KHRP interview, (non-politically-affiliated) Iraqi Kurd living in London, April 2006.
10. IDMC, 'Iraq: Sectarian Violence, Military Operations Spark New Displacement, as Humanitarian Access Deteriorates', 23 May 2006, <www.internal-displacement.org/8025708F004BE3B1/(httpInfoFiles)/5FF5134F8672E698C125717700492CAC/$file/Iraq%20Overview%202 3%20May%202006.pdf>.
11. Norwegian Refugee Council/Global IDP Project, 'Profile of Internal Displacement: Iraq'.
12. International Organisation for Migration (IOM) and United Nations Office for Project Services (UNOPS), April 2005.
13. Human Rights Watch, 'Claims in Conflict – Reversing Ethnic Cleansing in Northern Iraq', Vol. 16, No. 16(E), August 2004, <http://hrw.org/reports/2004/iraq0804/>.

20 CURRENT ECONOMIC/HUMANITARIAN ISSUES IN IRAQI KURDISTAN

1. 'Iraq: NGOs expand despite the security situation', OHRA, 8 December 2003, <www.cidi.org/humanitarian/hsr/iraq/ixl98.html>
2. Martin Walker, United Press International, 14 March 2003.

21 SELF-DETERMINATION AND AUTONOMY

1. For further information see KHRP, *The Safe Haven in Northern Iraq* (London: KHRP, 1995).
2. Full text of Resolution 1514 (XV) 1960 available at <http://ods-dds-ny.un.org/doc/RESOLUTION/GEN/NR0/152/88/IMG/NR015288.pdf?OpenElement>.
3. The Namibia Case, ICJ Reports 1971, 16.
4. Full text of Resolution 2625 (XXV) 1970 available at <http://ods-dds-ny.un.org/doc/RESOLUTION/GEN/NR0/348/90/IMG/NR034890.pdf?OpenElement>.
5. See James Crawford, 'The Creation of States in International Law' (1979), and Robert McCorquodale, 'Self-Determination: A Human Rights Approach', *International and Comparative Law Quarterly*, vol. 43, October 1994, 857.
6. Article 1 of the 1993 Montevideo Convention on the Rights and Duties of States lays down four criteria of statehood: (i) a permanent

population; (ii) a defined territory; (iii) government; and (iv) capacity to enter into relations with other states.

7. Crawford, 'The Creation of States'.

8. Michael Howard, 'Kurds Faith in New Iraq Fading Fast', *Guardian*, 21 October 2003, <www.guardian.co.uk/Iraq/Story/0,2763,1067275,00.html>.

9. Ibid.

10. Ibid.

11. For further information see <www.unmikonline.org/intro.htm>.

12. 'UN Transfers Final Government Responsibilities to Kosovo Institutions', News coverage, UNMIK online, 30 December 2003, <www.unmikonline.org/news.htm>.

13. 'Security Council, in Presidential Statement, Expresses Support for 'Standards for Kosovo', Welcomes Launch of Review Mechanism', Press Release SC/7951, <www.un.org/News/Press/docs/2003/sc7951.doc.htm>.

14. 'Security Council Backs Set of Written Standards for Kosovo', News coverage, UNMIK online, 12 December 2003, <www.unmikonline.org/news.htm>.

15. Jonathan Steele, 'Only the UN Can Give Iraq Security and Sovereignty', *Guardian*, 5 August 2003, <www.guardian.co.uk/comment/story/0,3604,1012360,00.html>.

22 KIRKUK

1. Mohammed Amin Zaki, *The History of Kurdish States and Emirates in the Islamic Era* (trans. from Kurdish to Arabic by Mohammed Ali Awni) (2nd edn, London, 1986), pp. 276–91.

2. Nouri Talabany, 'Iraq's Policy of Ethnic Cleansing: Onslaught to Change National/Demographic Characteristics of the Kirkuk Region'. London, 1999, <www.kirkuk.kurdishpoint.com/>.

3. Human Rights Watch, 'Claims in Conflict: Reversing Ethnic Cleansing', HRW Report, August 2004, <http://hrw.org/reports/2004/iraq0804/iraq0804.pdf>.

4. Ibid.

5. Ibid.

6. Ibid.

7. James Brandon, 'Kurds Quietly Angle for Independence – Oil Revenue Could Give Iraq's Kurds Greater Economic Distance from Baghdad, Experts Say', *Christian Science Monitor* 26 April 2006, <www.csmonitor.com/2006/0426/p07s02-woiq.html>.

8. Nechirvan Barzani, 'Why Kurdistan Insists on Kirkuk', 16 August 2005, <www.krg.org/articles/article_detail.asp?LangNr=12&RubricNr=&ArticleNr=5358&LNNr=28&RNNr=70>.

9. Solomon Moore, 'The Conflict in Iraq – Tensions Simmer as Kurds Reclaim Kirkuk Thousands Displaced by Hussein have Returned to Take Back their Homes and Government Seats. Arabs and Turkmens There Feel Marginalized', *Los Angeles Times*, 12 May 2006, <www.latimes.com/

news/nationworld/world/la-fg-kirkuk12may12,1,4687937,full.story>, accessed 19 May 2006.

10. Reuters, 'Iraq's Disputed Kirkuk Leads Property Claims', 24 April 2006, <www.alertnet.org/thenews/newsdesk/IBO459992.htm>.
11. Moore, 'The Confict in Iraq'.
12. Ibid.
13. Ibid.
14. Jonathan Finer, 'Shi'ite Militias Move Into Oil-Rich Kirkuk, Even as Kurds Dig In', *Washington Post*, 25 April 2006, <www.washingtonpost. com/wp-dyn/content/article/2006/04/24/AR2006042401560_pf.html>.
15. Andrew Lee Butters, 'Is Trouble Brewing for the Kurds?', *TIME* Magazine, 4 May 2006, <www.time.com/time/world/printout/0,8816,1190888,00. html>.
16. *Forbes* 'Kurdish Government Unites', 16 May 2006, <www.forbes. com/2006/05/15/iraq-kurds-krg-cx_0516oxford_print.html>.
17. Brandon, 'Kurds Quietly Angle for Independence'.
18. Ibid.
19. Lawrence Kumins, 'Iraq Oil: Reserves, Production, and Potential Revenues', CRS Report for Congress, 24 April, 2006, <www.usembassy. it/pdf/other/RS21626.pdf>.

23 THE TRIBUNAL AND THE VICTIMS

1. 'Justice for Iraq: A Human Rights Watch Policy Paper', 2002, available at <www.hrw.org/backgrounder/mena/iraq1217bg.htm>.
2. For example, the presumption of innocence, the right to a fair and public hearing, the right to be informed promptly in a language the accused understands, of the nature and reasons for the charges, the right of the accused to defend himself or herself or to appoint counsel of his or her own choosing, the right to witnesses, and the right to appeal.
3. For more information on the structure of the tribunal see Chapter 17.
4. 'Special Courts for Iraqi Leaders', BBC news, 8 May 2003, <http://news. bbc.co.uk/1/hi/world/middle_east/3010793.stm>.
5. Cited at Lawrence Smallman, 'Impartial Judgement for Saddam?', Al-Jazeera, 15 December 2003, available at <www.globalpolicy.org/ intljustice/tribunals/2003/1215impartial.htm>.
6. Edgar Chen and David Marcus, 'War Crimes Tribunal is Called For', seattlepi.com, 8 April 2003, <http://seattlepi.nwsource.com/opinion/ 116291_iraqwarcrimes08.shtml>.
7. Ibid.
8. Janet Adongo, 'Taking Stock of Sierra Leone's Truth Commission', 15 December 2003, available at <www.globalpolicy.org/intljustice/ tribunals/sierra/2003/1215stock.htm>.
9. Ibid.
10. 'Iraq Law Creating War Crimes Tribunal Flawed', Human Rights Watch, 11 December 2003, available at <www.hrw.org/press/2003/12/ iraq121103.htm>.
11. Cited in Chen and Marcus, 'War Crimes Tribunal is Called For'.

24 THE LAND QUESTION

1. Michael Howard, 'Kurds' Faith in New Iraq Fading Fast', *Guardian*, 21 October 2003, <www.guardian.co.uk/Iraq/Story/0,2763,1067275,00. html>.
2. Michael Howard, 'US Advances Bosnian Solution to Ethnic Cleansing in Iraq', *Guardian*, 24 April 2003, <www.guardian.co.uk/international/ story/0,3604,942302,00.html>.
3. CPA/REG/25 June 2003/05, full text available at <www.cpa-iraq.org/ regulations/REG4.pdf>.
4. 'IOM and Human Rights Protection in the Field: Current Concerns', IOM Governing Council Meeting 86th Session, submitted by Human Rights Watch, 18–23 November 2003, available at <www.hrw.org/ backgrounder/migrants/iom-submission-1103.pdf>.
5. Ibid.
6. Ibid.
7. Ibid.
8. Ibid.
9. Ibid.

Index

Compiled by Sue Carlton